Arthur Duke Coleridge

Eton in the Forties

Second Edition

Arthur Duke Coleridge

Eton in the Forties

Second Edition

ISBN/EAN: 9783337267155

Printed in Europe, USA, Canada, Australia, Japan

Cover: Foto ©ninafisch / pixelio.de

More available books at **www.hansebooks.com**

LONG CHAMBER.

ETON
IN THE FORTIES

BY
AN OLD COLLEGER
(ARTHUR DUKE COLERIDGE)

SECOND EDITION
REVISED AND ENLARGED

WITH NEW ILLUSTRATIONS
BY
F. TARVER

LONDON
RICHARD BENTLEY AND SON
Publishers in Ordinary to Her Majesty the Queen
1898
[All rights reserved]

DEDICATED

TO THE

VICE-PROVOST

OF

KING'S COLLEGE, CAMBRIDGE.

PREFACE

I AM indebted to two old collegers of my time, Green *ma*, K.S., and Green *mi*, K.S., for their contributions to this volume—an Eton scrap-book, no more, no less. The recollections of the last Montem, and of the assistant-masters fifty years ago, are reprints from *Blackwood's Magazine* and *The Churchman*. Sir George Elvey's 'Memoirs,' *The Windsor Chronicle*, and letters from former schoolfellows supplied me with more correct information, where memory and tradition were at fault. My friend, F. Tarver, has assisted me with some of the illustrations. If 'amongst Memory's hoarded treasures' there be found dross and rubbish intermixed, I ask the forgiveness of ancient and modern Tugs of the rank and file order to which I belonged.

The ideal essay on Shelley's summer afternoon on the Thames originally appeared in the records of the Shelley Society.

The Latin couplet under the portrait of Dr. Hawtrey was addressed in the first instance to Dr. Goodall, by Lonsdale, K.S., in 1806; it is equally true of and applicable to the many virtues of one of the best of Goodall's successors.

CONTENTS

CHAPTER		PAGE
I.	RECOLLECTIONS OF LONG CHAMBER AND OF SOME WHO SLEPT THERE FIFTY YEARS AGO	1
II.	THE LIVELY OPPIDAN—THE SCHOLARLY OPPIDAN—THE HIGH CHURCH OPPIDAN—THE GREEN OPPIDAN—THE MISCHIEVOUS COLLEGER	84
III.	THE FLOODS—TULL, THE LOCK-KEEPER—'HOPPY' BATCHELDOR — BAGSHAWE, THE FAMOUS SCULLER—AN EXCURSUS ON MR. JUSTICE MAULE	106
IV.	THE CAPTAIN OF THE BOATS — AN UNLUCKY CHALLENGE FROM WESTMINSTER — SOME SPECIMENS OF ENGLISH PROSE	127
V.	THE FIRST RACE BETWEEN ETON AND WESTMINSTER — A VICTORY AND A DEFEAT — ELECTION SATURDAY	144

CONTENTS

CHAPTER		PAGE
VI.	MY TUTOR'S DOGS—JACK SPARROW, THE WATERMAN—THE DUKE OF BEAUFORT'S DOGS—CHARLEY WISE—SPANKIE	152
VII.	ETON CHAPEL—ST. GEORGE'S CHAPEL	166
VIII.	THE PLAYING-FIELDS	257
IX.	THE PROVOST—HEADMASTER—UNDER-MASTER	346
X.	MORE ABOUT CRICKET AND MORE ABOUT FIREPLACE—ETON MASTERS FIFTY YEARS AGO	419

LIST OF ILLUSTRATIONS

		PAGE
LONG CHAMBER	*Frontispiece*	
JACK KNIGHT	*To face*	23
A FOOTBALL MATCH AT THE WALL	,,	30
FINMORE	,,	77
THE TABERNACLE	,,	171
PLUMPTRE IN THE PULPIT		175
SIR GEORGE JOB ELVEY		191
DR. ARNE		207
JOHN GRAY, PARISH CLERK		211
SILLY BILLY	*To face*	213
LORD JUSTICE CHITTY	,,	262
PICKY POWELL		273
A TOWN AND GOWN ROW		281
OLD TRANT		285
SPANKIE	*To face*	289
BOTT, 'THE HAPPY WARRIOR'		298
DR. KEATE		347
DR. HAWTREY	*To face*	364
ALFRED MYNN	,,	419
HARRY ATKINS		429

ETON IN THE FORTIES

CHAPTER I.

RECOLLECTIONS OF LONG CHAMBER AND OF SOME WHO SLEPT THERE FIFTY YEARS AGO.

THERE is no exaggeration in saying that some of the best men I have ever known ran a considerable risk of becoming the worst, from the ordeal of Long Chamber, as I remember that famous dormitory, more than fifty years since. Our forefathers, of yore, possibly fared rather worse than their descendants, but ours was a sufficiently stern baptism in the expiring days of Long Chamber; it was a Spartan training which required some stoicism to put up with, and one not likely to be forgotten by any who survived such a purgatory. The evidence of two old collegers in past generations accords with my own testimony and experiences. I quote a printed statement of Sir Edward Shepherd Creasy, formerly Chief Justice of Ceylon; my second witness is the late Provost of King's College, Cambridge, whose letter now lies before me. The Chief Justice and the Provost were not given to exaggeration or random statements, and this is their evidence, which confirms in most particulars my own recollections. 'The lads,' says Sir Edward, 'underwent privations that might have broken down a cabin-boy, and would be thought inhuman if inflicted on a galley slave.' Now for the Provost: 'My recollections of Long Chamber date from 1809. My master was a beast and a bully, and the reign of terrorism upon certain occasions was a horror I shall never forget. The following may be an old story to you, but it is not the less true:

'In July, 1826, contemplating matrimony, I went to the University Life Insurance Society for a policy. (It is always good for administrative personages to have a policy.) I went before the board—some sixteen men seated at a table covered with green baize — with friend Wray at the head. "You are a Fellow

of King's, I see, Mr. Okes, from your papers?"
"Yes, sir." "I infer, then, necessarily that
you were at Eton and in College?" "Yes,
sir." "How long were you in College?"
"Eight years." "Where did you sleep?"
"In Long Chamber, sir." "All that time?"
"Yes, sir." "We needn't ask Mr. Okes any
more questions." And they did not. You
may interpret this as you please. I thought
it meant, "If you passed the last eight years
of your youth in Long Chamber, and are alive
at the age of twenty-nine, you are a fairly
safe life."'

Long Chamber, seen even at its 'Election
Sunday best,' when decked with green boughs,
the grimy floor *frotté* by rug-riding,* was a

---

* Rug-riding was in fashion for a few days at the end of the summer half. An extemporized sledge made out of the coverlets of the collegers' beds in Long Chamber accommodated a single passenger. Strings were attached to either side of the rug; to these some half-dozen boys harnessed themselves, and ran up and down the floor of Long Chamber, dragging the sledge after them. It was a pleasant ride, though very damaging to the 'college clothes,' *i.e.*, fustian or corduroy trousers donned for the sake of economy and for the elegant entertainments of an evening. The old boards took very kindly to the annual polish.

rough barrack—now and then a chamber of horrors. There was generally one Torquemada amongst the upper ten, and sixth-form tyranny, though disapproved of, remained unchecked. Cruelty is sadly infectious. It is a matter of sixth-form and Long Chamber history that one of the best and kindest men (in after-life) ordered his fag to eat a tallow sandwich, by way of acquiring an extra relish for his own cold mutton at the sixth-form supper-table. I would not unnecessarily hurt the feelings of any old colleger, but one of them hurt mine very considerably, and if he lives and reads my anathema, he will see I have not forgotten him for scoring me heavily with a birch on that part 'which cherubs lack,' and indulging at my cost in other pleasantries of a revolting description. The offence supposed to warrant amateur scourging was that I had escaped the headmaster's *triste lignum*, often probably as I had deserved it. The captains of Long Chamber, Upper Carter's and Lower Carter's Chamber, were good and merciful, but they winked at the ruffianism of my tormentor, who, as a sixth-form boy, could do as he pleased. It pleased him to steal a birch from the headmaster's cupboard; it pleased him still more to wield the instrument of justice, and rehearse all the formalities of a public execution upon an unoffending victim. I have heard that this light-fingered gentleman was not too successful in after-life. Did a bully by instinct ever make a friend?

I know too well that at Eton, in Hawtrey's time, as in Thring's at Uppingham, 'the bully existed as a species. There were bullies as there are rogue elephants, but they had no fraternity.' The worst of it is that a single bully is more than enough to embitter the life of twenty or thirty boys beneath him. My man was a very active practitioner, with no humanitarian taint in his composition. He had a touch of Jeffreys' humour with his cruelty. After battering his fag, he would indulge in a quotation from the Psalter. 'Moloch,* call me to-morrow morning at six. I myself will awake right early.'

I saw the last days of Long Chamber, and

---

* 'Moloch,' alias 'Remphan,' is now a reverend gentleman who bears a name honoured in Eton annals. I suppress it as well as that of his master, who might with propriety have borrowed his fag's nicknames.

the first of the new buildings, and, in common with others of my unreasoning comrades, I cordially resented the change. Prince Albert laid the foundation-stone of these buildings, and at the function, B. D., our captain in College, addressed him in a Latin oration, which we youngsters, for all its classicality, thought a rather hypocritical performance. We had the most unaccountable prejudices against the Prince, founded on his supposed inability to take headers or dive in the Masters' Weir below Windsor Bridge. His abortive attempts to introduce a new hat for English soldiers, and his abrupt return to Windsor Castle for luncheon, in the middle of a run with the harriers, were high misdemeanours to our thinking. Such unsportsmanlike acts were discussed and condemned, *nemine dissentiente*. The Prince was as yet a novice in the royal art of laying foundation-stones, opening bazaars, etc., and at the actual moment of using the silver trowel, we were delighted to observe that he had forgotten to take off his gloves (lavender kid, and 'fitting like a second skin'), so that an equerry had to assist his royal master in getting rid of them, bedaubed as they were with untempered mortar. 'There goes three-and-six,' we said; 'serve him right!' Apart from his supposed incapacity as a swimmer, his bad judgment of head-gear, and non-following of hounds, some of us collegers looked on the Prince as a sort of Ahab 'troubling Israel's peace.' We felt instinctively that our theatricals in Long Chamber were doomed, likewise our Montem 'sure nights,' and our roaring songs and choruses, which dear old Hawtrey, a few yards off, affected not to hear. The rumour soon spread that Long Chamber was to be cut up into loose horse-boxes. This coming reformation of our lives and morals filled us with dismay. The beams of Long Chamber would cry out against the intended sacrilege; it was an insult to the college rats, the legitimate or illegitimate descendants of the Hanoverian vermin, whilom pursued or trapped by Porson and Goodall. The colleger of the last century must have been an accomplished rat-catcher. Porson was a regular member of the hunt, and possibly may have fingered some of the neck-of-mutton bones which were turned up by cartloads beneath the boards of Long Chamber as recently, Mr. Paul tells us, as 1858. Let no one suppose that the starved eighteenth-century colleger benevolently shared his supper with rats and mice! He used the mutton-bones as a bait to catch the enemy. If the rat was not trapped in a long stocking, set in front of his hole, and solemnly hung at a bedpost afterwards, he carried the sixth-form supper-bone to a cave beneath Long Chamber, which served as an underground larder and receptacle for stolen meats, and there he left the bones as interesting relics to the rats of a coming generation. I talked of Hanoverian rats; my belief is that Long Chamber rats were of Elizabethan pedigree, real Tudor vermin, rats with purple blood. Well, the fiat had gone forth—Long Chamber was to go—*Delenda est Carthago*. We might deprecate, we could not avert the impending sacrilege, so we wrote reams of lachrymose verses, by way of protest against the demolition of the sacred place. Some of us had shivered from the cold there, for the windows were usually broken, and the snow and wind found their way in beneath the heavy old shutters; but we heard whispers of intended hot-water pipes in the projected new prison, and this was an intolerable outrage. We suddenly discovered that Long Chamber was a holy of holies, a palace of comfort and luxury; there was nothing too good to be said for it, the home of well-fed, soft-sleeping generations of 'tugs.' So we enlarged in execrable Latin verses on the sweet, undisturbed slumbers enjoyed by ourselves and our fathers before us. Why disturb us, their successors? Two shocking bad lines have stuck to my memory:

> 'Horresco referens! impendet dira ruina,
> Iisdem sub trabibus procubuere patres,' etc.

That was our argument. Granted that the Augean stable wanted cleansing, still some very fine fellows had been stalled there. Hereditary dirt, once enjoyed by Lord Camden and Stratford Canning, was a savoury legacy we were proud of. We heard talk of a Winchester don who, unused to soap and towels in the days of his youth, declined the Order of the Bath in mature life. He prospered, and day by day plumped his unwashed face into velvet cushions in his cathedral, praising the Lord 'because it was so comfortable.' What cared he for the gibe of the Winchester boys?

> 'The Reverend the Dean
> Is not fit to be seen,
> And his son at thirty
> Will be just as dirty.'

We admired that soapless ecclesiastic, and shed crocodile tears at the prospect of order and cleanliness. We had heard of a very grubby man, but a good enough scholar for all that, who unconsciously expressed his habits in a Greek grammar which he printed and published. In a chapter on verbs, said he: 'λούω, I wash; λούομαι, I wash myself (but this is rare).' Why not leave us alone? Our basins are few, but we have the college-pump, and we can wash overnight if we please. Our appeals to the happy, contented state of primeval collegers were certainly demurrable. They were a rough lot, I doubt not. No fault of theirs, poor lads! if they were sniffed at by the fastidious Gray, who, heart-whole Etonian as he was, in most respects, is uncommonly hard upon the Foundation boys of his time. I possess a parody of his Ode, written in the last century, and a copy of a song, 'The fine old Eton Colleger,' which deathless ditty we sang as a chorus in 'Fireplace' in my time. The two compositions contrast rather oddly. I gather from them that the 'fine and old' one was a shade better off than his grandfather, under very similar conditions.

PARODY ON GRAY'S ODE ON ETON COLLEGE, ON A NEARER PROSPECT BY A COLLEGER, 1798.

Collegisse juvat.

1.

Ye chambers three, ye foul abodes
  Which filth and bedsteads line,
Where every instant adds fresh loads
  To Cloacina's shrine;
If gazing on your lofty brow,
Or if perchance the expanse below,
  One scene of dirt my eyes survey,
And many a spider drags along
Your window-shutter tops among
  His slowly winding way.

2.

My former rooms—ah! sorry change,
  A Dame, too, born to please,
Where once an Oppidan I ranged,
  A stranger yet to grease.
I know my gown when first it flow'd
An awkward majesty bestowed,
  When waving fresh each woolly wing,
That worn-out elbows serv'd to hide,
Or else to hold unknown, unspied,
  A loaf or pudding in.

3.

Say, almswomen (for you have seen
    Full many a college loaf,
Your perquisites that should have been,
    To *barracks* taken off),
Who foremost now delights to clear
With potent swigs a can of beer—
    Beer that your senses can't enthrall;
Pint after pint you drink in vain,
Still sober you may drink again;
    You can't get drunk in hall.

4.

Strong guts are theirs by mutton fed,
    Less pleasing when possest,
Sheep roasted well-nigh 'fore they're dead,
    Loins, shoulders, necks, and breasts;
There's knives and forks and plates but few—
Some white, some brown bread, seldom new,
    And swipes of malt and wormwood born,
Drunk the next day, made overnight
To make the rascals slumber light
    For 'sapping'* in the morn.

5.

Alas! the weekly stipend's doom,
    Some little debt to pay;
No chance have they of cash to come,
    Save on allowance day.
Ah! show them where in ambush stand,
To seize their prey, the dunning band,

---

* *I.e.*, getting wisdom, *sapientia*.

None from the schoolyard dares to stray;
Here Gilkes, Polehampton, Coker gape,
And Mother Carter looking sharp
    Observes each customer.

6.

Lo! the Carter's Chamber corps,
    A horrid troop, are seen;
The *barracks* ne'er had such before,
    No razors half so keen.
This sharps a fowl, this fetches bread,
This bites his nails, this scrubs his head,
    These in some deeper schemes are hot;
One *private* runs to fill a can,
Another takes the meat in hand,
    And boils it in a pot.

7.

To each his duty—all the men
    The colonel's justice own;
The meat's the major's; for their pains
    The *privates* gnaw the bones.
Yet, ah! why should they wash their face,
Or why despise their happy case?
    If cleanliness such joy denies—
Soap might destroy their Paradise—
No more: where beastliness is bliss
    'Tis folly to be nice.

Carter's Chamber* had a bad reputation. John Lonsdale, in 1812, writes to Hodgson in

---

* Carter's Chambers were divided into 'Upper and Lower.' The Bishop adopts the singular number in reference to the particular one which he occupied in college days.

the usual uncomplimentary style about it: 'Eton looks all lovely, always excepting Carter's Chamber, which is more beastly than ever.' Speaking from my experience as a humble tenant, I admit the impeachment of the fragrance of Carter's Chamber, though I must disclaim the imputation of being one of a 'horrid troop.' There were five of us in my time, and my brother and I were of the party. Foraging for illicit food was a sporting instinct greatly admired, if it resulted in something for supper. One day after twelve my brother noosed a hare in Windsor Park. It was a sudden act of inspiration and brilliant poaching in broad daylight, but he was not hot on a deep-laid scheme. We applauded his performance and jugged poor puss. How good she was without currant-jelly!

A great deal of the last century Ode comes home to the colleger in the first half of the present. It was the change from oppidan life, which is alluded to in the second stanza, that tried the neophyte to the uttermost. With very slight qualifications, I adopt the old colleger's benediction: 'A dame, too, born to please.' I was very happy at my dame's, though damson puddings several times a week ruined my taste for that fruit, and an occasional creeping thing in the salad has made me very cautious since boyhood in dealing with green-meat. Accidents will happen in the best regulated dames' houses. Ideal banquets, 'nights and suppers of the gods,' are not meant for beardless boys. It takes a full-blown Canon of Durham to invent a 4th of June *menu* for his Eton guests:

POTAGE ÉTANG DE BARNES.
Saumon à la Brocas.   Sauce Cascade de Boveney.
Agneau Rôti.   Pré Salé de Montem.
Canetons.   Château de Surly.
Pommes de Terre } au Savetier.
Petits pois }
Pouding à la Brozier.
Gelée à la Califano.
Fromage Suiche en Bloc.
Lapins des Galles aux cendres.*

VINS.
Sherry, Hanoverian Vintage, 1738.
Champagne, Premier Crû de Christopher.
Burgundy, Château Botham.

There was one beloved college almswoman in my time, Dobby by name, whom we would

* *I.e.*, Welsh rabbits. These were made by us when we toasted our college cheese under the stove in Hall. The sifting of ashes was very innocent.

not have robbed of her perquisites for a kingdom. She captained some half-dozen old female pensioners, who sat in a row, basins in hand, outside Hall, waiting for our mutton relics and broken meats, after we had picked the bones. We all liked Dobby, a thoroughly sympathetic old lady, who ate her scrag of mutton with simplicity of heart and very few teeth.

I suppose that Long Chamber was called 'barracks,' and the tenants thereof were 'colonels, majors, and privates,' by way of nursing the military spirit evoked by the constant threat of the invasion of England. Or—I hazard another guess—the parody may have been written in or about Montem year, when 'colonels,' 'majors,' and 'privates' abounded in the ranks of the boys who figured in that pageant. In the sixth stanza of the Ode occurs the name of Polehampton. I believe that Henry Polehampton, my old friend and schoolfellow, was descended from a family which, in the course of its history, had experienced many changes of fortune. In years gone by it had supplied a county with High Sheriffs, and in modern days a Polehampton, Fellow of King's, was private tutor to Isaac Williams, a distinguished Harrovian, who greatly respected his teacher. Therefore the hybrid pentameter line,

> 'Hot rolls and butter Billy Polehampton habet,'

which survived as a tradition to my time, must have marked an interval in the less prosperous days of the family. Whatever his ancestors, near or remote, may have been, no Eton colleger of my time lived or died more nobly than Henry Polehampton. I shall say more of him anon.

In the Lower School passage, near the entrance into the schoolyard, my friend carved his own name and the names of several of his comrades, that of my friend Brocklebank (*notus in fratres animi paterni*) among them. Let no Vandal obliterate this record!

We collegers were not actually sworn to secrecy in respect of the mysteries enacted in Long Chamber. A line and a half from Juvenal was printed in large black letters over the entrance-door. It ran thus:

> 'Nil dictu fædum, visuve hæc limina tangat
> Intra quæ puer est.'

And this was supplemented by a motto on the door of Lower Chamber:

> 'Ne fidos inter amicos
> Sit, qui dicta foras
> Eliminet.'

It had a binding force which the least willing amongst us invariably recognized. I never heard the name of the colleger who selected this Horatian warning, but it was a good choice, as texts go, for we knew our Horace, as the Westminster boys knew their Terence, pretty well by heart. We were overdosed with that poet. I have heard Lord Tennyson say that he, too, suffered in the same way, and he quoted Byron's line,

> 'Then, farewell! Horace, whom I hated so,'

with approval. 'I am sorry,' added the late Laureate, 'that they have made me a schoolbook at Harrow; the boys will talk of "that brute Tennyson."' I doubt it. As for blabbing, the Statute of Limitations no longer applies; after half a century, 'faithful friends' may blab with impunity, and the muzzle once removed, we can 'eliminate' without fear of consequences.

The orthodox number of collegers was

seventy; I remember in one year about half that number, and cannot wonder at it. There were fearless Spartan mothers in Windsor who, for economy's sake, launched their sons into Long Chamber, there to become hewers of wood, drawers of water, restless, fitful sleepers. A chance of Montem or King's was not to be despised, so there was always a small Eton and Windsor-born contingent in College. I found, in my scholar's days at King's, an old fossil Fellow, still living, Pote by name, a contemporary of Sir John Patteson, who left Eton in 1805. He was a curious, but not uncommon, specimen of the Eton tradesman's successful son. His father had been an Eton bookseller, who did a good business in 'description paper, derivation paper, letter-paper, wax.' (That was the invariable tag to the stationery 'order' signed by my dear old tutor.) At King's we were not very proud of our Pote, whose one mission in life seemed to be the shooting of partridges—a duty limited to about four months in the year. His Long Chamber education had made him neither useful nor ornamental. At one time he and Billy Hunt, a Senior Fellow, once Recorder of Bury, and a member of the

Norfolk Circuit, took to very frequent potations in our Combination room. They were a doubtful credit to their school or their College, and the better sort were decidedly shy of '*potus et exlex*,' as they were called.

The 'Up Town' collegers, presumably not born in the purple, were heavily handicapped from the first. The sons of Eton masters were received on equal terms, but the same privileges were not conceded to the sons of Eton or Windsor doctors or solicitors, royal servants, or successful tradesmen. The poor lad was pointed at; he began his career as a pariah,

'. . . Niger est, hunc tu, Romane, caveto.'

For some mysterious reason, the farther away from Eton a boy lived, the more he was respected; the nearer to Eton, the less he was esteemed accordingly. It was thought a brilliant piece of wit on Election Monday to ask the Windsor-bred boy, 'By what train are you going home?' the questioner knowing perfectly well that the lad's parents lived just beyond Windsor Bridge. This biting jest was supposed to come with extra force and acidity if hurled by a Scotchman or Northumbrian, whose long journeys were supposed to indicate long purses and ancestral acres. When the collegers were short in number (I remember less than forty, all told), the few lower boys amongst them were in constant demand as fags, and a stray, unconscious oppidan, hailed from a window in Long Chamber, was a godsend to the overtaxed Gibeonites in College. A small colleger would often assist as an extra cook and scullion. Our masters were growing lads with healthy appetites, and a competent fag would smuggle fish, kidneys, sausages, and lard into Long Chamber for their use and consumption. These *Delicatessen* were generally purchased some time before they were finally landed. I remember one old colleger with whom St. Vitus's dance was a trick, not an infirmity, and it was usually most active at the time of five o'clock lesson in school, if he had successfully stowed away in the pockets of his gown the raw kidneys or steaks intended for his late supper. The glimpse of the raw meat, provided by Thumbwood the butcher, the savoury prospect of *rognons à la broche*, set St. Vitus going, and my friend addressed the kidney thus: 'Oh, oh! my little kidney,

I've got you now,' in such loud and jubilant tones that Hawtrey, overhearing the unwonted apostrophe, exclaimed: 'Are you mad?' Our cooking was primitive, and the kitchen battery adapted by the Long Chamber Soyer was peculiar and fragile. Long strips detached from the coarse coverlets of our beds served as a suspending line for a duck, or a pike caught in Fellows' Pond or Perch Hole. The roasting and frying were simple processes, but the bird, I am afraid, was not always honestly come by, and on one occasion a farmer at Slough complained to our head-master that three of his ducks had been lamed by the slings and stones of fourth-form marauders. The school was summoned, and the head-master addressed us in the following terms: 'In the centre of our great Metropolis, on an artificial lake of water, surrounded with rare exotic shrubs, birds of an exquisite hue and plumage are to be seen daily. They lay their eggs, and rear their young, and float about in perfect security. But a mile from the most celebrated seminary in England, Eton boys— fourth-form boys, it is true, but still Eton boys—have forgotten themselves, and three

JACK KNIGHT, *alias* JOHN K(NOX),
Who drew out *molle feretrum* (mild beer) at the Christopher.

'He was a man, take him for half and half
I shall not look upon his like again.

ducks have had their legs broken.' [Unquenchable laughter.] Hawtrey: 'This is no *laffing* matter. Finmore, shut that door!'

Our chief amateur cook in College taught us, his underlings and assistants, how to prod the sausage or beefsteak with a fork, before trusting it to the pan. We watched the exuding juices with quite a professional pride, and sniffed them, as Thackeray's Alderman the coming turtle, 'with a hideous furtive relish.' The fags, on highly festive occasions, drank beer from a small portable cask, called, for what reason I know not, a 'governor.' Our masters were addicted to more fiery potations, consisting of brandy and cloves, or rum and shrub, smuggled into Long Chamber, with Jack Knight's* connivance, from the Christopher Inn. A very fatal concoction was that shrub punch aforesaid, brewed in the few washhand basins allotted to the upper boys, for the lower boy collegers washed and dressed, every morning, in rooms hired in Eton or Windsor. The statutory rights of the collegers had been ignored for years by the Provost and Fellows.

* Jack Knight, a good-natured Falstaff kind of man, presided over the tap at the Christopher.

Henry VI. never could have intended the poor scholars to pay for their own towels and Windsor soap; but washing was a formidable extra to the long-suffering parents, for it meant the compulsory hiring of a room outside the College precincts, and many incidental expenses. To me the escape from Long Chamber was a daily luxury, and I look fondly back on my room at Webber's, over Barnes Pool Bridge, as a city of refuge after twelve and after four. There I breakfasted in comfort, once a week, royally on twelve sausages, 'because it was allowance day,' and the hebdomadal shilling exactly covered the cost of the Monday's feast. That hired room indirectly fostered a loyalty in its tenant to all and everyone connected with the dear good Queen, for I could get up from the breakfast-table and watch our future King taking the air in an open carriage, with his governess, Lady Lyttelton, with one attendant, and a single outrider. Such occasions were frequent, and we were considerate enough not to waken the Heir Apparent from his morning slumber, reserving the full force of our lungs for his royal mother, whenever and wherever she appeared within hailing distance. Our boisterous loyalty must have tried the young Queen's nerves, though they had plenty of practice, for she and her Ministers repeatedly drove through Eton to the Castle, and it was our custom to run alongside the royal carriage, as near as the cavalry escort would allow us, and hurl our stormy cheers in her face.

There exists a letter from John Coleridge Patteson to his parents, describing the tumultuous loyalty and audacity of the Eton boys at the time of the Queen's wedding. Of course that was a very exceptional day, but I have witnessed many similar scenes, on occasions less conspicuous and important than our Queen's marriage, and shall be forgiven for quoting the language of my beloved relative, who, as a boy of twelve years of age, joined in the 'Eton shouts' which greeted the royal pair. 'In College, stretching from Hexter's to Mother Spier's, was a magnificent representation of the Parthenon; there were three pillars, and a great thing like this' (a not over successful sketch of a pediment), 'with the Eton and Royal Arms in the middle, and "Gratulatur Etona Victoriæ et Alberto." It cost £150, and there were 5,000 lamps hung on it.

Throughout the whole day we all of us wore large white bridal favours and white gloves. Towards evening the clods got on Long Walk Wall, and as gentle means would not do, we were under the necessity of knocking some over, when the rest soon jumped off. However, Fred and myself declared we would go right into the quadrangle of the Castle, so we went into the middle of the road and formed a line. Soon a rocket (a signal that the Queen was at Slough) was let off, and then some Life Guards came galloping along, and one of them ran almost over me, and actually trod on Fred's toe, which put him into dreadful pain for some time. Then came the Queen's carriage, and I thought the College would have tumbled down with the row. The cheering was really tremendous. The whole 550 fellows all at once roared away. The Queen and Consort nodding and bowing, smiling, etc. Then Fred and I made a rush to get up behind the Queen's carriage, but a dragoon with his horse almost knocked us over. So we ran by the side, as well as we could, but the crowd was so immensely thick we could not get on as quick as the Queen.

We rushed along, knocking clean over all the clods we could, and rushing against the rest, and finally Fred and myself were the only Eton fellows that got into the quadrangle. As we got there, the Queen's carriage was going away. You may fancy that we were rather hot, running the whole way up to the Castle, besides the exertion of knocking over the clods, and knocking at doors as we passed; but I was so happy!'

The traditionary privilege of bawling at the royal carriage, whenever it appeared on the way to or returning from Slough, seemed to astonish Prince Albert, in common with many foreign visitors, whom I have often seen dazed and bewildered at an Eton ovation. They don't do that sort of thing at Bonn or Leipzig. The German *Hoch, Hoch!* is a feeble thing. Our great capacity for noise impressed all foreigners, our Eton French master included; and under the word 'shout' in his big dictionary he paid us a well-deserved compliment by appending this sentence: 'I never heard anything approaching an Eton shout'—'*Je n'ai jamais entendu rien qui puisse se comparer aux vivats des élèves d'Eton.*'

Neither he nor anyone else, except 'the fine old Eton colleger,' ever heard anything resembling the cacophonous shouts in Long Chamber which formed our declamatory chorus in the so called college songs that cheered our winter evenings in 'Fireplace.' I give some specimens of those elegant choruses, half-spoken, half-sung, and amongst these 'The fine old Eton Colleger' must have the first place. His apotheosis dates, I expect, from some time in the thirties of the present century.

I. The Fine Old Eton Colleger.

1.

I'll sing you a fine old college song that was made by an old tug's pate
Of a fine old Eton Colleger whose chamber was his estate,
And who kept up this old mansion at a bountiful old rate,
With an old door-keeper to put down the young tugs that were late,
  Chorus : Like a fine old Eton Colleger,
    One of the olden time.

2.

His college desk, if desk he had, was plentifully filled
With Greek and Latin grammars, over which much ink was spilled;

And there his worship sat in state, in good old 'college clothes,'
And quaffed his cup of good old swipes to warm his old tug nose,
   Like a fine old Eton Colleger,
   One of the olden time.

3.

When winter old brought frost and cold, he'd freely drink with all,
And though so very, very old, he could outdrink them all;
Nor was the wand'ring lower boy forgetful of his call,
For while he hided all the great, he hided all the small,
   Like a fine old Eton Colleger,
   One of the olden time.

4.

But tugs, like dogs, must have their day, and years rolled swiftly past,
The resignation man proclaimed, this tug must leave at last.
He mounted on his four-in-hand, drove off without a sigh,
A solemn silence reigned around, and a tear bedewed each eye
   For this fine old Eton Colleger,
   One of the olden time.

5.

Now times are changed, and we are changed, and Keate has passed away,
Still college hearts and college hands maintain old Eton's sway;

And though our chamber is not filled as it was filled of yore,
We still will beat the oppidans at bat and foot and oar,
        Like the fine old Eton Collegers,
        Those of the olden time.

II.

Put your shirt on,
If you have one,
If you haven't one
Put your collar on ;
Stick your tail up,
Sip your ale up,
Drive the nail up,
    Go along !

III.

Brown bread all the week, pudding on a Sunday,
Because it is allowance day, porter on a Monday ;
    L, L, L, L.*   (*Chorus fortissimo ad libitum.*)

IV.

Have you seen football to-day ? Where, boys, where ?
'Twas kicking into goals, boys ; there, boys, there.
  (*Sung*) Collegers and sweet oppidans !
        Oppidans and sweet collegers.
  (*Shouted*) Hurrah ! Collegers !
        You stink like Russian bears !

---

* All these 'L's' stood for 'Lubberly,' 'Lazy,' 'Lousy,' 'Liberty,' and used to rouse great anger at the Liberty supper-table. 'Liberty' consisted of six boys immediately below the sixth-form ; they had a table to themselves, and when they heard the L, L, L, L shouted, they used to hurl a volley of coals at the singers.

A FOOTBALL MATCH AT THE WALL.

Why we told it out to the four quarters of the globe that we were so inodorous, I know not, but we delighted in emphasizing the fact.

V. Football Song: A Fragment.

Now football is over and finished the game,
      Fol de rol, etc. ;
For awhile, my brave fellows, forget that you're lame,
      Fol de rol, etc. ;
Your shins won't get better for making a fuss,
So I see no objection to having a lush,
      Fol de rol, etc.
Nor filled with more pleasure was Wellington's brain,
      Fol de rol, etc.,
When he saw England's banner float over the main,
      Fol de rol, etc.,
Than the heart of each colleger will be replete
When he hears the glad tidings of Snivey's[*] defeat ;
Then fill up to Joynes and then t'other Yonge,
A very good couple to end this here song !
      Fol de rol, etc.

VI. Mr. Simpkins.

I.

Mr. Simpkins lived at Leeds,
  And he had a wife beside,
Who because she wore the pantaloons
  She thought that she must ride ;

---

[*] Or whoever happened to be the captain of the oppidan eleven.

So she axed him for a horse, and
   He yielded to her folly,
'For, you know, I'm always mollified
   By you, my dearest Molly.'
      Fol de rol, de rol, de rol, de rol de ray.

2.

This horse he stood on six legs,
   As I will prove to you:
For he lifted up his forelegs,
   And still he stood on two.
Mrs. Simpkins tumbled off,
   And her loving spouse averred,
'Oh, my lamb's as dead as mutton, for
   She cannot speak a word.'
      Fol de rol, etc.

3.

So he put her in a coffin,
   And bade them nail her fast;
And in funeral array to
   The parish church they passed.
Says he to the pall-bearers,
   'Pray take it at your leisure;
For why, my dearest fellows, make
   A trouble of a pleasure?'
      Fol de rol, etc.

4.

At night a resurrection-man
   Resolved the corpse to raise;
So with pick-axe oped the coffin,
   And on the fair one gazed.

The voice awoke the lady. 'What,
  In Heaven's name,' says she,
'Are you doing with that pickaxe?' 'What
  D'you axe about?' says he.
    Fol de rol, etc.

5.

'Pray make haste, ma'am, and die, for
  I have no time to spare.'
'If I do, sir, I'll be hanged, sir!'
  Cried out the angry fair.
'Don't you see I'm sitting up?' 'Why,
  I cannot say you lie;
But if buried people live,
  Resurrection-men must die.'
    Fol de rol, etc.

6.

So up she jumped, he after her,
  And to the stable hied,
Where she found her spouse caressing
  The horse whereof she died.
Then in came neighbour Horner;
  Says he, 'I'll buy your beast,
If you think 'twill do for my wife
  As it did for the deceased.'
    Fol de rol, etc.

7.

'Oh no!' cried Mr. Simpkins,
  'I cannot take your pelf,
Nor sell a beast that promises
  Such profit to myself;

For though it killed my first wife,
   At that I am not vexed ;
As I intend to wed again,
   I'll keep it for my next.'
      Fol de rol, etc.

8.

'You wretch!' cried Mrs. Simpkins,
   And seized him by the hair.
'And now disown your lawful wife,
   You villain, if you dare !
I'm neither dead nor buried,
   And you cannot marry two,
And though you lived to bury me,
   I'll live to bury you.'
      Fol de rol, etc.

9.

Mr. Simpkins turned round,
   And beheld, alas ! alack !
A sturdy resurrection-man,
   Awaiting with a sack.
He axed him what he wanted.
   'Such a loving pair,' he said,
'Can never live together, so
   I'm waiting for the dead.'
      Fol de rol, etc.

10.

The digger looked grave, but
   His words came well in season ;
And though told by me in rhyme, yet
   They brought the pair to reason.

> Mr. Simpkins kissed his wife.
> 'I'm yours till death,' he cried;
> 'But when, my dearest Molly, will
> You take another ride?'
> Fol de rol, etc.

College songs died hard, but an attempt to resuscitate them in the new buildings was promptly suppressed by the master in College, my revered friend, the Rev. C. J. Abraham, lately a Bishop in New Zealand. He was quite right; they were, with a very few exceptions, not worth keeping, and only served to perpetuate a vicious taste. I heard, however, accidentally, of a ludicrous revival at Queen's College, Oxford, of 'Johnnie Coke, he had a gray mare,' under rather amusing circumstances. A superannuated colleger, of the name of Moffat, held a scholarship at Queen's College, in the days when Dr. Thomson, late Archbishop of York, was Provost. Some practical joker in the University had circulated a false report that Moffat numbered, amongst other gifts and accomplishments, that of an exquisite tenor voice, which had been assiduously cultivated, and would prove to be a fortune to its possessor. This *canard* obtained wide credence, and reached the ears of no less a person than Dr. Wilberforce, Bishop of Oxford. At a 'gaudy' feast at Queen's, the young Bishop was asked as the chief guest at the Fellows' table. He sat next to Dr. Thomson, the Provost, and after dinner questioned his host as to whether he was aware of a coming Rubini amongst the scholars, and was there a young man of the name of Moffat dining at the scholars' table? The Provost was surprised at the Bishop's superior information. He had heard nothing of the scholar's vocal accomplishments, but would call upon him at once to give the company a taste of his quality. A message accordingly was sent from the high table, to the effect that the Provost hoped Mr. Moffat would favour the company with a song. Poor Moffat —a thoroughly good-natured fellow—was about as musical as the inebriate gentleman who declared that he couldn't distinguish 'Pop goes the Queen' from 'God save the weasel.' He blushed and protested, but thought it churlish at Christmas time not to take up the unexpected challenge and to grant the strange request. 'I only know one song,' he said. 'You shall have it, if you like.' And, recalling the ancient strain in Long Chamber, he roared out :

> 'Johnnie Coke, he had a gray mare,
> Her legs were long and her tail was bare,
> Riddle dum, riddle dum, rido.'

The Provost applauded very faintly ; S. Oxon's information should have been tested before Moffat ventured on a solo.

Old Wykehamists are still to be found who defend 'tunding' as a wholesome form of chastisement ; they will never bring me round to their opinion. Eton borrowed many of the good customs, and some of the bad, from the older foundation of Winchester. Amongst the bad, I reckon a traditional connivance at tyranny, in which upper boys, armed with a little brief authority, could, with impunity, indulge. I do not admire even a partial and limited power of corporal punishment vested in the sixth-form of certain schools, and I think that any sixth-form is in a bad way if it cannot enforce discipline amongst the lower boys without a cane, and a traditional license to use it. This conviction was forced upon me in my first year as an Eton colleger. My tormentor operated on other subjects besides myself, and one evening took to battering a friend of mine about the face and head so savagely, that the poor lad was kept in bed for days, until his bruises were healed. I was a witness of that performance, and shall not forget it to my dying day. I marvelled at the sixth-form boys at their supper-table, conscious of all the brutality going on, and never lifting a finger to interfere with their comrade's all-licensed cruelty. The chief executioner was safe—safe from the vengeance of his fellows, who dared not interfere with the exercise of his power; safe from the higher authorities, who must have screened such iniquity, from the fear of a public exposure of the system. A more humane man never lived than Dr. Hawtrey, but I am convinced that he shrank from investigating the case; I suppose for no other reason than that he had been bullied in his time, and emerged none the worse for the purgatory; yet in public and private he was an eloquent champion of justice and kindness. I remember his sending for me one evening, to invoke my authority, as a sixth-form boy, on behalf of a lad whose notorious oddity and awkwardness seemed to mark him out as a butt for all professional bullies. 'They used to call Shelley "mad Shelley,"' he said. 'My belief is, that what he had to endure at Eton made him a perfect devil.' On one of the rare occasions when our headmaster was allowed to address us in chapel, he enlarged on the subject of the remorse which he had known to haunt in after-life the memories of men who had used their powers at school cruelly and capriciously. Never were truer words uttered — never was a message more faithfully delivered on behalf of the timid, the eccentric, and the unsociable, whose young lives can be made so miserable by an arbitrary exercise of power. 'By wanton abuse of authority' (said he), 'you may excite in the minds of the boys beneath you a lasting sensation of bitterness towards yourselves, which may, in spite of better feelings, sometimes be recalled in after-life. This will be the case with gentler natures, on whom injustice falls more painfully; but when you have to do with rougher and harder tempers, an injury which may be forgotten towards *you* will be treasured up as an example; and there are many who, at a later day, may suffer, from those whom you have roughly or unjustly treated, all and

worse than you ever inflicted, your example
being pleaded as an ample excuse; and then,
you may depend on it, that to many men who,
in after-life, have seen their error, who have
become kind and Christian-like in their deport-
ment, and use any authority which they may
possess in their new condition as if they were
well aware under Whose eyes they were acting
—you may depend upon it that to such men,
in their solitary hours, the recollection of such
youthful errors is a frequent source of very
painful and unavailing regret. There is not
one of them who would not undergo all the
little troubles a hundred times repeated, which
he thought to save himself by these petty
tyrannies,

> 'Turno tempus erat, magno quum optaverit emptum
> Intactum Pallanta. . . .'

though the day of immediate vengeance is long
past, though the injured has pardoned him, and
the rest of the world looks on him as if he had
never offended. But, then, he knows what
may have been—may even now be—the consequence of his boyish caprice, when perhaps
at the time he never meant harm, but yet did

enduring harm.' Assistant masters as well as catechumens warmed to the preacher, whose memories made him unconsciously eloquent; and after the lapse of fifty years and more since that address was delivered, I heard a famous teacher say that the Virgilian quotation was, in his judgment, the perfection of illustration. No one was better fitted to speak on such a subject than our headmaster. He had suffered himself and in after-life had heaped kindness on the head of the man who had been a terror to him in boyhood. No Eton man can mistake the pathetic truth of our headmaster's language, with the memories of Shelley and Sidney Walker still fresh in his mind. '... These are errors connected with authority; there are others which belong to mere strength of body, and these are more oppressive, more frequent, and always more mortifying to the sufferer. The objects of such kind of ill-usage are not those over whom there is any lawful or conventional right; they are the weak, the timid, the eccentric, and the unsociable. Sometimes those who have none of these failings, but who, from some peculiarity of character, are not acceptable to all, who are nevertheless capable of warm friendship, who are even possessed of no common mental powers which *might* be expanded into great and public usefulness, but which *may be* also compressed and concentrated in a sensitive mind, till they waste and devour it, till they lead to misanthropy, or perhaps to the more fatal error of doubting the justice of Providence, because man is unjust; of madly imagining that Christianity itself is a fable, because those who call themselves Christians have acted, in pure recklessness, as if they were heathens. Two such I knew in other days—one of them when I was too young to feel and understand what I *do* understand now. Both of them are long since gone to their account. The talents of the first, however abused, earned for him a reputation which will probably not perish while our language shall be spoken. But his life here was miserable from this kind of injustice, and if his mind took a bias leading him to error—which the Almighty may forgive; for He is all merciful, and makes allowance for His creatures which we in our self-approving severity seldom make —they who remember those days well know how that mind was tortured, and how much the wantonness of persecution contributed to pervert its really noble and amiable qualities. The other was known to a smaller circle, and was mercifully saved from the more grievous error with which the former sank into his untimely grave. But he, too, suffered as none ought to have suffered, and owed in a great degree the ills of a wayward and profitless life, though he was possessed of mental powers hardly inferior to those of any of his contemporaries, to unkind treatment he received as a boy from those who could not understand or appreciate him. To others who had the sense and humanity to take a different course with him, he clung with affectionate fondness till he sank, hardly regretted and almost unknown, to a less untimely and yet early grave.'

The allusion to William Sidney Walker has for me a pathetic interest, for that historical victim of permanent and unrelenting persecution shared with Hawtrey himself a rare magnanimity towards his tormentors, and not only forgave them, but in after-life numbered Eton among his

    'Goshen spots,
  Aye bright with spiritual sunshine.'

Walker, a born scholar, who, at the instance of Sir James Mackintosh, turned a page of the Court Guide into Greek verse, has recorded some of his few consolations in Eton days. 'My ode on Waterloo' (he writes) 'has received the honour of great approbation from the Duke of Wellington, which makes me stand five inches and a half higher.' Another crumb of comfort was the fact of his having shaken hands with the King of Prussia and Platoff, and he actually succeeded in touching the flap of Blucher's coat. He was so touched himself that he adds in a letter: 'I shall have this engraved on my tombstone.' His feelings must have been too deep for tears, when Marshal *Vorwärts* kissed Mrs. Keate before the whole school, who loudly cheered that act of gallantry.

Mercifully, there was a limit to the penal servitude imposed on every new colleger, and if—as was my own case—he was in the fifth-form, during his noviciate in college, one year was the period of probation. A good deal may be done in twelve months to break the heart and maim the life of a boy, though he may have spirit enough to round and trample on his tormentors. One such case came under my observation. I do not mention the names of my contemporaries in College who are still living, but a Bishop on the bench will forgive me—nay, he has already forgiven me—for reminding him, as I did on the day of his consecration, of the fact that I once entreated him to reconsider his resolve to write to his mother, begging her to remove him from Eton, rather than submit to the humiliations practised on him in Long Chamber, and how reluctantly he adopted my advice, and thanked me for it afterwards. It was a sore trial to my friend, for he had known, as a fifth-form oppidan, the sweets of power, and had wielded it generously. The sudden change to Russian serfdom had well-nigh spoilt his whole career; the near wreck of so valuable a life often occurs to my memory.

His taskmasters called the new tug 'a Jew,' and treated him accordingly, spitting on his gaberdine very plentifully, rolling him in the snow, after evening supper in hall, holding him under the college pump, to assist his digestion of the cold scrag of mutton, moistened with swipes from a tin 'tot,' and practising on him other pleasantries, not easily forgotten by the unoffending victim. Under these ordeals, cheerfulness and equanimity were required of us. We were expected to copy Sir Thomas More, and to speed merrily to our various punishments. Did not each executioner of the Jew, like Izaak Walton's ' Piscator ' baiting his hook with a live frog, ' handle him as though he loved him ' ? The forms of torture were varied and peculiar. ' Pricking for Sheriff' was a curious operation. The victim was laid across the lap of the chief executioner, face downwards, and into a very tightened and thin surface of small-clothes the assistant executioners ran pins, warning the patient that if he screamed louder than his predecessor he would be elected Sheriff and amerced in a bag of walnuts. I forget how I comported myself under this irritating ordeal, but I managed to escape the shrievalty, by a feeble effort to stifle a natural cry. The pin business was founded on the time-honoured process, recurring at the Law Courts every November, when three or four names of Sheriffs *in posse* for each county are agreed upon at the Court of the Lord Chief Justice of England. After that, the Queen, at a Privy Council, pricks with a golden pin, driving it into the page opposite the first effective name on the list. The walnut penalty is a family secret which must not be divulged.

'Seeing the stars' or 'turning up' had nothing to do with astronomical observation. Interpreted by the college Torquemadas, it meant that they—sweet creatures—would 'outwatch the Bear' until the Jews were sound asleep in their beds. That was their time for diversion, as by twos and threes they swiftly pulled out from the wall every bed tenanted by a snoring and unconscious Hebrew. 'The wretch in bed was warned to put his head under the pillow (which was attached to the mattress), then the bed was quickly pulled out and turned upon end, the head undermost. The movement was risky, and I have known a fellow much hurt by letting his head project at the side. It took a strong brute to draw out and turn up the heavy bed in a workmanlike manner. The patient was not jerked out; he was simply left, with his head undermost, and his other end or ends uppermost in the doubled-up mattress and bedclothes, to wriggle out sideways as best he could, shove his bed back and make it again. A second upset was never permitted on the same night. It was certainly a dangerous business. An old friend of mine, with a vivid recollection of the humours of Long Chamber, used to think Lower Chamber was the nethermost hell. There the Jews were mustered on their first appearance, and told off to their respective masters; there the sixth-form supped; there contraband stuff was handed in from Weston's Yard through the windows of the studies. There, too, was a murderous horizontal bar between two of the oak pillars, and a pair of ramshackle ropes suspended for gymnastics or torture of some sort. Lower Chamber, as an antiquity, was the most interesting of the four places. My friend had a horror of it, and stuck to the upper regions.' Less pleasant and more dangerous was the old-fashioned tossing in a blanket, an operation which *was said* to have disfigured my Cambridge tutor, Rowland Williams, for life. That brilliant and combative Welshman, who would have fought any one of his tormentors, had retaliation been allowable, was a historical victim to one of the amusements common in Long Chamber. 'Why is Taffy's head so like a top?' was asked by one of our scholars at King's, the answer being: 'Why, don't you know about their letting him drop from the blanket in Long Chamber?' That was the solution. The accident certainly did not affect his brain power.

Quite recently I have come upon the real version of the catastrophe, as described by the Rev. J. Wilder, Williams's tutor. 'Rowland Williams shared the fate of all others; but being small and of light weight, or more probably from some awkwardness or mismanagement in the officiating party, after the usual words,

'"Ibis ab excusso missus ad astra sago,"

he was thrown high into the air, and in a slanting direction, so that instead of falling straight down into the blanket, he fell with his head on the corner of a heavy iron-bound oak bedstead, such as was used in olden times, the result of which was that he was completely scalped. He was immediately conveyed to his dame's, and the surgeon was quickly in attendance. By a merciful providence it was found that neither was the skull fractured, nor was there concussion of the brain; indeed, beyond the pain of having the scalp sewed on again, and the natural irritation of the wound, he did not suffer at all, either at the time or in after-life.' The Rev. R. W. Essington, a friend of Williams and a witness of the scene, adds: 'Not one of those who stood round the bed expected any result except immediate death, and the alarm bell at the upper end of Long Chamber was rung in the greatest consternation. Happily the effects were not so serious as they appeared to be, but he remained under the doctor's hands for many weeks, and tossing in a blanket was never repeated whilst I remained at Eton.' Taffy was from first to last a 'dimicatory man.' His friendship with Essington began with a fight in the Playing Fields, and that friendship, cemented in blood, was never broken afterwards. We were fond and proud of our Taffy at King's, though I for one deplored his skirmishes with bishops and authorities. We saw him very rarely after he left Cambridge for Lampeter. I remember his preaching the University sermon in King's Chapel on the text 'After the way that they call heresy,' and old Shilleto bursting into guffaws behind his red bandana.

On the night before the collegers' and oppidans' football match there was a curious and, as far as we Hebrews were concerned, revolting ceremony called 'taking the omens.' A great heap of paper was piled up in a certain corner and lighted; then the Jews had to dance in flames, while the older tugs (or Thugs) observed the course taken by the sparks, and drew their prognostications therefrom. Poor Borrodaile, a friend of mine, not being a Vestris, and having a large hole in his stockings, or may be in his breeches, got severely burnt at one of these religious ceremonies. *À propos* of the football-match, I must be allowed a few lines of swagger, having been third man in the college eleven in our match with the oppidans in 1848. My *vis-à-vis* was my friend Blundell, whilom 'the Colonel,' and now a much respected M.P. Did an ancestor of his found Tiverton School, which has become illustrious by two such *alumni* as the present Primate and Colonel Chesney? If so, a fellow - Devonian feeling might have made him a trifle more tender to my shins; but fourteen shies for the tugs to the oppidans' nought vexed the soul of my opponent. I should have been equally complimentary, had we been on the wrong side. It was a hollow affair, and would have been an unsafe speculation for the Oxonian Malaprop, who, watching an evenly-balanced match, was heard to say to his friend: 'I'll bet you a pair of drawers that the game ends in a glove!' which, being interpreted, means: 'I'll bet you a pair of gloves that the game ends in a draw.'

It used to be thought a privilege for the new colleger to be told off to sleep in Upper Carter's or Lower Carter's Chambers, called so, as Mr. Lyte informs us, in compliment to a lower master in the early part of the eighteenth century. The privilege, if it were one at all, had its drawbacks. We were very much cooped up; 'an ampler ether, a diviner air' pervaded Long Chamber. I was 'lag' in Lower Carter's Chamber, and never relished the charwoman's duty, which was my daily fate for years, for no college servant slept on the premises, and our comforts largely depended on our own ministrations. There were only five of us, and we were captained by one of the most fascinating and gifted collegers of the time. Like his colleagues in Upper Carter's and Lower Carter's, he never interfered to protect a small boy from the Sheriff process or the lessons in astronomy. I do not blame him or cherish his memory the less, because he chose *stare super antiquas vias* like his predecessor, and to connive at much that in his heart he must have disapproved of. After highly distinguishing himself in classics, he had the serious misfortune to get Montem, ignorantly supposed to have been a windfall to the holder, instead of too often a dangerous temptation. I think that the evil wrought by Montem on its last representative had a good deal to do with Hawtrey's wise resolve to bring about its abolition. This he accomplished with wisdom and courage, and in the teeth of severe opposition. B. D.'s kindness to me, at Eton and at King's, is one of my most cherished recollections. He came to school in the year 1838. Gifted in mind and body beyond his fellows, he had the happy knack of brightening and enlivening everyone with whom he came in contact. Before he had been at school a week, he showed to an intimate friend a Latin couplet, in which he introduced the names, nearly all in school order, of all the upper school assistants of the time :

'Robora, Carbo, jugum, Crudelior et Cape gyrum,
  Oaks, Coal ridge, Wilder, and Pick a ring,
Et coquus ille vafer, Falle,   Bonumque vadum.
And Cook he sly, Dupe [us], and Good ford.'

Okes, Coleridge (called by Goldwin Smith in a Greek epigram ἀνθράκινος λόφος), Wilder, Pickering, Cookesley, and Goodford are intelligible to the average Eton mind, but 'falle' wants a special construe. College servants and underlings had a difficulty with the word 'Dupuis,' which they shortened into 'Dupus'; falle (dupe) therefore is the equivalent in dog Latin for the servants' misnomer. B. D.'s scholarship and varied attainments were the pride of his friends, oppidan and colleger; but, from a lack of moral fibre and tenacity of purpose, he failed to realize at Cambridge the hopes we so justly entertained of him. Some excuse must be made for him on the ground of ill health, but the initial causes of his falling off must be ascribed to the immediate command of the chance resources which Montem threw in his way. In this case the glories of Salt Hill were dearly bought, though it was natural for every old and impecunious colleger to pray for the captaincy of Montem.

'Aureus, ut spero, mons erit ille mihi!'

B. D. died prematurely at Madeira in 1853. His translation of the Eumenides of Æschylus, and an edition of the De Coronâ of Demosthenes

are all that he left for publication; but I must
be allowed to place on record the following
specimens of his scholarship. My opinion of
their merit is valueless, but the Alcaics (written
in Eton examinations) were greatly admired by
Provost Thackeray, and the Iambics (written
in the Senate House at Cambridge for the
University Scholarship) were praised by that
famous scholar, Canon Evans, who was the
successful competitor. The English verses
were twice repeated, in my presence, by Lord
Tennyson, who was greatly impressed with
them, and interested in all I could tell him of
my old friend's history. He asked me for the
loan of my manuscript copy, and proposed to
show it to a neighbour and friend at Fresh-
water, whom he was in the habit of constantly
visiting. No one who ever heard the late
Laureate reciting poetry which touched him
can forget the solemn cadences and modula-
tions of his voice; they haunt me still, whenever I turn to the old familiar passages of his
poems, which he would repeat at my suggestion. On the first occasion he read the verses
'On Illness' aloud to me, and on the second to
the friend upon whom we called.

Of old sat Freedom on the heights,
  The thunders breaking at her feet :
Above her shook the starry lights :
  She heard the torrents meet.

There in her place she did rejoice,
  Self-gather'd in her prophet-mind,
But fragments of her mighty voice
  Came rolling on the wind.

Then stept she down thro' town and field
  To mingle with the human race,
And part by part to men reveal'd
  The fulness of her face—

Grave mother of majestic works,
  From her isle-altar gazing down,
Who, God-like, grasps the triple forks,
  And, King-like, wears the crown :

Her open eyes desire the truth.
  The wisdom of a thousand years
Is in them. May perpetual youth
  Keep dry their light from tears ;

That her fair form may stand and shine,
  Make bright our days and light our dreams,
Turning to scorn with lips divine
  The falsehood of extremes !

      TENNYSON.

Olim insidebat montibus arduis,
Disjecta cernens sub pede fulmina
    Divina Libertas, superque
    Astra faces agitare vidit.

Et confluentes audiit undique
Amnes—operatis in penetralibus
    Exsultat, et ritu Sibyllæ
    Mente suâ latet involuta.

Sed vocis altæ fragmina præpetes
Venti ferebant—inde novalia
    Per culta descendens, per urbes
    Diva homines aditura venit,

Quo vultus ægros ante oculos virum
Sensim pateret : mox parit impigram
    Virtutem, et altari marino
    Suppositum speculator orbem.

Quæ seu Deorum more acies gerit
Dextrâ trifurcas, seu caput induit
    Regina regali coronâ,
    Expetit, insequiturque verum :

Quæ mille victrix experientiam
Collegit annos : O, Dea, si tibi
    Æterna, si dura juventa,
    Neu lacrymis oculi madescant ;

Sic enitebis, sic dabis aureos
Dies alumnis, aurea somnia ;
    Sic ore divino refelles
    Quæ properat malesuadus error.

                                            B. D.

Pomona loves the orchard;
   And Liber loves the vine;
And Pales loves the straw-built shed,
   Warm with the breath of kine;

And Venus loves the whispers
   Of plighted youth and maid,
In April's ivory moonlight
   Beneath the chestnut shade.

But thy father loves the clashing
   Of broadsword and of shield:
He loves to drink the steam that reeks
   From the fresh battlefield:

He smiles a smile more dreadful
   Than his own dreadful frown,
When he sees the thick black cloud of smoke
   Go up from the conquered town.
                          MACAULAY.

Vitem decorus Liber amat suum,
Pomona malos, stramineo Pales
   Laudabit in tecto morantem,
      Que pecudum calet aura flatu.

Venus susurros gestit amabiles
Audire, per quos sæpe iterat puer
   Dilectus et ducenda virgo
      Fœdera castaneâ sub umbrâ

Candente Lunâ: scimus ut æreas
Vibrare parmas et gladios amet
   Mavors, ut in pugnâ cruorem et
      Deciduam ut bibat ore flammam.

Risum ut timendus rideat arbiter
Contracta nec frons sævior imminet,
   Cernens triumphatas per arces
      Ignivomum volitare fumum.

                        B. D.

εἰ μὲν πρόσοψιν κρύπτεται τιμή ποτε
πτυχθείς τις αἰσχροποιὸς ἤκασται καλῷ.
αὐτὸς γὰρ αἰθήρ, ἄστρα, τ', ἐν μέσοις δε γῆ
ἔχουσι τιμήν, καὶ σέβας γεραίτερον
στάσεις δ' ἔχοισι καὶ δρόμους, χωρῶν μέτρα,
νόμους, τίλη τε, κυρίαν κατὰ στάθμην.
τοιγὰρ τὸ χρυσοφεγγὲς ἡλίου σέλας,
θρόνοισιν οὐρανοῦχος ὑψίστοις Θεὸς
ἄστρων ἁπάντων ἔξοχος καθίζεται
κύκλους τ' ἀπεχθείς, δυσπρόσωπα φάσματα
τρέπει παρ' οὐδὲν ὄμμασιν παιωνίοις·
χὤσπερ τυράννου ῥήματ' ἀγγάρου πυρὸς
αἴγλη κακοῖς τρέχοισα κἀγαθοῖς πρέπει.
ἀλλ' εὖτ ἂν ἄστρα συγκεκραμέν' οὐ φίλως
ἀκοσμία πλανῆτις ἐξ ὁδῶν τρέπῃ,
οἵας νόσους δὴ, τέρατά τ' ἠδ' ἀναρχίαν
ὁρῶμεν, οἵαν ποντίου βυθοῦ ζάλην,
σεισμούς τε γαίας, κἀνεμῶν φυσήματα.
φύσεως τ' ἀμοιβαί, δεινὰ δειμάτων ἄχη
εὔνοιαν ἀστῶν ἡσυχόν θ' ὁμιλίαν
διάστροφον κυκλοῦσι, καὶ πόλεις ἀεὶ
αὐτοῖς βάθροισι πρέμνοθεν διώλεσαν.
τιμῆς νοσούσης καὶ βίᾳ κινουμένης
νοσεῖ τε τἀγχειρήματ', οὐδ' ὁμηγύρεις
ἀνδρῶν πολιτῶν, οὐδὲ φρατρίαι ποτὲ
παίδων τε καλλιστεῖα καὶ γήρως σέβας,
στέφανοι δαφνώδεις, ἢ βροτῶν σκηπτουχίαι
τιμῆς ἄτερ σώζουσι κυρίαν στάσιν.

B. D.

'. . . . . . . Degree being vizarded,
The unworthiest shows as fairly in the mask.
The heavens themselves, the planets, and this centre,
Observe degree, priority, and place,
Insisture, course, proportion, season, form,
Office, and custom, in all line of order:
And therefore is the glorious planet, Sol,
In noble eminence enthron'd and spher'd
Amidst the other; whose med'cinable eye
Corrects the ill aspects of planets evil,
And posts, like the commandment of a king,
Sans check, to good or bad; but when the planets,
In evil mixture, to disorder wander,
What plagues and what portents! what mutiny!
What raging of the sea! shaking of earth!
Commotion in the winds! frights, changes, horrors,
Divert and crack, rend and deracinate
The unity and married calm of states
Quite from their fixture! Oh, when degree is shak'd,
Which is the ladder to all high designs,
The enterprise is sick! How could communities,
Degrees in schools, and brotherhoods in cities,
Peaceful commerce from dividable shores,
The primogenitive and due of birth,
Prerogative of age, crowns, sceptres, laurels,
But by degree, stand in authentic place?'
Troilus and Cressida.

On Illness.

1.

Thou roaring, roaring Sea !
   When first I came unto this happy isle
I loved to listen evermore to thee,
   And meditate the while.

2.

But now that I have grown
   Homesick, and weary of my loneliness,
It makes me sad to hear thy plaintive moan,
   And fills me with distress.

3.

It speaks of many a friend
   Whom I shall meet no more on Life's dark road ;
It warns me that here I must await the end,
   And cast no look abroad.

4.

Thou ever-moaning Sea !
   I love thee, for that o'er thy waters come
The stately ships, breasting thee gloriously,
   That bring me news of home.

5.

I cannot pray for grace,
   My soul is heavy, and my sickness sore ;
Wilt Thou, O God, for ever hide Thy face?
   Oh, turn to me once more !

                      B. D.

MADEIRA,
   November 30, 1853.

Barring 'Montem-Sure Night,' the orgies in Long Chamber had best be forgotten. The night of the twentieth day before Whit Tuesday was an anxious one for the expectant Captain of Montem. If, before the last stroke of twelve, no 'resignation man'* from Cambridge arrived at Eton with the news of a death or resignation of a Fellow of King's College, the spoils of Montem vested in the senior colleger, so soon as the time for the delivery of the message had expired.

We prepared for action, just before midnight, by hoisting our beds high in the air, and standing mute as sentinels, we listened to the clock from Lupton's Tower. At the last stroke of twelve at night, the beds were let fall with a loud crash, the shutters slammed, and Windsor and Eton audibly reminded that B. D. had got Montem. I have often wished that he had escaped that perilous distinction.

'Fireplace' was, on the whole, a laudable

* The 'resignation man' was the coachman of the Provost of King's. His office and duties were obviously copied from the Mr. Speedyman, so well known to Wykehamists. These officials were sent to Eton and Winchester from King's College and New College, to announce the voidance of a fellowship, either by death or marriage.

institution, for there were but two fires in Long Chamber, and a shivering, half-fed lower boy was at least well warmed for an hour or two, on an ordinary winter evening. There were strange mysteries incidental to the preparation of our supper and entertainment.

Two fags were told off to prepare the fire; this was an anxious duty, and very rigidly enforced by the Captain of Fireplace. The grate was quite of the baronial order, and the draught of the chimney so convincing, that I never saw Long Chamber clouded with any smoke but that of tobacco-pipes or cheap cigars. To select three huge lumps of coal, identical in size and height, and then deftly to fit them together on the top bars, sounds easy enough, but it was a ticklish operation, and we fags always dreaded the inspection of our performance. The Captain, armed with a rug string, measured each of the coals that formed the triple crown of our achievement, and after eyeing the intervening spaces between the lumps, gave a solemn verdict on the accuracy or the scamping of our duty. If he approved, and the ordeal by fire had been safely passed, at a given signal several beds were run out and placed in two parallel rows on either side, with a third facing the fireplace; this done, supper began.

The Captain of Long Chamber had a duplicate commission, for he was virtually Captain of Fireplace also, though the latter title has been ascribed to the first colleger out of 'Liberty' who led off the songs. His was the privilege of granting 'a half-holiday,' meaning thereby an extension of revelling time beyond ten o'clock, the hour for going to bed. Excepting on gala nights, bread and cheese were our only restoratives, washed down by beer, furtively imported into Long Chamber in small barrels.

Occasionally our entertainment was varied by what we were pleased to call 'a grill,' which consisted of bones and scrag ends of mutton, purloined from hall at eight o'clock, planted recklessly on the top of the three coals which had cost us artistic fire-makers such anxiety. When these lumps of meat were sufficiently charred and smoked, they were swallowed as succulent morsels.

I see, from Mr. Tucker's book, that the 'Legend of the Sow' which farrowed on the leads of Long Chamber was an article of the collegers' creed as early as the year 1811, or thereabouts; I am sceptical on the subject of that interesting event, and doubt if the pork suppers and the 'coy, bristly resistance of the crackling' ever existed, except in the imagination of some hungry colleger.

The idea of a hungry sixth-form boy fleshing his teeth, night after night, on 'pig and pruin sauce,' and finally sacrificing on the altar of his insatiate appetite the 'Niobe of Swine' herself, can never die out, since the legend, somehow or other, has crept into the late Laureate's poetry. I find that in the version of the legend which Tennyson followed the sow was *not* eaten :

> ' We took them all, till she was left alone
> Upon her tower, the Niobe of swine,
> And so returned unfarrowed to her sty.'

An equally improbable legend survived in my time of a colleger who, being blest with a Parsifal disposition, turned poacher, and after shooting one of George III.'s pet swans, served up the bird for supper. In the capacity of under-cook, I have assisted at the dressing of a pike and a duck in Long Chamber. These delicacies were very rare; small Dutch cheeses were good enough for us; if toasted, so much the better.

My good old tutor, who had known hunger in former days, fed his college pupils bountifully once every week. On Saturday evenings regularly, there arrived at the door of Long Chamber a servant, carrying an eleemosynary rabbit-pie, with a fruit-pie 'to follow.' These good things were distributed, share and share alike, from the highest to the lowest boy in College who happened to be my tutor's pupils. Each of us carved his two slices fairly and equitably. I don't know about 'eaten bread,' but eaten rabbit and cherry-pie are not soon forgotten. My tutor fed his house-boys magnificently; he was a household word for liberality, and we hungry outsiders had our turn also. Mrs. Hart (*clarum et venerabile nomen*) ought to have spelt her name 'Heart'; she had a true feeling for the collegers, and expressed it in unstinted hard-boiled eggs, nestling in delicious lairs, amid Ostend rabbits, and incomparable beef-steaks. On Saturday nights, the pale envy of lookers-on was the only drawback to our enjoyment. As a champion of the once a week eleemosynary pie-system, my tutor stood alone; I believe his example was applauded by his compeers, and, on occasions, followed by one of them.

'No song, no supper'; we had both in 'Fireplace,' such as they were. Our choruses in Long Chamber certainly contrast, very oddly and unfavourably, with the Harrow songs by Edward Bowen. Some of the more vulgar sort were redolent of music-halls and London cider cellars. Such was the ode to Thurtell, a ruffian very properly hanged, though he just escaped being drawn and quartered, in 1824.

We liked the fine Newgate flavour of the first verse, and 'gave it mouth,' as Dennis, the hangman in 'Barnaby Rudge,' exhorted his victims to do, when they made their dying speech before they were actually turned off.

> 'And then to Thurtell they did say,
>   You must for death prepare,
> For murdering such an honest man
>   As Mr. William Weare.
>
> 'His throat was cut from ear to ear,
>   His head was beaten in,
> His name was Mr. William Weare,
>   He lived at Lincoln's Inn.'*

---

* Altered by the boys from Lyon's Inn. Sir Walter Scott was much pleased with this song when it first came out.

Not that Mr. Thurtell was an equity draftsman. The wretch had served in the ranks, as a private soldier, and in a fustian speech, made for him at his trial, he talked in 'high falutin' strains about the evil fate that had spared him in the battlefield, and reserved him for the Dennis of the period.

'Had I fallen,' said the magnanimous gentleman, 'shame would not have rolled her burning fires over my memory.' I grudge him his niche, even in a college song, and the accident which has preserved his name in Carlyle.

It was at Thurtell's trial that a counsel asked of a witness, 'What do you mean by a respectable man?' Answer: 'A man who keeps a gig,' and the philosopher founded his contempt for a 'gig-like respectability' upon that strange definition.

Another funny answer is recorded. Mr. Thesiger, subsequently Lord Chelmsford, was the junior counsel for the prosecution in that famous case. 'Well, you saw them and heard them talking,' he said; 'what were they discussing?' Answer: 'Pork chops, sir.' The improved version is funnier still. A young woman was examined as to the house where the prisoners left the loin of pork which they had brought from London. They had put off the original time for supper, and counsel said to the witness: 'The supper, I believe, was postponed?' 'Oh dear no, sir; it was pork chops.'

I know by experience the ghastly effect of a Gilbert or Theodore Hook joke escaping from an unconscious witness during the trial of a capital case. The Crown Court of Hertford was rather unfortunate in Thesiger's early days. He used to describe a series of Under Sheriffs for Hertfordshire, all of the same family, and each of them with a nose of abnormal length— 'It was a fatality,' he said, ' a *damnosa hæreditas.*'

College songs must have grated, in old days, on the ear of a well-known poet, whose thrilling verses in praise of aquatics can be heard on the fourth of June in Calcutta, when Etonians will travel many a league to attend an anniversary dinner got up by old school-fellows. I should like to hear our Indian soldiers and civilians shouting the famous chorus by the author of 'Ionica.' Dry bobs and wet bobs will bless me for giving them what I believe to be the true and original version of the Boating Song which, happily for Eton, has become a classic.

SONG FOR THE FOURTH OF JUNE.

1.

Skirting past 'the bushes,'
   Ruffling over the weeds,
Where the lock-stream gushes,
   Where the cygnet feeds,—
Let us see how the wine-glass flushes
   At supper on Boveney meads.
Chorus: Jolly boating weather,
     And a hay-harvest breeze;
   Blade on the feather,
     Shade off the trees;
   Swing, swing together,
     With your backs between your knees.

2.

Thanks to the bounteous sitter,
   Who sat not at all on his seat:
Down with the beer that's bitter,
   Up with the wine that's sweet;
And oh! that some generous critter
   Would give us more ducks to eat.

3.

Carving with elbow nudges,
   Lobsters we throw behind;
Vinegar nobody grudges,
   Little boys drink it blind.
Sober as so many judges,
   We'll give you a bit of our mind.

4.

Dreadnought, Britannia, Thetis,
   Victory, Third Upper, Ten,
And the 'eight' poor souls whose meat is
   Hard steak and a harder hen;
And the end of our long-boat fleet is
   Defiance (to Westminster men).

5.

Rugby may be more clever,
   Harrow may make more row,
But we'll row for ever
   Steady from stroke to bow,
And nothing in life shall sever
   The charm that is round us now.

6.

Others will fill our places,
   Drest in the old light-blue;
We'll recollect our races;
   We'll to the flag prove true,
And youth will be still in our faces
   When we cheer for an Eton crew.

7.

Twenty years hence this weather
   May tempt us from office stools;
We may be slow on the feather,
   And seem to the boys old fools,
But we'll still swing together,
   And swear by the best of schools.

It was once my lot to sing that boating-song to a High Sheriff and some Grand Jurymen, at an Assize dinner, and the remark made by the first man in the county was: 'If I had been educated at Eton, that song would drive me mad.'

William Johnson (afterwards William Cory) won the prize for English verse at Cambridge in 1842. The subject was 'Plato.' He always insisted that Sir Henry Maine's unsuccessful exercise was a far more artistic performance than his own, but the examiners thought otherwise. This is Johnson's own criticism: 'Maine's poem on Plato shows wonderful thought, knowledge, and poetical feeling for so young a man. We, his contemporaries, thought he would be *the* poet after Tennyson, though Browning was then writing. The dons never discover a poet; the prize was given to Tennyson through a misunderstanding. Lord Brougham came down to Cambridge, and he pronounced Henry Maine to be an orator, though he spoke very little at our Historical Society, and not at all at the Union. . . . He became the Darwin of political science. He was also a capital writer of State papers; the Foreign Office wanted him to come to them to write their papers, but he refused. . . .'

I suppose that Johnson's poetry owed something—not much—to his Eton environment. He would have sung beautifully anywhere, under whatever conditions; surely he struck deeper chords than Moultrie or Mackworth Praed ever dreamt of.

Eton collegers were much addicted to theatricals in the days of Keate, as well as of Hawtrey. Speeches in upper school might have been supposed to foster the taste for acting, but the Ajax and the Brutus, clad in pumps, silk stockings, and knee-breeches, and swinging the right arm in semaphore fashion, were unreliable models for an aspiring Roscius. Plays were supposed to be illicit in Long Chamber, but the authorities connived at the performance. Twice I took leading parts on the stage in rooms hired at Slough and Windsor.

In my oppidan days at my dame's, our ambition soared to representations of 'Julius Cæsar' and Addison's 'Cato.' Levi, the Jew, in High Street, provided the dresses. To effect the loan of a dazzling cuirass, or a pair of greaves, was a difficult operation, for the Hebrew *costumier* preferred ready money to credit. Flannels and jerseys, cut and trimmed to Roman fashion, came in very usefully for togas; but the tin armour was a more expensive item. 'What shall we say for those two helmets, Mr. Levi?' 'Well, I won't be hard on you. Five on the nail, and four at sight.' (Shillings understood.) We clenched the bargain. I hope the 'four at sight' were realized by the confiding lender of the property.

There were a few good amateur actors when Keate was consul. He, like his successor, affected an utter ignorance of the preparations and rehearsals, and the boys in Long Chamber who took part in Sheridan's 'Rivals' flattered themselves that not a soul, except the invited guests, knew anything about the performance.

The day after, Keate, looking down on his division, which numbered over a hundred boys, called out, 'Lydia Languish, construe!' and up rose George Williams, blushing to the roots of his hair, bungled through a few sentences of Herodotus, and sat down again. The selection of George Williams for an *ingénue* was not a happy one.

He was tall, awkward, and ungraceful. In

University days some of his contemporaries called him 'the laughing camel,' others 'the tortoise on stilts.' Keate then shouted 'Captain Absolute,' and so on with the rest of the 'Dramatis Personæ.'

I never heard that George Selwyn, the Bishop of New Zealand, distinguished himself on the Eton boards, but he was fond of telling a story, which showed that he was thought by a first-rate judge to have one special qualification for a good stage presence. He happened to be travelling on the same coach with Liston, the famous comedian, who engaged him in conversation, in the course of which the actor observed: 'I would give five hundred pounds to have your chin.'

Our theatrical stars were two brothers who had French blood in their veins. This fact, as in Garrick's case, accounted for their versatility, and instinctive perception of stage effect. Both of them, I am persuaded, would have made their mark as professional actors, and those who have had the good fortune to see my friend, the younger of the brothers, in the leading parts of Molière's plays, will endorse my view.

Our theatre in Long Chamber was rather an

FINMORE.

elaborate construction; the setting up and the piecing of it together required at least a fortnight's preparation, before the actual performance. It was comical to see Hawtrey patrolling Long Chamber of an evening, preceded by Finmore, his servant, carrying a lantern in his hand. Master and servant walked, apparently in blissful unconsciousness, through the half-prepared scenery of 'A Midsummer Night's Dream' and 'High Life Below Stairs.' The pasteboard trees, the spangles and bits of finery, were curious frames for the two interlopers; but Hawtrey, after completing a very innocent police supervision, retreated, without ever asking a word about the new structural additions to Long Chamber.

I had a good soprano voice, and a smattering of music, from having attended Hullah's classes, so the songs were my contribution to the play. As Peaseblossom, I intercalated some of Shakespeare's songs, music by Arne and Bishop, unaccompanied, it is needless to say, for our orchestra consisted of one violin, played by Joel, brother of the football blower, and any extra musician would have been regarded as an insult by this monopolist.

The play-night was a great opportunity for the minor prophet. The entr'acte always consisted of Joel appearing in the middle of the stage, fiddle in hand, standing at the foot of a stunted tree, with an owl *à la* 'Freischütz' on the top of it. His song, 'The Howl in the Hivy Bush,' accompanied, Paganini fashion, on one string, was always boisterously encored. I think that three or four oppidans were surreptitiously smuggled into Long Chamber on the night of the play; anyhow, it was a very popular entertainment. Brian, one of the half-dozen vendors of 'church sock' at the wall, was our 'property' man. The ass's head, of ingenious construction, was his invention, and was voted a triumphant success. My gauze wings were made by a lady at Upton—rather a distressing fact for Levi, who was always sitting at the receipt of custom when theatricals were in the wind.

It is something to boast of that I heard 'Box and Cox' in its infant days; it was *the* farce of the time. Buckstone, Harley, Mrs. McNamara—that was the original cast at the Princess's Theatre. It was acted before the Queen at Windsor Castle. Her Majesty was in delicate health at the time, and she laughed so immoderately and convulsively that Dr. Locock forbade the repetition of the buffoonery until a certain event was over. Charles Kean, who had the management of the Royal Revels, told me this himself. Of course, we boys acted 'Box and Cox' *ad nauseam* on every possible occasion. I think Maddison Morton deserved a statue. People tell me that his farce is an adaptation from the French; if so, I should be glad to know the author.

The 'New Buildings' in Weston's Yard may have folded fewer black sheep than those which were penned within the walls of Long Chamber, but I consider that the collegers of my time were just the impecunious lads whose education and maintenance were the real objects of the founder's bounty. A short time since, I heard the present headmaster calling 'absence,' and when three aristocratic names were given out, I rubbed my eyes, like Rip van Winkle, and said to myself: 'Surely these fellows can't be tugs!' We collegers never affected purple blood in our time; such associates, cheek by jowl with the sons of Windsor tradesmen, would no more have amalgamated than the Rhine with the Rhone. I am not likely to be tried by a baronetcy or a peerage, but were I 'Sir Arthur,' or 'Lord Ottery,' I think I should pause before I claimed for my heir-apparent a colleger's education *à bon marché*. To be sure, democracy is forging ahead, but a young aristocrat in a serge gown is an anomaly not contemplated by the statutes of the Royal founder. I never knew a colleger who could pay for the luxury of a private tutor in schooltime. We were distinctly poor boys. One colleger of my time, and one only, succeeded to a large fortune, and, in that instance, the property was not left to him by his parents. Let me, as an old Kingsman, record with gratitude my sense of obligation to the memory of that friend. It is not every legatee that will disburse £4,000 on the adornment of his college chapel, years after he has ceased to be a member of the University. Stacey's presentation west window in King's College was as cheerfully paid for as his half-sovereign annual contribution to the East window in Eton Chapel was begrudged in former days.

I could make a goodly list of foundation scholars of my time, and immediately before it, who more than redeemed the bright promise of their boyhood. Let no one who remembers Mountain, Witts, Barrett, Rowland Williams, Balston, Thring, Marriott, Mathias, Bradshaw, declaim against 'The fine old Eton Colleger' as a myth and a delusion. It is gratifying to see on the bench, at the present time, a bishop and a judge who once knew the more than alphabetical distinction of K.S., and I gladly take off my hat to my own fag, who never dreamed as a 'little victim,' fifty years ago, of a Star of India and the accolade for his brilliant services in the East. We still have a colleger poet with us— Sir Alfred Lyall—and we had, until recently, a true genius in his way, my dear friend Henry Bradshaw, the Cambridge Librarian. But of the rank and file, the forgotten unrecorded collegers, I know of none worthier of special mention than Henry Polehampton. One of the treasures of my library is his copy of 'Poemata Italorum,' uninjured by the shot and shell that rained so fiercely on that 'fine old Eton Colleger' at Lucknow. Sir John Inglis, in a despatch that made the ears of Englishmen tingle, quoted my old friend's name as that of one of the heroes of that memorable time. In boyhood, his modesty and self-suppression made him doubly attractive to the few who knew him intimately. At Oxford, he rowed in the University crew, and became popular and conspicuous, in spite of himself. He is affectionately remembered by his old parishioners at St. Chad's, Shrewsbury, where he lived for a few years as a curate, loyal to his duty, loyal to his friends. But when the fiery trial came, the unassuming man of no special antecedents, of blameless, if undistinguished career, was found worthy of the confidences of such men as Lawrence and Inglis. As military chaplain, he was ubiquitous, during the agonies of those terrible Lucknow days, comforting the wounded, praying with the dying, 'a very present help in trouble.' There perished in that beleaguered city no nobler spirit than Henry Polehampton's. By one colleger, at least, his name will be always held in enduring remembrance. His epitaph, written by the most brilliant of his contemporaries in Long Chamber, is to be seen in the Parish Church of Hartfield, Sussex :

In Memory of

HENRY STEDMAN POLEHAMPTON, M.A.,

Scholar on the foundation of King Henry the Sixth
at Eton,
Fellow of Pembroke College, Oxford,
who, being stationed at Lucknow in April, 1856,
and wounded in the Garrison Hospital, July 8, 1857,
on the ninth day of the siege,
died of cholera, July 20, aged 33,
and was buried in the Residency
by those to whom
in a strange and fiery trial he had fearlessly ministered
as a good soldier and servant of Christ,

This Memorial

was erected by his brother, the
Rector of this Parish.

CHAPTER II.

THE LIVELY OPPIDAN—THE SCHOLARLY OPPIDAN—THE HIGH CHURCH OPPIDAN—THE GREEN OPPIDAN—THE MISCHIEVOUS COLLEGER.

THE art of bullying was not entirely monopolised by a few tugs. The two oppidan practitioners, whom I have reasons for remembering, were not of the coarse fibre of the college Tiberius, but were well-bred professors of horse-play. They called themselves very appropriately Burke and Hare, and I instinctively fled, in my fourth-form days, whenever B. and H. were on the prowl for mischief. I will say this for them—that they invariably warned a victim of their intended attack by giving a premonitory signal, 'Here we come, Burke and Hare!' so that a young swift-footed Achilles might save his hat by outrunning or dodging his pursuers, though the marauders, hunting in couples, and very lively and strong, had the best of it much too often. Their favourite hunting-time was in the winter half, just before five o'clock school, the results of their chase being of some importance to Sanders, the hatter, who profited largely if Burke and Hare succeeded in capturing a good bag of 'five o'clock lousers.' My readers should be reminded that economical fourth-form boys, conscious of the fleeting nature of head-gear at a public school, often invested in a couple of hats at the beginning of the half—an ante-meridian and a post-meridian Lincoln and Bennett. I could not afford such an embarrassment of riches. My rural 'tile,' shaped by a Devonshire tradesman, price 3s. 6d., and dear at the money, was not the stylish article that would have satisfied the late Earl of Hardwicke, but its capture and confiscation were favourite diversions with Burke and Hare. One cold, rainy evening the ruffians were close upon me in the school-yard. In full cry and at the best pace I made for the cloisters. Hare was leading, Burke somewhere about Lower School passage. Anyhow, they succeeded in 'purling' me or tripping me up on the hard stones at the base of the Founder's statue. I was so bruised and cut about the eye, that some pitying Samaritan took me off at once to my dame's, where Mrs. Hopgood—good old soul!—seeing me like the bleeding soldier in Macbeth, and fresh from a war of some sort, embraced me fervently for the first and last time in her honoured life. The *osculum pacis* bestowed on me by old Hoppy, coupled with some leeches applied by Surgeon Browne, and an escape from five o'clock school, softened my feelings of asperity towards my pursuers.

B. and H. preferred the open air and the large field of Eton for their practical operations. They fretted at the inaction imposed upon them by confinement within the walls of their tutor's house after 'lock-up.' Even there, however, their genius for mischief found opportunities, and they discovered one very curious instrument adapted to their purpose. Provost Hodgson was a short, fat man, about five feet eight in his shoes. Amongst the varieties of storage at the top of my tutor's house was a short, thick roll of cocoanut matting, which B. and H. godfathered and nicknamed 'the Provost.' It was about the height of that worthy, and bore some faint resemblance to him in shape, girth, and tonnage. The possibilities of this innocent *simulacrum* were not lost upon B. and H.; it would be useful for flooring little fellows running eagerly up the staircase at the cry of 'Lower boy.' Fags of the right sort, when thus appealed to, come on the run. 'Those also serve who only stand and wait;' but some exacting masters would summon from the depths several of the unemployed, and when these emerged from their rooms and hastened upwards on their mission, then did B. and H., spying their opportunity, gently tilt the 'Provost,' which, acquiring volume and impetus as it rolled downstairs, met the fags full across the chest, and sent them sprawling below. The ingenuity and inventive faculty of these 'Provost' rollers did not end here. They were very cunning at the art of 'dazzling,' an operation rather venerable and hallowed by custom, for it was in full vigour in the time of Keate, whose eyes, under that terrific movable penthouse of brows which Kinglake has immortalized in 'Eothen,' were made to wink by some audacious practical jokers, reckless of the consequence of detection, so long as they could blind the 'Baffin' by excess of light. The process, simple as it would seem, did not always succeed in the hands of a novice; but B. and H. were past masters in all irritating devices, and on a fine summer morning, with their two small looking-glasses held at a cunning angle of an open window, they would shout to lower boys on their way to the Brocas or cricket-field, who would suddenly turn, look up, and, staring full at the window, be half blinded for their pains. Old soldiers, bred at Eton, must have been reminded of this silly trick when the art of flashing signals became a part of the regular army drill.

If the state of the atmosphere neutralized the dazzling process, B. and H. would vary their diversions by fishing from the top story of the house, not with a dry fly, but with a large dry hook, for my tutor's geranium pots. It was a perilous sport, and certain of condign punishment if the anglers were caught, for E. C. was an accomplished gardener, and particularly fond of geraniums. Once safely hooked at the end of a fish-line, the pots, as they were hauled up, scraped audibly against the wall of ascent, and if the noise aroused the owner, B. and H., with their geraniums hanging in mid-air like Mahomet's coffin, stood a very good chance of being 'nailed.' After lock-up there was a short close time for practical jokes, though the 'Provost' was always at hand to be kept rolling. Burke, however, could not keep still during the evening prayers, which, but for his unseemly pranks, were an impressive service in my tutor's household. All the servants and all the boys attended. When the function was drawing to an end, Burke would creep on his knees under the long table, and, suddenly emerging behind a wooden bench at which the domestics knelt for devotion, would pull off the pumps of the under-butler and decamp with the spoil, leaving 'Cad George,' as he was called, to make his exit from the room shoeless. George was so used to these petty insults that he rather enjoyed the sport, if sport it can be called, and on the restoration of the stolen property the hatchet was buried at once. I, too, like George, have long ago forgiven though not forgotten the rowdyism of these two sprightly gentlemen, whose ingenuity never failed them, and, when not directed against one's self, was rather amusing than otherwise.

It seems strange, but it is a fact, that both Burke and Hare, with all their superabundant 'mus' (Eton abbreviation for 'muscle') and mercurial spirits, began to droop directly their school-days were over, and effervesced completely in the early days of manhood. They became shy, reserved, lonely persons, standing exceptions to the Wordsworthian doctrine that 'the child is father of the man.' Burke's ancient aversion to law and order cropped up on one single occasion after he left school, and that was on a flying visit to Eton, whither he was attracted, I suspect, by the fascination of the old hunting-grounds. His best friend could not call him devotional, but he perched himself in the organ-loft during an afternoon service in chapel. It was a commanding position in those days, and rather patronized by old boys as a convenient lounge. We distinctly heard the striking of a lucifer match in the upper regions. Burke was obviously the incendiary; he had lit his cigar as a soothing accompaniment to the chants and the anthem. I believe he was ejected. This supremely Bohemian act was too discreditable to be much talked about, but it is impossible for me, who nosed the tobacco and saw the smoke, to forget. I was favoured soon after this escapade with the sight of a letter of his to an Eton friend, describing rather graphically his visit to Newgate for the pleasure of seeing the execution of Hocker (a notorious criminal); but I believe the correspondence ended with this penultimate flash of interest in men and things. There was no repetition of the smoking concert in the chapel organ-loft. Burke vanished into space—clean forgotten; Hare's gambols ceased. Before the end came, the latter was quite altered, and died as the Hare with many friends.

In the same house with Burke and Hare there lived an oppidan of a very different stamp—my cousin, Herbert Coleridge, gifted beyond his fellows with intellectual qualities of the highest order. He was greatly distinguished in mathematics as well as classics, and he was strong in modern languages, including Icelandic. I was told, at the time of his death in 1861, that the progress of an Icelandic dictionary, to which he had contributed, was materially hindered by the loss of so brilliant a specialist. The late Lord Coleridge wrote an excellent obituary notice of him in *Macmillan's Magazine*.

Herbert and I were of the same age, and we were on terms of the closest intimacy up to the time of his death. He was Newcastle and Balliol scholar as well as double first at Oxford. The present Mr. Justice Mathew achieved the difficult task of beating Herbert in an examination for legal honours. That was in 1853, the year before my cousin was called to the bar at Lincoln's Inn.

Much of this brilliancy was inherited. About his mother the late Chief Justice wrote : 'I can truly say of her that, as I have never myself known any woman of learning and genius equal to hers, so I have very seldom known anyone of a character in all things more noble or more beautiful. Herbert Coleridge lost his father when he was at school, his mother when he was at Oxford ; but the impression made by them upon his character was deep and lasting. Most men no doubt are in most things what their parents and early teachers make them, and Herbert was no exception to this general rule. He had a great power of rapid and accurate apprehension, and a very strong memory.' After summarizing the few incidents of his career, the writer concludes : ' His life was uneventful, and if measured by the actual results of his labour, he seems to have left but little behind him to justify the strong impression of power and promise he made upon all who knew him well; but all who knew him well received this impression. . . . They, too, will treasure the memory of his warm heart and the affectionate disposition of his character and temper, softened from any harshness, and refined and purified from any selfishness into considerate and almost tender gentleness, by the affliction which he took as it becomes a Christian to take what it pleases God to send; of his religion, sincere and deep, thoughtful, as might be expected in the grandson and profound admirer of S. T. Coleridge, but remarkably free from pretence or display; of a man careless — perhaps too careless — about general society and ordinary acquaintance, but giving his whole heart where he gave it at all, and giving it steadfastly.'

I am told that American parents are sending heir lads to Eton, and that the interest in our public schools is no mere passing sentiment with them. Early in the Forties, Bristed, an American by birth, entered Trinity College,

Cambridge, distinguished himself, and on his return to the States, published a lively and interesting volume, called 'Five Years in an English University.' His visit to Eton, and his reflections thereon are pleasant reading, doubly so as coming from an alien in respect of the traditions and usages of English public schools. It seems not unlikely that his account of the school, and the value he set upon his friendship with a very eminent Etonian, may have had some influence on American readers; anyhow, Yankee parents have honoured us of late years with their attention, and I hope that they are satisfied with the experiment.

Shortly after my time, we had a colonial lad, born, I believe, at Sydney; at all events, he hailed from some place in Australia, and became one of my tutor's pupils. Foreigners localized for a time at Eton were never allowed to forget their origin. My own relative, William Reynell Coleridge, who was born in the West Indies, was nicknamed Bārbădŏĕs—a false quantity, of course, but it did for a Leeward Island of some sort or other. The young Australian had been duly cautioned in his native land on the subject of sharks. When summer and the Eton bathing season came round, he naïvely inquired 'whether there were any sharks at Cuckoo Weir.' This blissful innocence enchanted the lower boys, who would take care to remind the newcomer, and probably look him full in the face in chapel when the big fish allusion cropped up in the Psalm: 'There go the ships, and there is that leviathan.' The neophyte was certainly the greenest of the green, 'in verdure clad' from top to toe. Hardly had he been disillusioned on the subject of the Cuckoo Weir sharks, when in an unlucky moment he confessed to having shot a yellow-hammer without a license. This is the story:

'One evening, at the beginning of the summer half, just after Easter, some boys were talking together in one of the boys' rooms after lock-up, and the conversation turned upon shooting. The young Australian said that he had been staying at Tooting during the Easter holidays, and had shot a yellow-hammer, whereupon he was asked whether he had a game license. He said "No," and he did not know it was required. He was immediately told that a license was necessary for yellow-hammers, that he had got himself into a great scrape, and would probably be sent to prison. He asked what he had better do, whereupon J. W. told him that the only thing for him to do was to write at once to the Duke of Wellington, tell him what he had done, and ask his pardon, and that then, perhaps, the Duke might let him off. He did not feel quite sure about this being altogether accurate, and one of the boys then sat down at once, and wrote a letter to the Duke, telling him what the Australian had done. This was put into an envelope, properly directed and sealed up, and a lower boy was called in, and told to take it down and post it, with instructions, however, not to do so. The Australian thought it had been posted, and he was strongly urged to write at once to the Duke by the same post. Notepaper was produced, and he sat down at the table and wrote a letter as follows:

' " May it please Your Grace,

' " Has or has not a boy named J—— W—— written to Your Grace to say that I, G—— S——, have shot yellow-hammers without a license?

' " Your obedient servant,

' " G—— S——.

' " To His Grace
 ' " The Duke of Wellington, etc."

'This was promptly put into an envelope, directed to Apsley House, and sent downstairs and posted. The post went out, and afterwards the boys came down to supper, when this was all told to my tutor. He was immensely amused, and said to S.: "Well, at any rate, you are sure to get a reply from the Duke, and I will give you five shillings for it." My tutor was a great collector of autographs. The reply came by return of post:

'" F.M. the Duke of Wellington presents his compliments and begs to say that he has never heard of either J—— W—— or G—— S——."

'This was taken to my tutor, who looked at it, thought it was in the Duke's handwriting, and gave the Australian the five shillings. Some little time afterwards it was ascertained that the reply was wholly written by the Duke's private secretary, who, after the manner of the race, had come to imitate closely the handwriting of his principal. The ending was rather appropriate, for the Australian scored by getting his five shillings, which quite solaced him, and gave him ample compensation for the joke.'

Religious persecution was very rare at Eton. It happened, however, on one occasion, that a fifth-form boy of High Church proclivities had a fag of diametrically opposite opinions. He treated him with the utmost kindness, excepting once, when the lower boy refused to say 'Saint Charles the Martyr,' and was whacked accordingly. On another occasion a young nobleman interfered to protect a very earnest-minded younger brother in these terms: 'I won't allow you to bully my pious *minor.*'

Having betrayed some of my comrades, I feel bound not to spare myself, but to show that I had graduated successfully in the art of mischief, and flew at high game—no other than dear old Hawtrey himself. Twice in my career at school was I a ring-leader in worrying the best of men. It is never too late to blush: my confession will be a relief to me, all the more so as I got off scot-free on both occasions, at the expense of my weak, good-natured accomplices. My first offence against law and order was the result partly of my own vanity, and partly of the impecuniosity of a comrade, combined with the love of mischief in which, as a lower boy, I had been so thoroughly grounded by Burke and Hare. Spanky may have put in a distress on my friend's weekly allowance—very likely he was '*durus super*,' reduced to the 'four Joeys and a magpie' of the Artful Dodger, or in a state more elegantly described by B. D.:

οὐχ ἡμιστεφάνων ἐσθ' ἅλις ἀργυρέων.
(There is a dearth of half-crowns.)

Anyhow, the money had to be got. I hope I was not in the sixth-form at the time, but my accomplice and I were both of us up to the headmaster, which is tantamount to saying that we were game for any amount of monkey-tricks. My father had bought at a sale in Exeter a huge folio Virgil, and presented it to me on my birthday. It was too big a thing to keep to myself: I was bent on airing it and attracting the notice and admiration of the fifth and sixth-form: how was I to set about it? I wagered half a crown with my friend C. C. James, who accepted the bet, that he would not walk slowly the whole length of the Upper School to Hawtrey's desk, holding the monstrous tome in front of him, and apparently learning his lesson by heart in the usual way from an ordinary Virgil. One of the conditions was, that the march in slow time was not to be begun until the assembly of the divisions on either side of the Upper School was complete, and the derisive cheers a foregone conclusion, and certain to attract Hawtrey's notice. All went well. James stalked along at a funeral pace, reckless of the guffaws on all sides, and fulfilling the conditions of the bargain so conscientiously that he kept his book open until he started his repetition lesson to the headmaster. Hawtrey was down on the delinquent before he was half through the first line: 'It's perfectly obvious that that Virgil is too big for you to learn out of it,' and, after making this *fade* observation, the good man felt 'dooly quallified' (Hawtrey's rendering of 'duly qualified') to pass sentence. 'Write out your lesson twice, and bring it to-morrow *against* one.' So James won his half-crown, and was imprisoned next day, a martyr to my tomfoolery.

My second crime was more audacious; it almost amounted to *lèse-majesté*, and would probably have been treated as such by Keate, but Hawtrey had a fine, silent contempt for harmless folly, and very seldom made a 'Star Chamber' matter of petty infractions of school discipline. At eleven o'clock one summer morning it occurred to me that things were getting monotonous and the whole division sleepy, so I 'passed up' a message, 'Gills and kid gloves at five o'clock school,' never dreaming that this impudent and ridiculous mandate would 'catch on' with nearly every oppidan and colleger in the headmaster's division. At the hour appointed, we—with the exception of two or three renegades—who were held responsible for the discipline of the school, appeared before our *Magister Informator* gloved as if we were on the terrace at Windsor, and sporting extravagantly high and long gills *à la Plumptre* or the Ethiopian serenaders. Hawtrey took in the situation at once, and glaring at the buffoons ranged in front of him and on either side of his desk, thought for a moment as to whom he should pitch upon for his victim. The first to suffer was 'Ruby' M., an oppidan friend of mine with red hair and flushed face, for 'after four' he had been at some violent exercise, which left its mark on the new and curious toilette. His appearance testified to his loyalty to myself; it far surpassed my most sanguine expectations, for in his anxiety to fix his awkward paste-board gills, one of them, limp with heat, hung loose and flabby, while the other protruded far beyond the left cheek. Ruby looked rather like a lop-eared rabbit, with one ear very unnaturally high and at the point of attention. Hawtrey: 'M., put down that collar!' Down it went—to the floor beneath, I fancy, for the gill, of artificial construction, had no real continuity with Ruby's linen. After stammering through a few sentences of Herodotus, the inevitable 'Write out and translate the lesson!' was launched at Ruby, who, for all I know, was quite prepared to construe brilliantly. One serenader suffered after another. I, the arch-culprit, escaped, and like 'the rare exotic birds on the Regent's Park Canal which laid their eggs and reared their young and floated about in perfect security,' I enjoyed an ill-deserved impunity. 'Use every man after his desert, and who should 'scape whipping? . . . The less they deserve, the more merit in your bounty.' Exactly so.

The neatest score off a mischievous boy that

I ever heard of must be put to the credit of one Evans, the famous Greek scholar and Canon of Durham, who had been Goulburn's assistant master at Rugby, and was told off, on one occasion, to keep order in a room where a mathematical examination was being held. A boy of the name of Tawney, engaged on a trigonometry paper, and well knowing Evans's innocence of the subject, went up and asked him whether in one of the questions 'cot' had not been printed for 'cos.' Evans, catching the situation at a glance, said audibly: 'Well, Tawney, there is $\pi\rho\acute{a}\tau\tau\epsilon\iota\nu$ and $\pi\rho\acute{a}\sigma\sigma\epsilon\iota\nu$, $\tau\acute{a}\tau\tau\epsilon\iota\nu$ and $\tau\acute{a}\sigma\sigma\epsilon\iota\nu$, and so on. But, to go no further than your own name, there is Tawney and Sawney.' I think it more than probable that Tawney sat in sackcloth for awhile after this wholesome snub; I have certainly done long years of silent penance for those confounded 'gills and kid gloves.' We were young ruffians, 'and there's an end on't,' as Johnson used to say, though I like to think that he might have added: 'There's a courtly vivacity about the dogs that pleases me.' Were our predecessors more considerate to their pastors and masters? When Keate was barred into his desk in Upper School by *his* rowdies, and neatly vaulted over the prison-door, I am not to be told that future bishops and solemn M.P.'s refused to take part in the proceeding. Lord Hatherley, one of the best men that ever lived, at whose death Dean Stanley remarked that he felt as if a pillar of the abbey had fallen, was one of the ring-leaders in the so-called 'rebellion' at Winchester in 1818. I speak with less certainty as to Lord Seaton, peerless amongst Wellington's famous lieutenants, but I think that he, too, worried the headmaster of his time — I rather hope so, at all events. It comforts me to think that such great men no more lived up to the ideal of William of Wykeham than we did to that of Bishop Alnwick, who, in advising Henry VI., exhorted him to found 'a solemn school and an honest College of sad priests, and a great number of children to be there at his cost, and freely taught the eruditaments and rules of grammar.' How long did the school keep up its solemnity? How many 'sad priests' were to be found amongst the primeval tugs under Waynflect? My honest belief is that the solemn and sad ones would have had a hot time of it with their comrades if they had been found wanting in the orthodox ways of bullying the 'Head,' or niggardly in the purchase of 'Church Sock' before Mass and Vespers.

CHAPTER III.

THE FLOODS — TULL, THE LOCK-KEEPER — 'HOPPY' BATCHELDOR — BAGSHAWE, THE FAMOUS SCULLER — AN EXCURSUS ON MR. JUSTICE MAULE.

ETONIANS of my date loathe the very name of a house-boat, the Noah's Ark disfiguring the back-water, which joins the main stream below the railway bridge above the Brocas clump. We miss the punts, too, though there were good reasons for their abolition. In my time there was no bridge between Windsor and old Datchet bridge; the latter was a structure of several arches, each rather narrow; a boat could but just pass through without shifting or shortening oars. Boating below Windsor locks was generally against the rules of the school; but perhaps on this very account the stolen joy was sweeter, and boys of aquatic tastes were fond of making excursions to the Bells of Ouseley and to Runnymede.

The floods, a severe trial to the elders, were to us a delight. We heard of the trouble they caused, of cellars inundated, of punts needed for transit over what should be dry land; but as these inconveniences did not touch us, we rejoiced in the watery waste. The rise of the waters could be gauged by the woodwork of the locks just opposite the windows of the Fellows' houses in the cloisters. Gradually the river widened, creeping over the Fellows' eyot; then the water would soak through and enter the College garden—a slight rise in the ground and a low wall under the iron railings prevented it from pouring in. The Fellows' flower-garden was frequently covered, for the stream was considerable, even outside the river-bed; the waters fell as rapidly as they rose. We greatly enjoyed the inland ocean, and thought of the Tiber overflowing its banks, and the stanza from Horace, and all the anomalies of the age of Pyrrha:

> When whale and porpoise sought the hills,
>   When fishes hung in trees,
> Dislodging doves, while frightened deer
>   Swam o'er unwonted seas.

The two last lines in the original—

> 'Et superjecto pavidæ natarunt
> Æquore *damæ*'—

were, of course, the subject of a pun from our lower master, 'Dicky' Okes, who applied the word *damæ* to the various 'dames' in College. Barges often passed along the Windsor Lock-cut, which was beyond the natural stream, flowing down from the Masters' Weir; now and again would come a small steamer, a rare novelty in those times.

Tull, the lock-keeper of that day, had a stentorian voice, which in still weather could be heard in the Fellows' buildings, as he shouted to his helper or the bargee, or (it was said by some) scolded his wife. Tull was a privileged being, and when the humour took him, he would address the Fellows and assistant-masters by their surnames or Christian names. It was 'Well, Okes, how are you this morning?' or, 'John George, you 'ad a good dinner on Election Monday—you know you 'ad.' This free-masonry was never indulged in unless the surroundings were perfectly safe; no lower boy, except by accident, ever witnessed such curious greetings between the authorities and their employé. Tull, unlike Justice Stareleigh, who hesitated as to the entry of 'Sam Veller' or 'Sam Weller' on his note-book, had no hesitation about changing his V's into W's. When F. Vidal, the chapel Conduct, was talking with him in the lock, and discussing old days and scenes incidental to the Masters' Weir, Tull, pointing to some alders, said, 'Me and Selwyn planted them trees, *Widal!*'

There were, too, notable runs with the Royal staghounds which were still talked of in my early days at Eton. On the Thames, as on the Teith in 'The Lady of the Lake,' it might be said that :

> 'From shore to shore
> The gallant stag swam stoutly o'er.'

Once he ran into the playing-fields, made for 'Sixpenny Corner' (the angle between the Slough road wall and the wall of Ward's garden), and there turned to bay, the whole hunt coming up. Once the quarry came into Windsor, and ran up the 'Hundred Steps' from the foot of Windsor Hill into the cloisters adjoining St. George's Chapel, where, finding an open door, he entered, mounted a staircase, and penetrated to the drawing-room of one of the canons, the redoubtable Dr. Keate himself. Not far from the confluence of the Sheep's Bridge stream with the river was a coal-wharf, and a dwelling-house close to it, in which lived Major Brine and his family.

Batcheldor (nicknamed 'Hoppy' because of his one short leg) was the fishing authority, a cunning angler; from the shingly islet opposite the lower corner of the eyot he was often seen taking large chub with an artificial fly.

A dry-bob should approach the subject of aquatics with modesty and reserve, for in most instances his scientific knowledge of rowing is about as elementary as Mr. Winkle's of the outside edge backwards on the ice. 'Mr. Winkle probably knew as much about skating as a Hindoo,' and we all remember with approval Mr. Pickwick's lofty command to his faithful Sam, 'Take off his skates. Sir, you are an impostor!'

My admiration for W. L. G. Bagshawe has never waned, from the days of our early friendship, when we boarded together at Evans's. I rejoiced in his unbroken succession of triumphs on the river; he was pre-eminently the boating-man of my time most fondly remembered by me, and I have reason for believing that many of his contemporaries shared my enthusiasm. Of course he rowed in the 'eight,' but his greater fame rested on his reputation as a sculler. The last two lines of a stanza by the Eton poet—

> They toil at games and play at books;
>   They love the winner of the race
> If only he that prospers looks
>   On prizes with a simple grace—

are specially applicable to my old friend. Bagshawe bore his victories meekly, and he was honoured accordingly.

The races in my time were always from the 'Brocas' round the 'Rushes.' It was a very strenuous contest; in the powerful stream just above 'Athens' many a rowlock gave way; sometimes through bad pilotage an oar was broken, and the rower or sculler was credited with superhuman exertion, reaping a fictitious glory from a mere accident, for a dash at the bank in a flurried moment or an entanglement of the blade of the oar in a bunch of weed might have caused the catastrophe. But if Bagshawe was in the race, the defeat of his boat seemed impossible. The direst mishap in the early stage of a contest failed to put him out, or seriously imperil his chances of ultimate victory. I believed in him as implicitly as betting men were wont to believe in 'Ormonde with Archer up'; and whenever Bagshawe raced, I yelled at him from the bank, roaring myself hoarse from start to finish, giving him well-meant but execrably bad and gratuitous advice. Riparian tactics must be very bewildering to the party most concerned in the race. 'Go it, Bags!' 'Pull your left!' 'Shift your right!' 'Look ahead!' 'Mind your eye!' 'You'll be swamped!' 'Barge coming!'—totally superfluous counsel, seeing that Bagshawe knew his business thoroughly, and we did not know it at all; and if we left him well alone, he was as sure of victory as Nelson himself. Bagshawe 'shook off our zeal as a seal throws off water.' He paddled his own canoe; the harder the race, the more he enjoyed it. He was not 'one of those who like the palm without the dust.'

A reminder of the discipline enforced by a Cambridge trainer of a racing crew as far back as the year 1845 has recently appeared in print;

it confirms me in the idea that Bagshawe was wise to disregard advice from the shore. Here is the account of the race, and none of my readers will begrudge an old Kingsman the pleasure he feels in recording a victory so honourable to his College.

'K.C.C.,
'*April* 24-25, 1845.

'Our boat is almost an absorbing interest this week, because of the races. We have achieved a complete conquest over the unkind prejudices of our elders in the College, who at first threw some cold and not very clean water on the project of the revival of the boat-club. Wednesday was to be the first race, and we practised at 7.30 in the morning, and then had to race twelve hours afterwards. And greatly rapt I was about it all day, thinking about it as keenly and qualmishly as I used to about one of our national struggles at football. We had to start last but one, because we had so recently entered. It was the wildest scramble— we had to change our place at the last moment, but started advantageously. You know *we are not allowed to look on the bank* (much less at the pursuing boat), but keep our eyes straight aft and *think* about every stroke; nothing could be wilder than pulling thus with a dozen unseen partisans on the bank shouting to us, "Go at them!" as if we were bulldogs set at a bull. In about 200 yards one might infer from the noises that we were close on the quarter of the Emmanuel boat. Going round a corner, with not light enough to steer by, we found our oars digging into the sedge, and the boat going one-sided; one or two lookers-on holloaing to our steerer (a very young but marvellously cool-headed being) to steer out (to give us room). Luckily he disobeyed, and persisted in making for their inside; so in a few strokes more we were bumping them most decisively, and stopped and hoisted our flag, having had not enough work to give us a breathing—the Emmanuel eight looking sulky at being caught so early by a six-oar . . . One feels quite a professional interest in fulfilling all that our jockey has taught us; and the improvement in health resulting from all this careful and vigorous life is a great reward for the surrender I make of puddings and parties and conversational walks.'

On one occasion only I trembled for Bagshawe's success on the river, and that, I think, was in the first heat for the Sculls in 1847. There was a large fleet of starters; the best men were heavily handicapped by their being posted a long way behind the foremost leaders of the flotilla; the danger was that in getting through the ruck off Bargeman's Bush the favourite might be swamped, and so out-distanced in consequence as to lose all chance of competing in the second or final heat. This fatality actually happened to Bagshawe, whose boat was so cannoned against and bumped by the awkward squad at the turning-point that it sank and disappeared, whilst the favourite had to swim with one hand, dragging and pushing to the bank his swamped ship with the other. To bail out the water, rearrange the floating boards, and begin the race again when the fleet was nearly out of sight, would have tried the equanimity of most men, but Bagshawe was no ordinary man. After his historical wreck, Robinson Crusoe was all in favour of fronting his misfortune then and there by a bit of practical work. What was the good of crying? 'It was in vain to sit still and wish for what was not to be had; and this extremity roused my application.' Our man, too, may be said almost to have re-made his ship, which was in a very leaky condition after its complete submersion. We—Evans's boys—watched the whole scene in deep dejection, but were greatly comforted when Bagshawe, in dripping jersey and oozing shoes, rejoined his boat, seized the sculls, and sang out, 'All right—I'm all right!' Away he went, and after catching up and passing the flotilla, ultimately came in third or fourth—I am not sure which—but quite early enough to secure his right of competition and ultimate victory in the crowning heat. It was a remarkable performance. So uniform a course of victory on the Thames at Eton fully warranted Bagshawe's entry for the University Sculls at Cambridge in his earliest days as a Trinity undergraduate. Old stagers regarded this challenge as highly presumptuous, and the 'two to one bar one' people waylaid my friend one day as he came out of hall, and aggressively backed the field or their special favourites, laying heavy odds against the upstart Etonian. Bagshawe, no gambler as a rule, quietly took the bets—it was said to the tune of £200. Of course he won the race, pocketed the money, and was rusticated for a short time. We— immensely proud of his achievement — were anything but *mærentes amici*, and the banished one was regarded as an *egregius exul*.

I never saw him after he left Cambridge, but the tragedy of his unavenged murder has not been forgotten on the Midland Circuit, to which I have the honour officially to belong. The trial of the seven ruffians who did poor Bagshawe to death took place at the Derby Summer Assizes in 1854, before Mr. Justice Maule, whose notorious aversion to the game laws and the preservation of pheasants or salmon made him a special favourite with poachers of all kinds. The prisoners had been reported, on good evidence, to Bagshawe, as trespassing on his river in pursuit of salmon, and he went instantly to the *locus in quo*, attended by his brother-in-law, the late Sir Henry Halford, with the intention of apprehending them. From my experience of Bagshawe's character, I think it likely enough that he was in high spirits at the prospect of a row; I also think that he would not have hesitated to initiate the fray, but it was seven to two against him, and the poachers succeeded in trampling my poor friend's life out in the river. I have often talked with Midland Circuit men who were present at the trial. There was but one opinion among the experts, and this was, that the evidence, if not strong enough to warrant the conviction of one and all the prisoners on the capital charge, was quite sufficient to sustain a verdict of manslaughter, and that of a very aggravated kind. From first to last the Judge—a powerful and determined one—was against the prosecution; it was plain that he meant the accused to escape, and they were acquitted. I think it was Maule's last appearance on any Circuit; he certainly never appeared again upon ours. His name in Derbyshire *non redolet sed olet*. With all his scorn of popularity-hunting, I doubt if he would have faced another meeting with the gentlemen and magistrates of Bagshawe's indignant county. In those times the invitation to the Grand Jury dinner, given by the judges to the magistrates on the first business day of the assizes, would have served as an opportunity for snubbing the Judge. Hecatombs of fatlings and oxen would have failed to appease the wrath of Bagshawe's friends and admirers, with whom and their descendants the bare mention of Maule's name is to this day 'maranatha.' No one has ever attempted to palliate the Judge's conduct in my hearing.

I am tempted at this point to 'travel out of the record,' as lawyers say, and to give my readers a few particulars concerning the Judge whose prejudices were stronger than his impartiality. His cynical and witty sayings, though casually and imperfectly recorded, are more familiar in legal history than his great attainments as a scholar and a mathematician. Everyone knows that he was Senior Wrangler and Fellow of Trinity, Cambridge — such honours are lifelong certificates of college distinction; few are aware of his classical attainments. The late Lord Coleridge told me more than once that, when he was acting as his father's marshal on circuit, Maule being the junior judge, the latter offered to 'coach' him in the 'Agamemnon' of Æschylus. 'I was reading for my degree at the time,' he said, 'and Maule's lecture was the best I ever had on the subject.'

The biography of this eminent man is wretchedly meagre. It has been suggested that there was some mystery connected with his youth. I venture to think that the early death of a younger brother, to whom he was devoted, and whose education he had assisted by frequent correspondence with the lad in undergraduate days, prematurely soured him, and made him on the Bench an object of terror to young practitioners. At the Bar, too, he certainly was an awkward customer. No judge could muzzle him in his Oxford Circuit days. He bearded Baron Parke at Stafford as remorselessly as Erskine flew at Buller in the famous libel case at Durham. The Baron chafed, snorted, and puffed out his cheeks in vain: to repress Maule was a hopeless task. If the judge was loud and fierce, counsel was louder and fiercer. Some wag in court, fresh from the humanities of the University, recorded his impression of the *mauled* Baron in two quaint Iambics:

ἤκουσα πρώην ἐν δόμοισι κορτίοις
φωνὴν βαρῶνος ἐντόνως μεμαυλμένον.

He was often on the Midland Circuit in his judicial days. Though fearful of warming up 'old chestnuts,' I am not aware that the three following stories have ever been seen in print before; two of them are incidental to the records of Warwick and Coventry assizes. Maule's appearance in court, if the weather were cold, was almost grotesque, his scarlet robes being frequently overlaid with a short, old-fashioned blue cloak, with brass clasps. No outsider would have divined for a moment that the wheezy, asthmatic, parti-coloured magistrate before him was a genius in his way, intellectually inferior to none of his contemporaries on the Bench, though 'there were giants on the earth in those days.' Some Justice Shallow, in the person of a Warwickshire magistrate, had committed a little boy for 'highway robbery with violence,' and Maule was never happier than in reducing things to absurdity, if the occasion offered, and there was a good and appreciative gallery. The case was called on, and the prisoner summoned to appear. A very small head, supposed to represent that of a big desperado, Joseph Johnson by name, was faintly discoverable over the front of the dock.

'Where is he?' grunted Maule from the Bench. 'I can't see him. Stand up, Highwayman Joe!'

Joseph's release from bondage was a certainty from the moment that Maule, with assumed difficulty, had realized his existence. I believe it was on the Midland Circuit that Maule's summing-up of evidence to character in a particular case was thought to be a model of brevity and incisiveness. On the trial of a man caught *flagrante delicto* stealing a ham, counsel called several witnesses to the character of his client for honesty. The Judge sat listlessly until his turn came, and this was the summing-up: 'Gentlemen of the jury, here is a man of irreproachable character who has stolen a ham. What do you say?' The owner of the ham was speedily avenged.

Coventry has for many years ceased to be an assize town — I beg Coventry's pardon, I should have said 'city.' At the time I speak of, the Judges' lodgings were so unhealthy and ill-drained that the subject became a common topic in judicial charges on the first day of the assizes, though nothing was done to remedy the evil. Maule watched for his opportunity. He was presiding in the Crown Court, and the civic authorities *pleno ficu* were in attendance. A sheep-stealer was summoned to the Bar.

The skin and some part of the carcase of the animal were produced in evidence. It was a hot summer's day, and the stench was intolerable. Maule, holding his nose, said :

'Take that skin to our drawing-room at the Judges' lodgings; it won't matter there!'

One would have thought that this very palpable hint would have spurred the magistrates to action, but no alterations were made, and the sheepskin failing to deodorize the 'ancient and fish-like smells' which had nauseated the Bench for years past endurance, it fell to the lot of Sir J. T. Coleridge to give Coventry the *coup de grâce*. He fined the Sheriff £500, and the city of Godiva saw no more of the judges of the land. There are many consolations left to the citizens, whose fortunes have varied in different ages. For the moment bicycles, canaries and cheap watches are valuable and popular investments there. New courts, new lodgings, and more fragrant, may be built, and Judges of Assize in the twentieth century, travelling on 'bykes' or flying to Warwickshire in balloons, may once more send justice to Coventry — who shall say? If Creswell's method of summing up to a rustic jury was described by a casual listener as 'the Almighty lecturing twelve black-beetles,' it may be assumed that Maule's estimate of the four judges who were to listen to his argument was not much higher. By way of training, he ordered for luncheon a beef-steak and strong beer, and to a friend who expressed surprise that any counsel should indulge in such solid fare with an afternoon of hard work before him, replied: 'You see, my dear fellow, I must eat and drink myself down to the level of the judges before me.' The words, passing swiftly through the walls of the common room, were hawked about by reporters and gossips. Though the river of Lethe is said to flow between the Bar and the Bench, they were soon wafted across the stream, and reached the ears of the four inferior gentlemen so lightly esteemed by the well-fed advocate who was addressing them. One of these was equal to the emergency. This was Sir Edward Hall Alderson, Baron of the Exchequer, Senior Wrangler, and Chancellor's Medallist, whose Cambridge antecedents are to this day the legitimate boast of Caius College.

Maule came before him a few days after his

beef and strong beer *pronunciamento*, and there was a very pretty duel between the two logicians. Maule was beaten, and at the close of the argument, Alderson added quietly: 'You have not had your beef and beer to-day, Mr. Maule.'

One more story, and positively the last. My authority for it was the late Mr. Justice Denman; the episode belongs to the Western Circuit. Some county magnate, with a bad cook and an inferior cellar, was rash enough to invite the dyspeptic Maule to dinner. It was about as jovial an entertainment as the Chancellor's breakfast, for which Lord Bowen in 1883 thus prepared himself by soliciting a seat in Mr. Justice Mathew's brougham to take him to the scene of awful mirth.

'COLWOOD,
  'HAYWARDS HEATH,
    'SUSSEX.

'My dear J. C.,
  Will you be free
  To carry me
  Beside of thee
  In your buggee
  To Selborne's tea?
  If breakfast he
  Intends for we

> On 2 November next (D.V.),
> Eighteen hundred and eighty-three,
> A.D.
> For Lady B.
> From Cornwall G.
> Will absent be,
> And says that she
> Would rather see
> Her husband be—
> D dash dash D
> Than send to London her buggee
> For such a melancholy spree
> As Selborne's toast and Selborne's tea.'

After dinner was over, he called, or rather grunted, for brandy.

The host, quite alarmed: 'Is there anything I can send for for your lordship? You are ill, I fear?'

Maule: 'Not at all; it's only the effect of a little wine upon an empty stomach.'

I ask pardon for this digression anent the eccentricities of the Judge, whose administration, or maladministration, of justice in the *cause célèbre* of the Bagshawe murder has never been forgotten in the county of Derby.

CHAPTER IV.

THE CAPTAIN OF THE BOATS—AN UNLUCKY CHALLENGE FROM WESTMINSTER—SOME SPECIMENS OF ENGLISH PROSE.

THE uninitiated can but faintly appreciate the glory, ephemeral though dazzling, which radiated from the captain of the boats, stroke of the *Monarch* (more popularly called the *Ten-Oar*), and supreme arbiter of all questions incidental to aquatics, and to the races in the summer half. His influence was felt outside the various crews who bowed to his jurisdiction, for he used to play *ex officio* in the annual cricket-match between the collegers and oppidans, and, in return for this distinction, now and then took into the crew of the *Monarch* a 'courtesy,' meaning thereby an inefficient oar in the shape of a popular dry-bob. I remember being greatly excited and pleased by an invitation sent to my friend Cheales and myself to row in the *Victory* on a 'check night';* it was meant as a compliment, and accepted as such.

Arundell was captain of the boats in my first year at Eton, and in his admiral's uniform, cocked hat, and gold-laced trousers on the fourth of June and Election Saturday, he loomed so largely in my imagination as partially to divide my homage with Emilius Bayley, the captain of the eleven. The latter was my chief idol, for the cricketing instinct was dominant in my family for two generations; five of us Coleridges were in the eleven, only one in the eight, though the late Lord Chief Justice was in the first flight of scullers both at Eton and Oxford. His brother Henry, too, was a very pretty bat, and only just missed getting his 'blue.' Though deprecating the fetish worship of athletics, 'perfections which are placed in bones and nerves,' I remember with wholesome pride the brilliant lads who scouted the very idea of being *fainéants* and loafers. It was delightful to

* So called because of the check shirts worn by the rowers.

read in Lord Blachford's 'Memoirs' of Arthur Hallam taking a 'header' from Windsor Bridge, a feat very seldom attempted by any but professional experts. When the news of Ferrers' Senior Wranglership arrived at Eton, Stephen Hawtrey's pupils cheered to the echo, none the less lustily from the fact that the mathematician's undeniably fine 'headers' at 'Athens' were the admiration of his contemporaries, and in some mysterious and unexplained way were supposed to have helped him in trigonometry and conic sections. We trumped the Harrow boast of Byron's swimming the Hellespont with Sir John's Patteson's historical swim from Windsor to Staines—an exploit to which the old Judge often alluded in my hearing. 'Angelo's* water-rats' were famous in their day, and Bishop Selwyn, a sort of tutelar god of the river in my time, was the successor of Thomas Sherlock, Bishop of London, a contemporary of Lord Townshend, Henry Pelham, and Robert Walpole. Pope in the 'Dunciad' calls him 'the plunging Prelate'; he was violently attacked by Bolingbroke in the

---

* Angelo kept a dame's house.

'Dissertation on Parties' for defending the measures of Sir Robert Walpole, who used to relate that when some of the scholars, going to bathe in the Thames, were standing shivering on the bank, Sherlock would plunge in immediately over his head and ears.

Speaking generally of captains of the boats, I have no wish to vilipend the order when I say that in most instances they were not distinguished outside their special vocation. They seldom initiated, though they frequently initialled themes and verses. If a 'purple patch' occurred anywhere, it was the work of one of the many henchmen who were always at the beck and call of the stroke of the *Ten-Oar*. I fear it was a boating-man who was guilty of the hexameters on Daniel in the lions' den:

' Cras rex Solque simul surgunt, rex advenit antrum
Et voce exclamat magnâ, " Nunc, si potes, exi ! "
Respondet Daniel, " Rex, vive in sæcula cuncta."'

If the quality of the boating-man's Latin verse was of an inferior order, his poetry in the mother tongue was usually on the same level. The captain of the boats generally godfathered a 'Vale' of some sort, and confided the poetical embodiment of his sorrows on leaving Eton to more than one auxiliary bard. There was a stock phrase for collecting this patchwork of vicarious emotion; it was called 'taking the hat round,' and when the contributions had filled the hat full enough of lugubrious verses, some expert was employed to piece the motley poem together, and to conceal the stitches as best he could. Posterity has not lost much by the suppression of these 'Vales,' which were watery in every sense of the epithet. The author was supposed to drop the tributary tear over Bargeman's Bush, Brocas Clump, Upper Hope, and the Rushes. Perhaps two stanzas would do for promontories, eyots, Windsor Bridge, and Clewer. The ducks and green peas would probably have a stanza to themselves, and there would be a passing allusion to Henry VI. as he appeared in a blaze of fireworks. The 'sitters' were sure to be commemorated if they had been liberal with their Perrier Jouet, or Heidseck's Dry Monopole, called by my friend Canon Kynaston '*ficti doloris pocula*'

—*i.e.*, 'cups of sham pain.' I saw this fragment in a 'Vale' on the desk of a tutor's pupil-room :

> 'Farewell unto my studies, too,
>   Though I confess my knowing
> Has chiefly been confined unto
>   The principles of rowing.
>
> If summer half's a Paradise
>   Which everyone is sweet on,
> All I say is, if I have one,
>   I'll send my son to Eton.'

Talking of 'sitters,' we small boys were taught to believe as a fact in Eton history that Canning had honoured the *Ten-Oar* as a 'sitter' on June 4, 1824. Through the kindness of Mr. Arundell, with whom it has been my good fortune to exchange several letters, I have now ascertained that for once in our lives we lower boys were correct. From information supplied in a Boating Calendar, I find that Canning 'sat' in the *Ten-Oar* on June 4, 1824, and that he was in great excitement at the danger of being bumped as the boats rowed through Windsor Bridge. We were credulous enough to expect that the Prince Consort would follow his example, assist at the 'cold collation' at Surley, and watch the members of the different crews handing over their shoulders eleemosynary lobster-claws, or fragments of pigeon-pie, to their younger brothers or friends. We were assured and piously believed that Arundell felt awfully nervous at the prospect of his responsibilities, and at this distance of time I think the state of his nerves, if they really were agitated, highly creditable to him, for the captain and the 'sitter' were close to one another in the boat. The soundest-timbered old *Ten-Oar* might spring a leak and go down like the *Royal George;* and what if His Royal Highness, like Admiral Kempenfeldt, went down also? If the Prince could not take headers, it followed in our minds that he could not swim; so pity and admiration were bestowed without stint or a particle of reason on the captain of the boats in the face of coming events which cast purely imaginary shadows before them. A contemporary of mine, of whom I inquired if he remembered Arundell, replied: 'I remember him in a brown and brass coat at speeches.' How oddly this would strike the present black-coated generation! I myself remember my hero as a strong-built powerful Cornishman, his arms all 'mus.' This was a quality so highly esteemed at Eton, that a pocket Hercules, kneeling in chapel, would nudge his neighbour in a slack moment of devotion and whisper to him: 'I say, Stephen, feel my "mus"!' and, doubling up his arms to make the muscles protuberate, would challenge the future Judge's admiration. If Arundell was an ordinary sample of the bulk of Cornishmen, I understand how it was that Lord Exmouth, in 1793, stipulated for an importation of eighty Cornish miners as the crew of his frigate the *Nymph*, and after drilling them for the space of one week, went forth and captured the French frigate *Cleopatra*, the crack ship of France, 40 guns and 320 men, commanded by Captain Mallon, one of the ablest officers in the French marine. 'We dished her up,' Pellew wrote, 'in fifty minutes, boarded, and she struck her colours.' It was a glorious action. 'I never doubted,' said Lord Howe, 'that you would take a French frigate, but the manner in which you have done it will establish an example for the war.' The smoke of St. Vincent, the Nile, and Trafalgar, have blinded the eyes of the nation to the glory of Lord Exmouth's victory as completely as Quatre Bras and Waterloo have outshone 'the beautiful battle of Sauroren.'

Singularly enough, in one of his letters Mr. Arundell himself describes an accident to the *Ten-Oar*, which he stroked for two years consecutively. These are his words: 'The "sitters" in my time were Lord Ward and my father—in the latter case he was in an awkward fix, for coming down from Surley we swamped a four-oar (which got directly across our bows under Windsor Bridge), cutting the boat in two. The crew managed to land on the cobbler. Our boat was not much damaged, and we had to get to Tolladay's raft in the best manner we could—all our toggery, and the governor's, too, rather soppy!' So, as I said before, the fourth-form imagination was not so baseless as usual, seeing that the ducking of H.R.H. *vice* Arundell *père* was a possible if not probable contingency.

In Keates' time no master went to the riverside on June 4 or Election Saturday; but it was supposed that they came *incognito* to see the fireworks. For the river was out of bounds, all but the sixth-form having to shirk the masters, and all lower boys to shirk the sixth-form.

Since 1860 boys have been free to go where they like within certain restrictions of time. Keates' innocence of the display on the Brocas was as complete as Hawtrey's of the theatricals in Long Chamber. He addressed the captain of the boats thus: 'You know I know nothing—I have *heard* you are in authority. Lock-up time will be twenty minutes later than usual; it is your customary privilege.' In the early days of the present century a waterman stroked and drilled all the crews, except those of the *Monarch* and the *Dreadnought*. The *Hibernia* was reserved for Irishmen. In 1821 the second boat was called the *Nelson*, and before 1814 the rowers sported the most extravagant fancy dresses, appearing as Highlanders, Swiss peasants, galley-slaves. I suppose that when real business began, in the first race with Westminster in 1829, all these follies were banished for ever.

It was said that there was a captain of the boats in my time who had the misfortune to compromise the character of wet bobs as men of letters by deputing Billy Goodman, a boat-builder on the Brocas, to write the answer to the ordinary challenge sent by Westminster. To go to Billy Goodman for literary inspiration on an occasion for a more or less public letter was an error for which we were sorely punished, seeing that Eton's answer was carefully preserved. It will be seen that Billy Goodman, the oracle, and the captain who consulted him, had not modelled their style on Addison. The fatal document provoked the satire of *Punch*. Here are *Punch's* observations :

'*Correspondence between Eton and Westminster.*

'These two great nurseries for British Statesmen have been corresponding through two of their senior pupils on the glorious subject of a rowing match. Westminster writes a tolerably business-like note, but Eton soars far, very far, above the trammels of Lindley Murray. It is true that public schools teach only Latin and Greek, which may account for the fact that Eton cannot write English. We give from recollection a specimen of the style of Eton, and we beg the public to bear in mind that a lot of Eton boys are the chief characters in Mr. d'Israeli's young England novel of "Coningsby." Westminster having written to inquire whether Eton will enter into a rowing match,

Eton, in the name of one of its scholars, thus replied to Westminster :

'" DEAR SIR,

'" I don't know what you mean to say when I read your letter, which I think very absurd. I don't suppose you wrote what you have said in your note, because the match, in the way you propose, is a very strange manner of doing things, which all who have seen it say they think as I do. I hope you will tell me you did not write your last letter, because then if you do, I shall be able to understand it better than if you did, which I must say I do not, nor do I see very well how you could have thought how that I ever could.

'" Believe me, dear sir,

'" Yours very truly,

'" ——.

'" ETON."

'To the above communication the Westminster captain pithily replied that he retracted nothing, and would publish everything. Considering that Eton gives so many members to the Senate, can we be surprised at the wretched manner in which those who speak in Parliament are often found to express themselves? It is to be regretted that Sir James Graham did not on this occasion practise his letter-opening propensities, for if he had intercepted the Eton part of the correspondence he might have saved the credit of the College. We should suggest that every Eton grammar should have stitched on to the end of it a copy of the "Complete Letter-Writer."'

There was no race at all in consequence of these blunders, and of the bad management of our illiterate captain, whose performances have been recorded by a Westminster contemporary in language which is studiously moderate and courteous. 'The Eton captain attributed his refusal of the challenge to the inability of two of his selected eight to row, and met the Westminster suggestion that they were prepared to row Eton with any number of oars, or in any denomination of boat usual in matches, with a stolid *non possumus*, which annoyed his own school as much as his challenger. His second captain offered to get up an eight to row Westminster—an offer which of course had to be declined, but worthy of the chivalrous reputation of the great school.'

Billy Goodman, as ship-builder, was no more reliable than he was as a despatch writer, for in 1845 he persisted in building a racing boat on antique principles; when it appeared on the course, London watermen reckoned it 'not a bad boat for a provincial.' The Westminster eight appeared in a new out-rigger, fifty-five feet in length, and about two and a half in the beam, constructed by Noulton. A Westminster bard had prophesied our defeat:

> 'Let Eton boast their Luttrell dear,
>   His style, his strength, and eke his weight;
> We hope to find the captain here
>   Quite Good-enough to suit their eight.'

July 19, 1845.

He suited our crew much too well, for we were badly beaten.

I have seen holiday tasks, written nearly half a century later, which rival Eton prose, as represented by Billy Goodman, in the Forties. The writer of the first seems to have been asked a series of questions, the subject being

Lord Clive.

1.

2. 'Clive was born in the South of England, in the county of Dorsetshire, at a town near

the south-east, which is not particularly famous nowaday. The year of his birth was about Anno Domini 1750, from which time he was always particularly enterprising. His father was a private gentleman in the county of Dorsetshire. He was in the occupation of a farmer, but the old man's descent was not very high. In after years he behaved very badly to all his relatives by taking them prisoners in his wars, and slaying some of them even, so that he behaved very badly to them.

3. 'Lord Clive was connected with the Tower, where he kept several of his prisoners. This great and venerable building is in London beyond the City end.

4.

5.

6.

7. 'Lord Clive was a very bad manager in his money matters, as he was somes very scrupulous, and at others spent his money a random.

(i.) 'With regard to himself, he spent lots, bought everything he could think of for himself, and always thought of himself.

(ii.) 'With regard to the servants of the Company, he was very stingy, and so he got very disliked. He would never see that anything was wanting which anyone else thought, and so got into trouble.

8. 'Lord Clive visited India three times, twice by sea, once by land.

9. 'Lord Clive killed himself.'

HOLIDAY TASK.—THE REFORMATION.

'England at one time was very bad. You found gentlemen drunk early in the morning, and you used to see men rolling about the streets. The reformation took place in the time of Henry the Eight. The morals and manners of England was also very bad in Henry's reign.'

HOLIDAY TASK.—WARREN HASTINGS.

'Warren Hastings was born from a man of low degree, who had risen into the world a little by labour and honesty. His father was a very poor man when he first married, but, as I have said, gained money by labour. Warren Hastings rose to be Governor of India by honesty, and making himself known to all the chief men of England and Scotland, and was elected 1751. Warren Hastings, says Macaulay, was of good reputation in the state.

He was pleasant, talkative, and temperate, but he liked to have his own way in some things, which was a great pity, as it spoilt his other good faculties. He was very sober, never drinking much.'

This last specimen of a boy's essay was shown to me by a brilliant Etonian, *donatus rude* as an assistant master, but the author, I fancy, hailed from a private school.

'Breath is made of air. We breathe with our lungs, our lights, our livers, and our kidneys. If it wasn't for our breath we should die when we slept. Our breath keeps the life going through the nose when we are asleep. Boys that stay in a room all day should not breathe—they should wait till they get outdoors. Boys in a room make carbonicide, carbonicide is more poisonous than mad dogs. A heap of soldiers was in a black hole in India, and carbonicide got in that black hole, and killed nearly every one afore morning. Girls kill the breath by corsets that squeeze their diagrams. Girls can't run and holler like boys, because their diagram is squeezed too much. If I was a girl I rather be a boy, so I can run and holler and have a good big diagram.'

CHAPTER V.

THE FIRST RACE BETWEEN ETON AND WESTMINSTER—A VICTORY AND A DEFEAT—ELECTION SATURDAY.

I HAVE never ceased to regret the abandonment of the old historical race of Eton and Westminster; the winning of the Ladies' Challenge Plate at Henley, or a victory of our lads over a Brazenose crew, kindles but a spark of emotion in us old fellows. Here is an extract from *Bell's Life*, describing the first race between Eton and Westminster on July 27, 1829:

'The Etonians and their friends arrived at Putney in a commodious carriage, with four handsome bays; the Westminster scholars in an open barouche, with four grays. Brumwell, of Vauxhall, steered the Westminsters; Mr. T. Honey, of Lambeth, was coxswain for Eton. This latter circumstance had a material effect on the betting, for it was well known that no individual could be appointed to the station who possessed more scientific knowledge in "handling the lines" than Mr. Honey. . . . Forty or fifty gentlemen on horseback accompanied the crews along the whole line of the towing-path. Eton won by a quarter of a mile; the course was from Putney Bridge through Hammersmith Bridge, and down through the centre-arch of Putney Bridge.

'Both parties had been some time in active training—the Eton gentlemen in the *Britannia*, built by Archer of Lambeth, and the Westminster scholars in the new eight, which was built by Searle for the Cantabs in their late match with the Oxonians at Henley. Heavy betting took place in favour of the Westminster gentlemen previous to the start, and the interest which this juvenile contest excited among the numerous relatives and friends of the contending parties was, perhaps, never surpassed on any similar occasion. Both parties appeared full of confidence. Six o'clock was the hour named for the start, but it was some time after that hour before the parties took their stations. . . . The Etonians pulled up to the bridge in broad blue-striped Guernsey frocks, and dark straw

hats with blue ribbon—true sailor fashion—
with the celebrated Mr. T. Honey as coxswain.
The Westminster scholars appeared at the
bridge in very neat trim, the whole wearing
white shirts and straw hats, Brumwell acting
as steerer. The toss for station having been
won by the Etonians, Mr. Honey took his
place from a pier on the Middlesex side. On
the signal being given, they went away in style,
accompanied along the whole line of the towing-
path by between forty and fifty gentlemen on
horseback, the majority of whom wore a piece
of blue ribbon in the buttonhole of their coats.
The Westminster gentlemen went ahead at
starting by about a boat's length, and continued
the lead up the river for nearly half a mile, when
the Etonians came opposite their opponents,
and by some well-timed exertions on the part
of the rowers, and a degree of science on that
of the coxswain, the *Britannia* was brought out
in a slanting direction; and notwithstanding
the skill displayed by Brumwell, who nearly
succeeded in bringing the nose of his boat on
the quarter of that of the opposite party, as she
was shooting by, the Eton gentlemen went
well ahead, and maintained it throughout the

distance, gallantly winning by about a quarter of a mile.'

Now for the sad story of our defeat on June 20, 1837, as told by the late 'Billy' Rogers:

'This was a memorable race; Eton had never been beaten before. The King was present, and declared the Eton boys lost because Dr. Hawtrey was looking on. The Eton boys, in their turn, said their defeat was the immediate cause of the King's illness. On the morning of the race, His Majesty had said to Lord Howe, "What carriage shall I have to-day?" The answer was: "Your Majesty ought not to go out; you are too unwell." But he meant, he said, to see the match. I remember well his figure seated in a closed carriage, wrapped in a white great-coat, about a hundred and fifty yards from the bridge. As soon as he saw that the Westminsters were ahead, he pulled down the blinds and drove back to the Castle, which I do not think he afterwards left. The race was at Datchet, and Westminster won by six or eight boats' length.'

The last Summer half! Who can forget it?

'Oh! dass sie ewig grünen bliebe
Die schöne Zeit!'

A friend of mine, attending the service in Eton Chapel on Election Sunday, heard a pathetic sermon addressed more particularly to the boys on the eve of leaving school; some of them wept—none rebuked them nor thought them childish. The *fête* on Election Saturday which, in my day, was an exact repetition of that on June 4, had more pathos for me than brightness. There were many farewells—no presentiments as yet of Crimean War or Indian Mutiny, where Eton blood flowed freely, but a dim feeling of Paradise lost, vague uncertainty, darkness ahead. Outsiders may call it sentimentality—they are welcome to the sneer. The author of *the* Boating-Song is the best interpreter of the conflicting emotions so common to all Etonians in the closing days of their last Summer half.

'*Election Saturday, July* 25, 1868.

' I went at 8.15 in the glow of sunset up the river to meet the boats coming down. I met swarms and lines of boys coming down. For the most part I escaped them by keeping to the right, favoured by the twilight; but some of them saw me. However, I went on like a ghost, silent, looking at no one, bent only on keeping my freedom, my right to go against the stream, my right to see the pretty sight of the long boats and their curtseying flags come out of locks in the light that suits my eyes; all the vulgarity of their singing did not kill the beauty of their movements. The band—a vile band—played the old 4th June tune which Scott Holland used to like. There was a half-moon on the right, queening it in spite of rowdies; and I saw a dear form in a light-blue coat standing up to take the Henley crew through the crowd of inferior boats. I stood alone, watching, listening, rehearsing the part of a discharged usher. They got clear of each other, and with my glasses I followed their curves of movement far down the dear river. I thought of young men quartered in Indian hill-forts, droning in twos or singly through a steaming night, miserably remembering their last row at Eton, pining and craving for lost youthfulness. I, all the while, know that I am as youthful in feeling and in enjoying as the noisy lads in these boats. Presently I was in absolute solitude, sitting on a well-known stile, watching the rockets cross the breadth of South

Meadow and Brocas. Now and then a fixed firework blazed up so as to show what I knew to be a mass of people looking on from the bank, and their cheers were transfigured into pure joy at that distance. Clewer Tower in the background; behind a spiritual after-glow; on my right lady-moon; wind up stream, letting the little meteors fall slowly, well above the crowd.'

Election Saturday was undoubtedly a time of reconciliation for thoughtful boys, who, 'if a cloud had supervened on their original amity,' recognized the fact that now or never would that cloud be dispersed. It would soon be too late—Smith must go to India, Brown to China, Jones to Woolwich, Cooper to an attorney's office. Assuming two of them to have been Collegers, and the other two Oppidans, and that they had mercilessly hacked and shinned one another at football, or cherished apparently incurable antipathies—still the last hours of their last half not seldom culminated in a day of atonement. It was 'a gracious and a hallowed time,' belying a famous pentameter by my friend Canon Kynaston:

> 'Non est multus amor perditus inter eos.'

But the leave-taking of the members of the same pupil-room, in the presence of their tutor, has been sketched by a masterly hand:

'A. and others stayed a good time, talking in the ordinary way—no confessional—and one by one they shook hands; first, N. L., veiling his grief at leaving school in his quaint, hard, stoic manner, shaking hands with X.; they used to hate each other, but have been great friends this summer. Then R. H. spent some time with me, copying out two of his honoured exercises into my book whilst I did business. M. L. came, and his shyness did not prevent my saying what I wished to say to him. But to H. I could say nothing: now that I am writing about it, I cannot bear to think that he is lost.'

CHAPTER VI.

*MY TUTOR'S DOGS—JACK SPARROW, THE WATERMAN—
THE DUKE OF BEAUFORT'S DOGS—CHARLEY WISE
—SPANKIE.*

My recollections of the boat-races at Eton would be incomplete without a few words anent Bear, my tutor's famous dog, who, from the time that he could run, never missed a boat-race during his long and well-remembered career. My tutor brought him as a puppy from the monastery of the Great St. Bernard; he was buried under the sycamore-tree on the lawn of the old house (now Ainger's) in Keate's Lane. Why, with such a majestic animal before us, the prejudices of some few should have been in favour of small dogs, I cannot say, but I remember that at my dame's, and at Cambridge afterwards, we grew rapturous over two little mongrels called Crab and Tigser, palliating the absurdity by crediting these two curs with a purely fictitious pedigree. Crab and Tigser were declared to be 'well-bred' dogs, which of course they were not, whereas Bear was a real St. Bernard without a blot on his scutcheon, and such a public character that Landseer came all the way from London to Eton on purpose to paint him. I should like to have witnessed his introduction to my tutor, who was hand and glove with his neighbours, the painters Evans and Nesfield, and greatly affected the society of all artists. George Richmond was a constant visitor at his house. My tutor's drawing-room was resplendent with Turner, Stanfield, and Mulready. He certainly did not welcome Landseer after the fashion of the King of Portugal, who began conversation thus: 'Delighted to make acquaintance with you, Mr. Landseer, for I am very fond of all kinds of beasts.' My brother remembers seeing the painter at Eton dip his fingers in an ink-bottle, and without a pen, much less a paint-brush, leave on a sheet of paper a finer representation of a dog than any photographer could aspire to make. In the picture which Landseer and his brother were commissioned to paint for my tutor were three of my cousins, one of them sitting astride old Bear. The pet of the Coleridge household was a prime favourite with all 'wet-bobs,' for on the evening of a boat-race, directly after the gun was fired as a signal for the start, Bear rushed off with the runners on the bank, and yelled and barked his approval at the winning boat directly it forged ahead of the adversary. He had no sympathy with defeat, and knowing that the crucial moment of the race was at the turning-point of the Rushes, reserved his loudest barks for the winners, at the moment when the danger was passed. Bear was so devoted to aquatic sports that no distance prevented him from attending the Eton and Westminster boat-race. His appearance at Maidenhead, Datchet, or Putney, was a matter of course, and on one famous occasion he had the good luck to meet some triumphant Etonians, who decorated him with a light-blue rosette, and sent him off to Eton at best pace, the first ἄγγελος to announce our victory. He had a great ovation; everybody liked him—some tried to draw him, and illustrated the Greek oath, μὰ τὸν κύνα, by sketching him on the margin of their Phædo. A more ambitious illustrator would embellish the words '*odora canum vis*,' or '*Molossus aut fulvus Laco*' with pictures of the smaller dogs— Pepsy, Toby, Dash, Dandy—familiar to everyone who haunted Keate's Lane. None of these, however, attained the old dog's measure of popularity, though they were frequently seen of a summer's morning, as they lagged at the heels of Charles Coleridge, on his way to the Playing-Fields and the Masters' Weir for his morning bath. At the sixth-form Bench the punt was in waiting, manned by Jack Sparrow, ready to take the intending bathers across to the Masters' Weir; the small pack of hounds always swam across as best it could. Good old Jack! of course his name was fatal. We called him *Passer, deliciæ meæ puellæ*, and if he stumbled in his punt, overcrowded as it was with gudgeon fishers, some wretch would call Hamlet to the rescue, and observe that 'there was a special Providence in the fall of a sparrow.' He was my favourite waterman. It was pretty to see him resign the punt-pole to Bishop Selwyn, so often his own Palinurus in Pacific seas, and now, after long years in New Zealand, revisiting the old Bush over which he used to take his headers into the Weir.

Two of my tutor's dogs died prematurely, and on one special occasion the peace of the household was disturbed by a rumour that Brenda had been poisoned by a tramp, or by some one maliciously inclined. She had been done for—so much was certain, for what was once Brenda lay lifeless at the foot of the steps of my tutor's pupil-room, and some of us were present at the funeral oration. The upper boys had been reading in 'private business' Pericles' funeral oration in Thucydides' and another section the 'Ajax' of Sophocles; so the dear tutor's lament was a curious *mélange*, dashed with hearty anathemas of all dog-haters, and regrets tinged with classical allusion. On a hot summer's afternoon my tutor and Cookesley would exchange the black coat for a light dressing-gown, and, thus clothed, would sit in their studies, looking over themes and verses. It was in this costume that E. C. appeared, surveying the corpse of poor Brenda. I remember one sentence: 'If money can track thy slayer, dear dog, it shall be forthcoming!' and there was more in the same Sophoclean strain. We were prepared for a tag from the grand finale of Pericles—' And now let everyone, having mourned as much as is becoming, take his departure '—but it would not have had much effect. Brenda's demise was not keenly felt; our heart was in Bear's grave.

Toby died suddenly and unaccountably—so mysterious was his exit, that a post-mortem was peremptorily ordered by the owner. The result of the autopsy was peculiar, for poor Toby had made a meal off one shirt or more, illustrated with pictures of Taglioni the *danseuse* and choked himself in the process. This form of suicide was reckoned so abnormal and diverting that we admired the dog's originality; so, far from eclipsing the gaiety of the pupil-room, poor dear Toby added to it very considerably. The funny dog is usually an unconscious animal, not the poor mesmerized, half-starved creature which goes round sniffing in a circle, picking out the ace of spades at the bidding of a cruel owner. My dear friend Archbishop Benson had a dog called Watch. One night, at prayers in the private chapel attached to Lambeth Palace, the animal had stolen in unobserved amongst the servants and others forming the domestic congregation. The Primate took part in the service by reading a few verses from Scripture, and he paused with a natural accent over the words, 'And what I say unto you I say unto all, *Watch*,' whereupon the dog emerged at a bound from his hiding-place, and, suddenly presenting himself before his master, seemed to say: 'Well, it's rather odd you should want me here, but here I am!'

Good old Bear's attachment to Eton and Windsor had been anticipated, some few years before his time, by an aristocratic pair of dogs which were smuggled into College by the then Marquis of Worcester, the present Duke of Beaufort. His Grace, writing to the *Times* quite recently, tells an interesting story about the homing instincts of his contraband pets. 'In the summer of 1838 I was a boy at Eton; I had two bloodhounds, a dog and a bitch, both four or five years of age. I kept them at a livery-stable. I received a hint (from Harry Dupuis) that I must not keep them. So I wrote to a friend at Brighton, who agreed to receive them. I settled with the coachman of the Windsor and Brighton coach to take them. They were slung on the hind axle in a large hamper. Twice on the road he gave them water, the last time, four miles from Brighton, where the road from Leatherhead and Dorking joins the one from Horley and Crawley. When the coach got to Brighton the hamper was empty. Between eight and nine the next morning both the bloodhounds were in my room at my dame's in Eton.' The return of the prodigals will be fully appreciated. There's no place like home, particularly if that happens to be at Eton—a kennel with Charley Wise to look after it, and an occasional visit to the 'room at my dame's,' were the limits of earthly felicity to those well-bred patrician animals.

Who was Charley Wise? When I say that he was the one livery-stable-keeper at Eton, his unique position will be better understood. All 'horsey' boys, all the coming dragoons and hussars, all followers of the 'wily animal,' paid willing homage to C. W., and 'man,' Southey says, 'is like a trout, and can be caught by tickling.' So Charley sniffed up the admiration of the youthful sportsmen, who regarded him as Sir Oracle in all questions affecting cavalry manœuvres, favourites for the Ascot Cup, etc. We thought much more of him than of Admiral Rous as an infallible handicapper or judge of horseflesh. Charley, with his piercing eye for hock and shoulder, was supposed by us to detect in an unclipped Yorkshire filly the Flying Dutchman or Beeswing *in futuro;* and from his more than Papal infallibility in racing matters he was equally esteemed as a judge of cavalry tactics. On review days in Windsor Park the gifted livery-stable man was sure to be present, strenuously enforcing his candid criticisms of the cavalry manœuvres on fourth-form questioners. Charley was quite equal to slating a Murat, Sir Stapleton Cotton, or Hussey Vivian. 'I say, Charley, don't the Lancers charge splendidly!' 'Lor', bless ye, that Colonel Pennycuick, as they call him, don't know 'is business, and as for them Blues and Cherubims, why, they're hall hover the place! Never see'd such a mess in my life!' All of which froth and blather passed with the lower boys for sound military criticism.

My faith in Charley Wise was once rudely shaken, though I think it likely enough that my amateur coachmanship of his hired cattle brought about what the lawyers call 'contributory negligence.' At the end of the summer half in 1847 it occurred to H. Aitkin and myself—the oppidan and colleger captains of the eleven—that it would be a sporting and possibly useful thing for one of us to drive to Harrow and watch the play of our adversaries in a match on their own ground. So Buckleigh *mi.* and I—having got leave for our expedition—chartered a dog-cart, and a young horse warranted by the oracular Charley as several degrees quieter than a lamb. All went smoothly enough on our way to the scene of action; it was at Slough, on our return to Eton, that the lamb's home instincts, apparently for no rhyme or reason, lashed him into a furious gallop, and he made for the distant towers like a racer. I urged Buckleigh to shout and warn any carts or carriages that might collide with our machine, which dashed through the High Street, mercifully encountering no obstacles, and ended by crashing full tilt through the Windsor Bridge turnpike. The lamb was caught at the top of Windsor Hill. Buckleigh and I were thrown out of our carriage on opposite sides, each supposing the other to be killed. We were within an ace of a serious catastrophe—so serious, indeed, that my old friend, Frank Tarver, refused to caricature the situation, though frequently applied to. The accident was on a Saturday, and on the following Monday Charley Wise was interviewed and examined as to the lamb's antecedents. I think he admitted that an older and more pious animal, his neck less charged with thunder, should have been selected for the Harrow expedition; but he declined to bate materially on the question of consequential damages to the dog-cart, and my father was mulcted in the sum of £5. I was popularly supposed to have escaped by my thick hair or 'wool' as my friends called it; anyhow, on the top of my wool was my hat. I fell on the flagstone, straight on the crown of my 'tile'; it saved my life, and I have blessed the abused chimney-pot ever since.

I believe that Charley Wise really did visit Badminton. None of us doubted that His Grace of Beaufort had a kindly liking for the old livery-stable man. I have sometimes speculated as to the high probability of Lord Cardigan having had a chance interview with Charley Wise before the Crimean War, the leader of the Light Brigade being put up to a thing or two on cavalry tactics, and the merits of this or that subordinate officer. I hope that Charley had a kind word for Tremayne, Roger Palmer, Morgan, Wombwell, Percy Smith, and other Etonians who took part in the battle of Balaclava. I dare say he swaggered a little about his friendship with Scarlett — an old Etonian I rejoice to say—which fact is not forgotten by Kinglake in his description of the glorious charge of the Heavy Brigade.

'General Scarlett's old Eton experience' (says he), 'of what used to be called a "rooge," was perhaps of more worth to him than many a year of toil in the barrack-yard or exercise-ground. Close wedged from the first in an enemy's column, and on all sides hemmed in by the Russians, he was neither killed nor maimed, for the sabre which stove in his helmet was stopped before reaching his skull, and the only five wounds he received were, each of them, so slight as to be for the time altogether unheeded.'

Now for another old Eton boy 'grown heavy,' for he commanded the 4th Dragoon Guards in that superb fight, all the nobler because fought *secundum artem!* I mean

Lieutenant-Colonel Hodge, who steered the *Victory* in his boyish days on the river, and his Dragoons to victory in the Crimean Valley. 'There used to be a terse order which came to his lips as often as the boat crossed the river; and now when he had come to be so favoured by Fortune as to find himself at the head of his regiment with no more than a convenient reach of fair galloping ground between him and the flank of the enemy's column, the remainder of the business before him was exactly of such a kind as to be expressed by his old Eton word of command. What yet had to be done would be compassed in the syllables of "Hard all across!" (the direction given by the steerer to the crew of an Eton longboat when about to cross the Weir).' Scarlett's three hundred have a fascination for us Eton fellows; surely his was an artistic performance, and would have passed muster with Charley Wise. Cardigan's ride with his six hundred was magnificent, but 'it was not war'; they were 'all over the place' according to Charley.

Lord Cardigan was at Harrow—for a short time. We naturally prefer our own man, '*qui coatum Scarlet habebat.*'

The Duke of Beaufort, amongst patricians,

was not alone in his loyalty and kindness to Eton underlings, tradesmen, 'cads at the wall,' *i.e.*, the low broad wall west of the Upper School, who have no successors, I am sorry to see. Spankie (of whom more anon) was a prime favourite with 'Jack Savile,' before he became Lord Mexborough, and one evening, at a large dinner-party given to old Etonians in Yorkshire, the old 'sock' provider was specially retained for the surprise and amusement of the assembled guests. No one ever dreams or dreamt of Spankie without his tin and the inferior tarts inside it, so J. S. served him with a *subpœna* to bring himself and his inevitable appendage all the way from Eton to the North of England. None of the invited guests were in the secret of the entertainment until the time of dessert, when folding-doors were thrown open, and Spankie was discovered with the old tin under his arm, as if on the point of starting on one of his fraudulent crusades in Upper Club, of a match-day. He called out the old familiar challenge: 'Any tarts, cakes, sweets, strawberries, gentlemen?' Roars of applause. Spankie's health drunk with Kentish fire *ad lib*. This Yorkshire feast was Spankie's apotheosis; he was very proud of it.

CHAPTER VII.

ETON CHAPEL—ST. GEORGE'S CHAPEL.

THE religious teaching in my schooldays was not a strong point, either in or outside Eton Chapel. Sermons so inaudibly delivered as to be, in some instances, little more than dumb-show, a hebdomadal dose of Secker in school, varied with the meagre commentaries of Burton and Valpy on the Greek Testament in pupil-room, were a spiritual diet not robust enough for intended divines or Christian heroes. Eton was near enough to Oxford to be affected by mutterings of the great Church upheaval, and the phases of the Oxford movement were absorbing topics of interest to more than one of the assistant masters. Hodgson, our Provost, formerly Archdeacon of Derby, a high and dry divine, with no taste for controversy or faction, whether dominated by Newman or Arnold, kept rigorously aloof from the vexed questions which agitated many at Oxford and some few at Cambridge; and our headmaster, Dr. Hawtrey, a man of letters, and the friend of literary men, was indifferent as Gallio to the '*Credo in Newmanum*' watchword which awoke the suspicion of some alarmed Protestants in the cloisters of Eton. We boys had no Goulburn or Vaughan, still less a Lightfoot or Westcott, to keep us straight. Plain expositions and lectures on the Greek Testament would have been a more wholesome study for some of us than Archdeacon Manning's sermons, which were too frequently substituted, in my tutor's pupil-room, for the ordinary subjects of private business. These sermons, with all their beauty of style and language, veiled but imperfectly the restless and dissatisfied mind of their author, and I am persuaded that, at a time when the '*Tendimus in Latium*' cry was at its loudest, they were perilous reading for boys of an emotional turn. We attached a dangerous importance to them, and when the Archdeacon 'went over,' his flag followers saw their mistake. The future Cardinal bought up the four volumes which had made the Chichester Cathedral pulpit so justly famous, and we were taught too late to discover the elements of slow poison in teaching for some time warranted sound by our guides and instructors.

Eton, like other places, caught the contagion of church restoration, and the old chapel, offered a fine field for transformations of all kinds. Many years elapsed before the chapel, 'in the very decent manner in which it now appears' (such was the quaint formula applied to King's College Chapel, and annually repeated by our Provost, on Founder's Day), emerged, free of the old wood panelling, the hideous reredos, and the great boxes set apart near the east end for the male and female servants of the College. It was never known whether the gift of a new East window was the spontaneous suggestion of some of the upper boys and leading spirits in the school, or the result of some hint dropped by one of the tutors or authorities. It would have required but a spark to kindle into a blaze such devotional minds as Marriott's and Patteson's, but there ought to have been more foresight and care in the initial stages of the enterprise, before the authors of it bound their successors to a scheme involving the yearly expenditure of sums of money wrung from the pockets of anything but cheerful givers. That East window was a terror of long standing, a running sore to generations of boys. I myself, for a year or two, had the odious duty thrust on me of collecting 'window money.' Tax-gathering is not a pleasant office, but I was less odious to my comrades as a collector of 'candle money'* than of 'window money,' which, half after half, found its way to Newcastle, the home of our highly-paid creditor. This person was reputed to be the foremost man of his profession, and he pieced together his staring, garish window by instalments of stained glass which arrived at long intervals, and were severely criticized by his employers. When we boys had got together a round sum, a fresh and ugly Apostle, half paid for, was added on the flanks of the three central lights. If there was one thing that the school in general, and the lower boys in particular, loathed, it was this East window, which taxed the pocket-money of

* 'Candle-money' was a contribution levied on every house, tutor's or dame's, for payment of the lighting of schoolrooms in the winter evenings.

hundreds of Etonians, after the originators of the first idea had become bearded men. Irreverent jokes were made about 'the straw hat and leaving book'—a fourth-form equivalent for the nimbus and the Gospel; I do not defend them, but I maintain that we were not quite fairly treated, and that the artist's name should never be added to those of Eton's benefactors. I have been told that, when this questionable ornament in the chapel was completed, and the much-enduring school supposed to be free of obligation, a little supplementary account was sent in, which the headmaster at the time, rather than that the boys should be worried or bothered any further, discharged by drawing a cheque of his own and relieving the school from further responsibility. If money, lavishly, recklessly bestowed, deserved its proper equivalent, *sumus facti pro* in two particulars—our East window and our organ. The Fellow of Eton who paid for our new organ got no fair equivalent for his money, for, years afterwards, when it was eviscerated by a cunning musical anatomist, it was found to have next to no stomach; and we boys looked upon our East window as a transparent failure.

THE TABERNACLE.

For one year, during which time the chapel was closed for restoration, we attended service in a wooden tabernacle, which was run up in a field adjoining Barnes' Pool. It was said to have been originally intended for a missionary building, to be used in the Colonies; I am afraid it added more to our amusement than our edification. The tabernacle was a fragile, unsubstantial structure, with boards and benches so loosely put together that they were constantly giving way. In the summer-time the wasps, finding out the weak points, built a nest in the interstices of the building, and this was a matter of great discomfort to Plumptre, the Fellow of Eton who happened to be in residence during the summer half when we first worshipped in our temporary chapel. I should like to have compared notes with the Rev. James Lonsdale, whose biography—the joint work of two of my contemporaries, Russell Duckworth and the Hon. G. C. Brodrick—has won the gratitude of all loyal Etonians. I could have added considerably to his *répertoire* of subjects chosen for sermons, though I believe that he had a large stock, compiled from memories of his old Eton days, long before the tabernacle discourses. He remembered the old Fellow, that ancient ecclesiastic, whose monosyllabic texts were famous. 'Shout!' was one of them. Another text, declaimed by one of Plumptre's colleagues, made a lasting impression on my friend and schoolfellow, the late Sir James Fitzjames Stephen, who records the fact in his diary: 'It rings in my ears after the lapse of more than forty years.' The text was this: 'The subject of my discourse this morning, my brethren, will be the duties of the married state.'

Before Plumptre's time the Eton pulpit was occasionally occupied by an old Fellow, not 'happy and careless,' but 'cappy and hairless.' On one Sunday his text was: 'My sins are more in number than the hairs of my head.' As he had not a single one and was as bald as a coot, the text convulsed the youthful congregation. Here are some of Plumptre's texts:

1. 'And his mother made him a coat.'
2. 'Wash.'
3. 'This thing was not done in a corner.'

I have been told, on high authority, that Plumptre had an extraordinary command of Scripture language, though his studies of the Concordance could not restrain him from quaint and grotesque applications of it. Thus, when inveighing against Lord Melbourne for having introduced Professor Owen to the Queen, he said that Owen had made 'Blastus, the King's Chamberlain,' his friend. A famous text of his was the single word 'Woman,' which introduced an invective against Mariolatry. My correspondent, who has a vivid recollection of the comic effect produced, adds that the assistant masters were obliged to duck down behind their desks to conceal their laughter. But the old man reached his climax in the 'fetching a compass' sermon, *i.e.*, a funeral discourse on the death of Charles Wilder, brother of the late Fellow of Eton, our great benefactor. Wilder, during his last illness (I think in 1838), was moving about from place to place in Italy and Sicily. I believe he died abroad, and his body was brought to England. Anyhow, Plumptre described his last wanderings in this fashion : 'And departing thence they came to (say) Palermo, and after three days they took ship and came to Naples (or perhaps Parthenope, for Plumptre was fond of classical allusions), and from thence they fetched a compass and came to Rome (pause), the mother of all spiritual adulteries.' This cadence was given with great emphasis, for so ardent a Protestant was 'Plumrum' (as my tutor called him) that he could never let Rome pass without a wipe. The finale was as queer as the opening movement: 'And now he rests by the banks of his own Jordan.' This was supposed by the congregation to mean the Thames at Eton, but poor Wilder was buried at Sulham; 'Jordan,' therefore, must have been intended for the river Sul, or a brook of that name.

In the pulpit, Plumptre always held his glasses an inch or two in front of his face. When the wasp interrupted a full view of his manuscript, or playfully seemed disposed to settle on the preacher's nose, and leave his mark there, the old gentleman appeared to be playing a miniature game of racquets, backhanding and volleying with his tormentor. There was a huge cushion on the pulpit, and Plumptre's first idea, after placing his cap upon it, was to turn up each end of the cushion, and peep under it, as if he expected to find some lurking foe; then he planted his head in his cap and glared with his swivel eye

PLUMPTRE IN THE PULPIT.
DR. HAWTREY LOOKING OVER EXERCISES.

at the congregation. His text on one occasion was, 'Whether it be to the King, as supreme.' He accented the last syllable of 'supreme,' and pronounced the word 'shu-preme'; and we had sermons from him twice at least on the same theme. The popular opinion was, that the Provost remonstrated with him, as he proposed taking the same text for the remainder of his course, and that as he refused to give in, he was not allowed to preach the other two sermons; but I fancy there would have been a row in the chapel, if he had been forcibly prohibited from giving us the rest of his lucubrations. The sermon itself was a 'cento' of Biblical phrases, which the preacher adapted as describing the happiness of the English people under Queen Victoria. 'And the land is at peace, and every man sits in his own garden of cucumbers.' He called the Queen 'a mother in Israel,' and made some passing allusion to the Society of Friends. Anxious that the school should understand the allusion, he paused, and broke the universal silence with an ejaculatory jerk pitchforked at us—'The Quakers' (it sounded like 'The Quakersh'). We had a very memorable discourse on the

Sunday after the Queen had been shot at. Plumptre's indignation at the attempt made on her Majesty's life found vent in his sermon, in which he gave a *précis* of the transaction. 'After the shot had been fired,' said he, 'who should appear upon the scene but pedestrian Peck? Pedestrian Peck seized the assassin, and handed him over to a Life Guardsman.' Peck's promptitude and courage seemed to have impressed the preacher greatly, for he laid strong emphasis on 'pedeshtrian Peck,' and evidently considered him as a protagonist in the scene. Owing to his grotesque mannerisms, and Spurgeonisms, we were highly delighted whenever Plumptre ascended the tribune. When Long Chamber was broken up into cubicles, I doubt if Plumptre half liked the alteration, but he made an occasion of it, and we enjoyed his text: 'And Elisha said, Let every man take unto himself a beam, for the place we have made is too strait for us.' I have heard quoted, as one of his pulpit gems, the sentence: 'Your hearts are like gooseberry-tart without sugar,' but I doubt the genuineness of this story, which is probably the invention of some imaginative fourth-form boy.

Some of the old Fellows kept to the ancient custom of knee-breeches, buckles and shoes—the hat a shovel or church dignitary hat, very high collars, voluminous folds of neckcloth—frilled shirt-fronts, spotless and fine. Bethell always wore a 'Spencer,' *i.e.*, a double-breasted jacket of thick cloth used as an overcoat, the swallow-tails hanging down from underneath it. These should have been supplemented by breeches and stockings, which would have carried off the 'Spencer.' We quite erroneously credited him with parsimonious habits, and quoted an address of his to a waiter in a country inn parlour, 'Give me a glass of water and a tooth-pick, and d——n the expense!' I wish I could agree with an old schoolfellow who reminds me that the school gained some dignity from a canonical chapter of old Etonians who loved Eton. There were excellent old-fashioned scholars amongst them who had served as assistant masters from twenty to thirty years, and Sir Edward Creasy, a first-rate judge of such matters, upheld his old tutor (Green) as the best and most sympathetic of his time; but the melancholy fact remains that the influence of the Fellows in the pulpit was, with two exceptions, practically *nil*. Doubtless we were ignorant of their antecedents, and did them scant justice. Many years elapsed before I became aware of Plumptre's excellent scholarship; I am glad to have been favoured with the two following specimens of his skill in Latin verses; the Sapphics commemorate a visit of Jenny Lind to Worcester, where she sang for a local hospital; the 'longs and shorts' are on old Gray, the clerk of Eton chapel:

I.

' Suevici cantûs decus, et theatri
  Sis licet virgo (Philomela seu tu
  Audias hibernæ, libentiusve
      Lindia) felix.

' Sospes accedas Agape's propago
  Dii tui guttur liquidum annuerunt,
  Ut salutari medearis arte
      Unica morbis.

' Rebus et fractis eadem patrona
  Pauperem solere, Famesque Pestisque
  Exulent tectis; tibi tale vocis
      Est iter udæ.

' Illa quæ vicit populos sub Arcto,
  Asperum linquens genus, æsculetis
  Suevicis audita, Vigornienses
      Mulceat aures.'

II.

Gray Minor's Elegy in a Suburban Churchyard.

' Qui tot composuit terrâ, componitur idem
Sic, quâ crediderat lege, requirit humus,
Quod bene dixit Amen toties ad busta paratus,
Ne dictum elato tam grave desit.—" Amen." '

Here is an English version by my friend Edward Stone:

' Many has he laid in earth, where now himself is laid;
The soil reclaims its own, the debt is duly paid.
"Amen!" he promptly said, and well, o'er many dead,
O'er his own grave to-day the grave "Amen!" be said.'

As an assistant master, Plumptre had detected the rare classical attainments of his pupil, John Lonsdale, when the future Bishop of Lichfield was still a youngster. 'Sir,' said Plumptre to the Bishop's son, 'your father was a poet in his fourth-form days.' He was proud, and justly proud, of having tutored that distinguished man. It may be doubted if Shelley's poetical development was materially assisted by his tutor, Bethell, *vox et præterea nihil*. Frederick Tennyson, the Laureate's eldest brother, was Green's pupil.

Plumptre adored the memory of George III., the Royal House of Hanover, and Protestant succession. For one whole night he walked round and round the Eton cloisters, praying and waiting for the expected news of the defeat of the Roman Catholic Emancipation Bill. He never, to his dying day, forgave the passing of that measure. A kinder and more narrow-minded ecclesiastic never lived. I should like to have heard him on the subject of Bishop Lloyd's celebrated vote.

Temperate in all things save his maledictions of the Pope and the Radicals, Plumptre enjoyed his glass of port with a moderation not known to some ecclesiastical canons of those days, who were loaded with grape up to the muzzle. His doctor on one occasion had prescribed two glasses of port-wine a day. At his next visit the patient observed, 'I have taken the liberty, sir, to drink the fourteen glasses at a sitting, once a week!'

The Fellows of Eton, judged as a corporate body, were kindly men, conspicuous for watching the interests of their relatives and dependents; is it a libel on their memory, or the simple truth, to say that, with two exceptions, they were useless and superannuated, as preachers not only ineffective, but at times very ridiculous in the 'wood'? They contributed in a full measure to the poverty-stricken services which were then unhappily the fashion in Eton Chapel.

'Catechism' was a form of Lenten penance confined to collegers of a certain age and standing; twice I endured the infliction, and it fell to my lot to repeat the three fearfully long-winded solos in answer to Bethell's question of the meaning of the Lord's Prayer, and the two separate duties prescribed to all youthful catechumens. I never could understand why Bursar Bethell was told off to officiate at this annual church-drill. To be sure, he had a penetrating voice, and was credited with one original and comprehensive question in the Upper School, when he was an assistant master: 'Who dragged who how many times round the walls of what?' When he started the Communion Service, the 'Our Father' was called by Cookesley 'the Paternoster *row*,' and impressed a rural listener to such an extent that he remarked after the service: 'Good Lord, how he made all the spiders run into their holes!' Bethell was no doubt an articulately-speaking man, and Homeric to that extent only. His sermons were audibly delivered, but as for their matter our sensations were those of the crowd in the Court, when Mr. Skimpin opened the pleadings in the famous case of Bardwell *v.* Pickwick: 'Mr. Skimpin proceeded to open the case, and the case appeared to have very little inside it when he had opened it.' Catechism followed the anthem on a Sunday afternoon, when the clearance of the choir of St. George's had been effected, and some ten or twelve of us collegers stood up, ranged in a single row to front the Bethell artillery. It was a trying ordeal, even for the most brazen-faced amongst us, who were not old enough to have appeared in silk stockings and knee-breeches at speeches in the Upper School. Most boys profited by that experience, but with the constitutionally timid, bravado expired with the short fizzle of the speech itself. Lesser men than the poet Cowper have trembled at the prospect of reading a printed document in public, *à fortiori* of reciting a passage committed to memory before a large assembly. To a friend of mine—Page by name—the publicity of Catechism before six hundred oppidans, with upturned faces, most of them eager for a breakdown, was real torture. I hope he got off with the short Commandments. The stare of a single pair of eyes at Page would make him blush to the roots of his hair, or, as we called it, 'make him *smoke*,' and this infirmity once ascertained, it was the fashion in chapel at the words in the Psalm, 'If He do but touch the hills they shall *smoke*,' deliberately to lower our Prayer-Books and fix our cruel eyes on 'sweet Anne Page,' the sight of whose cheeks, suddenly turned into flaming beetroot, amply rewarded us for our hideous cruelty. When Bethell opened fire with 'What is your name?' some irreverent oppidan below the catechumens would mutter, ' M. or N., Melbourne or Norton, as the case may be,' in allusion to a *cause célèbre* which agitated the school, from the high position of the litigants. Our interest was really intelligible, for Mrs. Norton, Sheridan's gifted niece, was often seen by us in Eton Chapel. Two of her sons were my contemporaries, and her illustrious nephew, Lord Dufferin, was nicknamed by his tutor 'the Orator,' by way, I suppose, of reminding him that the Sheridan relationship involved serious responsibilities. I remember Lord Dufferin rowing in the crew of the lag-boat on June 4. Little did he dream of his great future as a statesman, or that he would live to be canonized by Tennyson, for in those days his Lordship was very much as other boys, with an occasional Irish taste for lawlessness, and quite ready to pay the penalty by what Lord Bramwell used to call 'special indorsement.' The executioner and the victim became great friends. Here is Lord Dufferin's own testimony in a speech made in public. We, his old schoolfellows, can realize the scene of Hawtrey's salaam and the youthful nobleman's sense of the altered relationship. 'I remember, two or three years after I had left Eton, meeting Dr. Hawtrey, the well-known headmaster, in the streets of Paris. I shall never forget my dismay and embarrassment when he stood uncovered at my approach. (Laughter.) The recollection of the occasions when I had stood uncovered before him, though in the opposite sense, so overcame me that I was quite incapable of returning his salutation with proper dignity.'

'*Quo, Musa, tendis?*' I am forgetting my

Catechism. The ceremony, a few years before my day, opened in a manner very gratifying to the oppidans, who always rejoiced in any form of humiliation inflicted on a colleger. The unhappy Coriphœus was Kirwan, K.S., whose Christian name was 'Hyacinth.' I believe there was nothing floral about him; he had no hyacinthine locks, and collegers in the football half were seldom very fragrant. He was own brother to 'Wacky' Kirwan, a terrific underhand bowler in 1834 and 1835, given to 'daisy clippers' which were the terror of Harrow and Winchester batsmen. He became a distinguished Hebraist at Cambridge, where he won the Cross Divinity Scholarship. Then he went to India as chaplain, and died of fever at Lucknow in 1858. The 'Charles' or 'John' next to him amongst the catechumens should quietly have exchanged places with Hyacinth before Bethell's peremptory 'What is your name?' was flung at poor K. How the poor lad, turning as crimson as his prototype was purple, must for the moment have loathed his godfathers and godmothers! It is too cruel to launch a boy into a public-school with a *prænomen* which he would give his eyes to be rid of. I have known the names of two reverend clergymen in different generations who must have smarted in their time for the thoughtlessness of their parents and sponsors — the Rev. Cicero Rabbits and the Rev. Paschal Lamb! The Rev. Cicero became the subject of a jest one evening in the Trinity Combination-room at Cambridge, and Professor Sedgwick, rebuking the Fellows for their jokes about the 'conies being a feeble folk,' added: 'We have really no business to laugh at Cicero Rabbits when we have got our own Julius Hare.'

In the course of my forty years' experience of Circuit life, I have stumbled upon every variety of Christian name in use among jurors and witnesses. Hannibal, Erasmus, Jedediah are rather trying; but the first time I invoked a gentleman called 'Wellington Waterloo,' it fairly took my breath away. After a while I missed this gentleman on the accustomed beadroll, and then I was Paul Pryish enough to make some inquiries—these resulted in evidence that the *culte* of the great Duke was so inveterate in the family that W. W. had actually named some of his children after the Peninsular victories. My grandfather, an old soldier, had such a veneration for the sister service and its great Admiral, that he called one of his own boys 'Nelson,' so I have no right to be squeamish; but, as a matter of choice, I am rather glad that I had not an Uncle Toulouse nor an Aunt Salamanca.

I fear that the disfigurement of many anthem books testified to the constant *ennui* of the worshippers, which must in part be ascribed to the lugubrious services in Eton Chapel. My dear friend Bradshaw kept one of these as a souvenir, and if he were in low spirits or in want of a laugh, he would turn to the curious volume as others would to some favourite page of Dickens or Thackeray. The indices to these anthem books, with the names of the authors annexed to the various compositions, were embellished with quaint sketches or arabesques, and there were often epigrams or questions on the margin. Of course Charles Lamb contributed :

> 'Cannot a man live free and easy,
> Without admiring Pergolesi?
> Or through the world with comfort go,
> That never heard of Dr. Blow?'

If an anthem was headed 'Bless my soul' (*Dupuis*), 'Harry' or 'John George' would be pencilled as a prefix. 'Praise the Lord' (*Bird*), and the composer would be christened 'Cock i olly.' Then there would be 'Plead thou my cause' (*Cutler*), because Cutler, Q.C., was so good a musician, even in his boyhood, as to be called 'Mozart.'

On Sunday morning we had no music; in the afternoon, and on Saints' days, the College borrowed the choir of St. George's Chapel, and we had a mongrel performance, miserably inferior to that in the Royal Chapel itself. It was said of our organist that he was an eminently charitable man, 'for his right hand knew not what his left hand did'; and the contrast between the two players was so humiliating, that not a few of us were frequent worshippers in St. George's, where we were sure of services and anthems in the grand style.

Sir George Elvey, the Windsor organist, a worthy contemporary of Wesley, Goss, and Walmisley, is gratefully remembered and honoured by all musical Etonians of my time. In the winter half, when 'lock up' was early,

SIR GEORGE JOB ELVEY.

and attendance at the entire service at St. George's, on a Sunday afternoon, an impossibility, Coley Patteson and I often listened in the Windsor cloisters, at the key-hole of the chapel door, and after catching the last notes of the anthem, we rushed down the Hundred Steps, and, with all the alacrity of Pedestrian Peck, contrived to get to our houses in time to answer to our names at 'absence.'

The hour of our afternoon service at Eton made it impossible for the members of St. George's choir to stay beyond the second collect and the anthem which followed immediately after. When that was finished, the chorister boys and men filed out of our chapel, and started off for their service at Windsor. This unseemly proceeding was inevitable, so long as the College was forced to depend upon outsiders for a choir, and it vexed the righteous soul of one of our assistant masters, who gave vent to his feelings on the subject in a short speech, made at the Founder's Day dinner, when he was called upon to return thanks for the toast of 'The Assistant Masters.'

'Mr. Provost,' said Harry Dupuis, 'this state of things is intolerable. I for one protest against our having only a moiety of Mudge.'

Mudge, a tenor singer in St. George's Chapel, became historical from that moment. The words 'a moiety of Mudge' were such a shock to Provost Hodgson and his brethren, that the College passed a decree in favour of undivided, unpartitioned Mudges, and I hope that Eton choristers, native to the soil—Chalvey Ditchers, Brocas Clumpers—may flourish and abound, ripening in time to emulate the Colets and Lord Tenterdens, who started in life as 'canaries.'* How I envy the present generation of youngsters their musical opportunities, their skilled and earnest Choragus, and the genial sunshine of approbation that smiles on a young Jubal, or a coming Rubinstein! May the time be far distant when a bust of Hubert Parry will adorn the walls of the Upper School! There it will be for certain, for I anticipate no difficulties or questions, as in poet Shelley's case. Eton morality is not too discriminating. We were allowed to look at Fox's portrait without fear of its arousing our gambling instincts; but our sensitive orthodoxy was on

* The Eton term for 'chorister-boys.'

no account to be imperilled by worshipping the bust of the author of 'Queen Mab.'

One of Shelley's eccentricities at Eton was to pursue the cook at his dame's with a roasting-spit; his chemical experiments were the terror of old Bethell, his tutor. The Shelley Society did well to print a masterly paper by William Johnson, in which he drew an imaginary picture of Shelley's 'After Fours' in the summer half. I recommend this essay to all lovers of the river as we knew it, before house-boats, steam-launches, railway bridges, and other horrors brought chaos to the Thames.

SHELLEY'S RIVER HAUNTS AT ETON.

'When Shelley was at Eton, the bridge that linked Eton to New Windsor was a wooden one, like the old Putney Bridge, and many others that have been in my time replaced by structures of stone and iron, only it seems, from an engraving by Cooke, after Owen, to have been unusually homely and frail—in fact, Owen's drawing of this spot is to me far less easy to identify with what I saw when I first went thither in 1832, than his other drawings, of such places as Cliefden, Staines, and Harleyford, are with the places as I knew them. However, it is certain that there were picturesque, old-world things of wood on the Thames, at the point at which one crossed over from Mercia into Wessex, or, in other words, from Bucks to Berks. The Thames was still a traffic-line for heavy goods, brought up and down in barges dragged by horses; and at the spot of which we are thinking, there was a meeting of commerce with pleasure, of rude, irritable bargemen with frolicsome boys from Eton School, and lounging privates of the Staffordshire Militia, which guarded Windsor Castle.*

'Shelley on a summer day, after his run up the long street, and his escape from his "baiters," would plunge into Brocas Lane, pass a hot den where clay pipes were made, dodge the curved beaks of boats under repair in a little crowded builder's yard, scamper down a rickety stairstep on a single plank that ran out into the river, undo the rope or the chain

---

* I have heard my uncle, who was half starved in the College, talk of the great pleasure it was to hear the trumpets of this regiment sound at nightfall; it cost him a smart run between barracks and school.

that held a skiff or a funny to the rail that was parallel to the plank, and jump into his "lock-up" (season ticket) boat, or into his "chance boat," which, unlike the lock-up, required a race and a scramble for priority, and shove off without stopping to see whether there was rain-water under the bottom boards; for of course he could bale out for himself, if he got away from the world of well-dressed people and reached an eyot or a creek fairly out of sight. Would he scull up or down stream? There was a boy thirty years after who, when beginning to learn—what looks very easy, but is not—the art of steering a boat while looking sternward, and plying long-handled sculls without jamming his fingers, used to go down-stream, carefully avoiding the "cobbler," or "coblair," into the artificial "lock-cut," which served as a sort of groove of direction, since he had to keep either scull just a yard clear of its bank, and work both hands equally.* But he that made that

* This lock-cut was pictured by Heffner in the exhibition at the French Gallery, Pall Mall, a poetical representation of a bit of ground that many people might despise for its straight lines, cut slopes, and pollard willows.

mechanical use of a straight slice of water, cannot imagine the skylark boy of 1805 deigning to bear such limits.

'Shelley would be sure to cross over beyond the eyot, which then served for the fireworks, and round which the big boys in their long boats used to have lubberly bumping races, sometimes ending with a regular challenge to a fight on land, stroke against stroke, steerer against steerer, a whole Irish crew against a British crew. He would hurry up the unfrequented bargeless right bank, pass the Clewer fields, behind two more eyots, where the Windsor people in modern days bathe, almost in sight of Brunel's railway bridge, where, in the first forty years of this century, one might lie in a punt, screened by willows if it was hot weather, or set up a mimic battery of cannon in mid-autumn, and fire away, till the bank began to crumble under the shock. There is one alive who can well imagine Shelley's enjoying, most innocently, the early escape from ushers and boobies, which could be secured by a rush to those bowers, that lay over against the well-known clump of elms which the railway, forty years ago, was compelled to spare. And then, just above that was a fascinating "back-water" that led up to Clewer mill, and below the mill there was a tumbling-bay, and you could let the refluent eddy sweep your skiff in a curve up to the bottom of the little cataract, and, poising the sculls, let the white water hurry you along some twenty yards. Then you could find an easy slope on the left side of the mill, lift the boat out, if you had a mate, carry it, whilst the miller was at dinner, across a bit of tame land, only a few steps, launch into the mill-stream where it was really dangerous, above the wheels, and then wander up a natural meandering stream, with grand high banks; and one may be sure that Shelley saw these banks all alive with hawthorn in blossom, saw and attacked with scull or with boat-hook the harmless water-voles that lived in holes amongst the roots of the overhanging trees, saw, perhaps, once or twice. the sudden blue gleam of a kingfisher, and then hunted for the fish-bone nest.*

* Campbell of Isla, who wrote well, some thirty years ago, about ice-scratched rocks, says, in his book about Normandy, that when he was a boy at Eton he found king-

'Passing out of the Clewer mill-stream, the trespasser would, within an hour after his parting with his tormentors, come in sight of their beloved pot-house, Surley Hall, and he would there, if he had enough cash, pay a shilling for negus, and give sixpence to the waiter; for was he not a gentleman? In those days, the Eton boys did not drink beer at taverns; beer was for bargees; negus, punch, bishop, were the drinks for gentlemen, and if they could not pay for such luxuries, they went without drink. Just above Surley Hall there was, in Owen's days—that is, about the time of Shelley's early manhood, and there may have been in his boyhood—an attractive

---

fishers' nests in sequestered waters close to the school, probably near 'Black Potts,' Walton's fishing cottage.—*Note by W. J.*

Some doubt has been suggested to me as to 'Black Potts' having been Walton's property, or even in the possession of Eton College. Where is there distinct evidence of this? Izaak Walton says, 'I often fished with Sir Henry Wotton,' and the old Provost, when past seventy, wrote a poem 'on a bank as I sate a-fishing.' This was presumably at Eton. Wotton also asks Walton to come and 'let him enjoy his delightful company at Eton, in the approaching season of the Fly and the Cork.'—*Note by A. D. C.*

villa called The Willows. Owen's drawing presents something that is a little more poetical than what one found on the same spot in the reign of William IV. This was the only touch of smartness or gentility on the banks for some miles. It used to be reckoned a six-mile course from the bridge to Surley Bay and back, and the greatest race was rowed over these six miles, "be they more or less"—probably a good deal less. There was no lock at Boveney; the stream was strong just there. This was all in favour of an "Alastor"; for there could hardly be a crowd above the place called "The Shallows," where the navigation up-stream was difficult. It was here that beginners required help, and had even to hire a waterman in their early trips.

'There was another thing in favour of "the spirit of solitude": bathing went on unmethodically. Instead of having to resort to regular bathing platforms, with their ladders, punts, and liveried warders, a boating boy, or pair of boys, could stop at a tempting point, and, with no ceremony, with nothing but a casual towel, would plunge or sneak in. The strange historical truth is, that the river was out of bounds, though some recognition of swimming, as an extra accomplishment, was given in the accounts forwarded to parents and guardians by tutors and dames. The authorities hardly ever walked along the towing-path, much less did they row, punt, or sail, or swim, except at a distance from the boys. Early in this century a boy was drowned close to Boveney Meads, in the presence of many big schoolfellows, of whom not one could dive to bring up the body, that was plainly seen by those who stooped over the sides of the gathered boats. But for the breadth of beam of the craft, and the reasonable lightness of the human load, many would have perished; but the notion never entered our heads.

'If Shelley was like some other unsociable boys, it may be guessed that he delighted in the danger of sailing in a skiff, if it had a hole in one of the thwarts for shipping a mast. Alastor spreads his cloak aloft on a bare mast; less sublime persons have made shift to scud before the wind, a little faster than the stream, by the help of an arrangement of bottom-boards tilted on end, with sculls or oars raised at various angles, and presenting their blades to the breeze; this gave one a sense of repose. But if we were intemperate in our laziness, we stealthily tied the boat to a downward barge's rudder and were towed. Bargees did not mind it down-stream, so long as we did not refer to "the puppy-pie eaten under Marlow Bridge"; one went into "kef," and woke only when the boat, by the barge's yawing, went hard at a pier of Windsor Bridge. All this was in the compass of the ordinary two hours between the fixed points of school obligations. But there were some rare delights of insubordination that broke the two hours' limit. Fixed points were not merely hours of lessons, and chapel services, and twilight barring of house-doors. A summer afternoon was cut in two by a roll-call at 6.15, and, for the juniors, by another roll-call at 8. These inspections were, in Shelley's days, and long after, left to the burdensome prerogative of the headmaster, and though he might be expected to know, by force of habit, the voice of every one of his hundreds of subjects, his mind might slacken at times, and a "doubleganger," reserving his countenance, protruding his hat, and conventionalizing his "Here, sir," might personate one that at 6.15 was miles away from the school-yard arcade, or from the big elm which, in the cricket season, was the place of muster at that hour. Even Shelley must have found it easy to get "a fellow to answer for him at absence," provided he did as much for Dromio, on another similar occasion; and unless Ascot races were going on, the chances were greatly in favour of the caller being taken in, from mere weariness. By help, then, of a brilliant mendacity, Alastor could get nearly five hours, and he could go alone as far as Bray, with mates as far as the handsome bridge that carried rank and fortune across the Thames between London and Bath—the bridge beyond which one got the treat of seeing Taplow and Cliefden woods. Now, it is to be stated that between Boveney and Bray there were two halting-places. There was Water Oakly, the very pink of rusticity, with a pot-house that had settles and ingles, a hamlet unembellished by gazebo or shrubbery; here you could hob and nob with waggoners, and, as we used to say, "study human nature." But Alastor would rush on, through weeds and the haunts of swans, pass Queen's Eyot, up the right bank, to the stone steps that dignified the right side of Monkey Island. I hope and believe that this fairy-tale spot was in 1805, as in 1835, uninhabited and yet not ruinous. It, was, as Keble says of the Canaanite gardens, when Joshua came to them, "a fearful joy" to venture into the deserted summer-house, whose walls presented monkeys behaving like so many Herveys and Churchills; to sit on the floor with the back against a frescoed wall, and there eat the biscuits and fruit brought from Surley Hall. One had not a notion how near one was all the while to that farm, with its mossed thatch, which stands on the Bucks side, just below Bray Lock. The island was out of the abhorred mean world in which formalists held dominions; and yet there was that consciousness of trespass which we could not enjoy if we were in Eden.'

Let us return to Hubert Parry, whose early achievement in taking an Oxford degree in music, whilst he was yet a boy at Eton, was a more rare event than that of any contemporary winning a Balliol scholarship straight away from school. Will not his 'Blest pair of Syrens' outlive many classical achievements?

To have wedded Milton's verses to music worthy of them is, indeed, no ephemeral distinction. Dr. Arne is quoted by Creasy, in his list of eminent Etonians, so he will not 'die altogether,' but I fear such compositions as 'Water parted from the sea,' 'In infancy our hopes and fears,' and 'The soldier tired' are at their last gasp. Handel, it is supposed, had a sneaking fondness for him, as he calls him his 'goot Gustavus.' Judging by his portrait on the walls of the Cloister Corridor, the Doctor looks like a cross between Sir Hugh Evans and Mantalini. It reminds me of Professor Sedgwick's satire upon a Trinity exquisite: 'For chains and chitterlings, for curls and cosmetics, for rings and ringlets, no man was like him. He was indeed a finished and a fragrant fop—a very curious coxcomb.' Arne had his merits; the author of the songs which I have quoted as moribund, if not actually dead, knew what melody meant, but a glance at the head of the older, and at that of the modern, composer, which so curiously resembles that of 'immortal William,' as seen in the Stratford bust, will satisfy any impartial observer of the very different capacities of the

DR. ARNE.

(*Done from an original sketch by F. Bartolozzi.*)

two Eton musicians who represent their various epochs. There are little tinkling, tuneful rills in 'Artaxerxes,' but in Parry's noble music to 'Job,' 'that grandest poem in the world,' according to Tennyson, 'one deep calleth to another.' With so great an example before them, I am full of hope, and have no fear for musical aspirants at Eton. As executants, the Uppingham boys were, a short time since, far ahead of other Public Schools—all honour to their trainers!

The demeanour of the Eton boys in chapel, as I remember it in the forties, would not warrant Dr. Boyd's favourite epithet, 'uplifting.' We were a cold, stagnant, mute congregation. Of course, all Englishmen, men and boys alike, are insular and undemonstrative, but that is no reason why a lad who makes an audible response at Divine service should be regarded as a curiosity. The ordinary defence set up for us is, that the arrangement of the seats in chapel is the real hindrance, and that if the boys faced all one way, as at Harrow, we should be a very sympathetic and responsive congregation. I doubt the soundness of this plea. There are the ordinary congregational opportunities, if the boys will but take off the padlock from their mouths.

We ought, from sheer malice prepense, to have drowned old Gray, the clerk, with his horribly distinctive solos all through the services. He had been at his dreary recitatives ever since 1809, and all those years had not taught him one spark of reverence. His manners were repulsive. Ten minutes before service began, we saw and heard him expectorating on his hands, before he pulled the chapel bell-rope, and the unlicensed hawker repeated these performances during service, as if his 'Amens' were not far too audible already. Latterly he became very deaf, and being obliged to make a guess at the part of the Creed orally given out by the officiating Provost, or Fellow, who was at some distance from him, and frequently inaudible, the result was that the parson and clerk generally finished it one before the other. The effect on a boyish congregation may well be imagined. We always looked forward to old Gray's performance in the service for the Queen's Accession, when he canonized Queen Victoria twice in the same verse of the psalm. This was his

JOHN GRAY, PARISH CLERK.

SILLY BILLY.

reading: 'And blessed be the name of Her Majesty for ever, and all the earth shall be full of Her Majesty. Amen and amen.'

Another grotesque character in chapel was Silly Billy, *alias* 'Foolish William,' *alias* 'Mr. Leggett.' So far from being *parcus Deorum cultor et infrequens*, he attended every service that he could possibly get to in Eton and Windsor. He was chaffed and worried by the lower boys, at whom he hurled his anathemas, as he shuffled up the church steps. In chapel, and at St. George's also, we always knew when the first or second lesson was finishing, for at the last verse Silly Billy always rose to the occasion, and he was credited—and, I believe, with perfect justice—with knowing by heart every verse in the Bible.

In the old days, before the restoration of the chapel, a very absurd distinction was conferred on the noblemen in the school, for the Marquises, Lords, and Honourables were allowed to sit in stalls, and to look down on their humbler brethren. I was never impressed or awed by the sight of this noble contingent, though I had an eye for the bearer of a historical name, and stared very unbecomingly at the Henleys, Darnleys, Grosvenors, and Talbots of the period. The newest stall-holder, when he succeeded to the dignity of a special seat in chapel, marked the event by sending a packet of almonds and raisins to each of his brother noblemen already installed, and the Honourable this or that was often seen to empty his pocket, and flesh his patrician teeth on this 'church sock' whilst confessing his sins vicariously through droning old Gray.

Twelve of these purple-blooded youths were selected to act as pall-bearers at the Marquis Wellesley's funeral. They behaved with propriety on that occasion, but on ordinary days some, who were leading aquatics, were not conspicuous as devotional models. Their irreverence was rather oddly evoked by Handel's first chorus in the 'Messiah': 'And the glory of the Lord shall be revealed, and all flesh shall see it.' A series of good, swinging, short, detached phrases, sung *fortissimo* at the end of a chorus, was a favourite with the boating men. They foisted in the names of watermen, and the loafers on the Brocas, who were ready 'to go anywhere and to do anything for sixpence,' and the crew of the *Ten Oar* or *Victory*, or the profane ones amongst them, would sing far too audibly :

> 'Jack Haverley,
> Bob Tolliday,
> Row all the day
> Round Surley Bay!
>   Amen.'

Everybody affected a faint connoisseurship in music; everyone had his pet anthems and services, his pet aversions also. Randall, K.S., grandson of the Cambridge Professor of Music, who was a friend of Gray, the poet, and set one of his Odes to music, had the rashness to murmur to me at the opening of the *Magnificat*: 'Arthur, my grandfather's service in B flat.' This was too good to be kept to myself, though I wished no harm to the poor fellow, but ever after, if a chant or anthem jarred upon the ears of any colleger, it was 'passed up' in chapel, that after service ' Randall will be licked for his grandfather's bad anthem,' etc. What ruffians we were! I have heard that a canon of Westminster's inordinately long sermons so vexed the souls of Westminster schoolboys, that they devised a method for attempting to shorten their weariness by promising condign punishment of the preacher's son, 'If your governor preaches fifty minutes next Sunday.' Forewarned, the preacher was a little less prolix for once, at all events.

I was present in chapel at the funeral of the Marquis Wellesley, and had the good fortune to be seated very near to the chief mourner, the great Duke of Wellington himself. The Duke was, naturally enough, an object of adoration whenever he appeared at Eton. I remember, on the occasion of the French King's visit to Eton, that our Queen and Louis Philippe were almost deserted in the school-yard, for directly the Duke on his white horse was seen in the procession that followed the Royal party, both Queen and King were forgotten, whilst masters and boys mobbed the old soldier, who was luckily mounted on a quieter animal than Copenhagen. This visit was duly recorded in a Parisian newspaper, by a correspondent whose ideas of geography and of English institutions might have been improved upon; here is his special report:

'After the ceremony of the investiture, the

King of the French received the Corporation of the City of London, who presented their addresses to His Majesty. Then the King went to visit the College of Eaton, as he had promised. This college, one of the most ancient in England, and *a dependence on the University of Oxford*, is situated in the vicinity of Windsor. Built not far from the Thames, and on the old road which led from Windsor to London, its old walls *are seated half-way up the hill*, on the summit of which stand the slender turrets of the Royal Residence. The visit was, therefore, only a short and agreeable walk for their Majesties and their attendants, for Eaton is contiguous to the park of the Castle. Their Majesties were received by the *Honourable Dean*, who did the honours of his college, celebrated among those of Great Britain for the numerous and brilliant assemblage of youths who congregate thither to study, sa well as for certain privileges and immunities which the pupils enjoy at the periods of the examinations. It is at the College of Eaton that almost all the young men who belong to the opulent families of England are instructed. *It is also at this college that some of the sons* of the noble, but poor, families are gratuitously admitted.

'In order to meet the expenses incurred for the maintenance of these indigent youths, a custom of a singular nature has been introduced. At certain periods all the scholars of the college *take a bag, and go to the neighbouring highways*, to beg of passengers and travellers, who always answer the demands graciously and generously, *and thus supply the necessary means for the support of the college.* Every year, it is said, large sums are collected by this affecting (*touchante*) custom, and new exhibitions (*bourses*) thus founded, for the advantage of those youths without fortune who bear honourable names. As to the privileges (*immunités*) of the scholars of the College of Eaton, they extend widely at the time of the examination; thus, for instance, at that happy period, *they may abandon themselves* in the City of London to all the eccentric vagaries of youth without any fear of the constable's forming an obstacle. They may break furniture and smash windows without the police interfering. If a police-agent happens to come in the middle of the havoc (*dégât*), the Eaton scholar has but to show his card, and immediately the constable drops his staff respectfully, which he had raised to interpose between the rioters.'

The sight of a great soldier or sailor at Eton stirred us more than the familiar presence of Royalty. Such enthusiasm is hereditary. Stratford Canning writes home: 'A much greater man than George III. was here yesterday—Lord Nelson. The Admiral wrote to Dr. Goodall, asking for a holiday for the school.' That letter has been religiously preserved at Eton as a sacred relic.

I glory in the careers of two of my contemporaries, and although at school I never exchanged a word with either soldier or sailor, that I can remember, yet I record with pride and gratitude the names of Lord Roberts and Admiral Tryon. I well remember our delight at the escape of Arthur Hardinge — 'little Arthur'—who rode by his father's side at the battle of Ferozeshah. The headmaster suggested our signing and sending a round robin of congratulation on his escape in that famous action. This curious document was sent to India at the instance, I should think, of Dr.

Hawtrey himself, who was known to be a great admirer and friend of Lord Hardinge.

The author of 'Eton of Old' has given us a really new and authentic story of the Duke, whose victorious Guards, shortly after the Waterloo campaign, feasted and sang in the Long Walk in Windsor Park, the Eton boys watching them. I wish he had remembered the whole of the Waterloo song, from which he quotes this verse :

> 'Likewise that General Ponsonby,
>   Which grieved my heart full sore ;
>   I saw him lie
>   As I passed by
>   Like Pompey in his gore.'

'A few weeks after the battle of Waterloo, the great Duke, with his laurels still fresh on his brow, appeared at Eton. When I first saw him, he had jumped upon, and was running along, the Long Walk wall, followed by his two young sons and a body of young noblemen and gentlemen's sons, whose fathers he knew. He was dressed in top-hat, coloured tie, brown cutaway coat, and top-boots, and walked on, or stood laughing and chattering to the boys, and the boys laughing and chattering back, until he jumped down in the midst of them, the veriest boy of them all.

'The solemn historian, of course, could scarcely believe it; and how he managed to escape the Provost and Head in their robes and persuade them to be contented with an informal visit, I have never been able thoroughly to understand, seeing what he was to the English world at the time. But so it was; and then he hurried off in the midst of all his boys to his old Dame's, or Dominic Raguenau, not to call upon the old gentleman, but to run to the kitchen-door, where in his youthful days he had cut his name or initials; he had a great desire to see that effort of youthful talent.

'He stayed in Eton about an hour, and went back to Windsor. But there was no fuss made about him by the authorities. His tastes were always simple; he probably had enough of that in the greater world, and no doubt thoroughly enjoyed his Long Walk wall.'

Applause or hisses never disturbed the Duke of Wellington's unruffled calm; he had heard plenty of both. I watched him very narrowly at his brother's funeral, and he certainly showed no emotion whatever. He had acted as chief mourner, years before, when the fiery Crawfurd was buried in the trench at Ciudad Rodrigo, where he had so gloriously fallen. There also he sternly repressed any outward display of feeling. I only remember to have read of three occasions when human nature got the better of him; two of them are recorded by the brothers George and William Napier, the third by his friend and physician, Dr. Hume. When the list of the slain was read out to him after the murderous assault of Badajoz, 'the iron nature gave way, and the Duke burst into a flood of tears.' Precisely the same thing happened in the early morning after Waterloo, but to my mind Sir George Napier's equally authentic but less well-known story is the most touching of the three. I am quoting from the Diary of Sir George T. Napier, K.C.B., an anecdote which will bear repetition.

'At the battle of Orthez, Lord March, who had left the staff and joined his regiment, the 52nd, was desperately wounded. A sergeant came running after me, saying: "Oh, sir, Lord March is killed!" I went to him, and found my gallant, high-spirited young friend lying with his head in my brother William's lap, to all appearance a lifeless corpse. . . . Lord March was conveyed to the town of Orthez, to a quarter there, as it was made the hospital for the wounded. The next night after he was wounded, he was in so dangerous a state that Dr. Hair, of the 43rd, who attended him, had given positive orders that no noise should be made, and that, as he should himself remain up all night with Lord March, if anyone wanted to come into the room, they should not speak, but be as quiet as possible. About the middle of the night, as Dr. Hair was sitting dozing in a chair opposite Lord March's bed, who had fallen asleep, the door of the room gently opened, and a figure in a white cloak and military hat walked up to the bed, drew the curtains quietly aside, looked steadily for a few seconds on the pale countenance before him, then leaned over, stooped his head, and pressed his lips to the forehead of Lord March, heaved a deep sigh and turned to leave the room, when the doctor, who had anxiously watched every movement, beheld the countenance of Wellington, his cheeks wet with tears. He had ridden many a mile that night, alone, to see his favourite young soldier, the son of his dearest friend. He then returned to his headquarters, having first made every inquiry respecting the sick and wounded, and given such orders as were necessary. Does this betray a want of feeling in the Duke? It needs no comment; the fact speaks for itself.'

There was a fourth occasion many years afterwards, when the Duke was visibly moved to tears, and this was in the House of Lords, when he paid a tribute to the memory of Sir Robert Peel, the great statesman, whom he loved and revered. Will it be believed that an Eton pentameter like the following was actually shown up to an assistant-master:

'Lapsus equo campo, Peele Roberte, jaces'!

Lord Wellesley's letters to his brother in the Indian days were addressed to 'dearest Arthur,' but the Iron Duke was the least emotional of men, and a little less stolidity on the part of the chief mourner would have been welcomed by us, who watched the old soldier narrowly, and were disappointed at his seeming coldness and indifference. Neither of these illustrious brothers was given to the melting mood, though the Marquis, in his famous epitaph, begged for a tributary tear from Eton herself. We all know the lines; I only cite the last four, and the late Earl of Derby's English version:

> 'Si qua meum vitæ decursu gloria nomen
>   Auxerit, aut si quis nobilitavit honos,
> Muneris, alma, tui est, altrix da terra sepulcrum,
>   Supremam lachrymam da memoremque mei.'

> 'If on my later life some glory shine,
>   Some honours grace my name, the meed is thine;
> My boyhood's nurse, my aged dust receive,
>   And one last tear of kind remembrance give!'

The night before the funeral of the Marquis Wellesley, the coffin rested at the Provost's lodge, and we were taken by batches of twenty or thirty to see it. I remember Hawtrey's delight, when the Duke, a short time after the ceremony, sent the MS. epitaph, which he had found amongst his brother's papers, to the Eton authorities.

The famous hook-nose and impassive face were very familiar to me. The Duke was a frequent visitor at Windsor Castle, and he constantly appeared on Sunday afternoons on the Terrace, or accompanying the Queen and Prince Albert on the slopes. There it was our privilege to stare at Royalties at the shortest distances. I never wearied of watching the old hero, marching in slow time with his Royal host and hostess. In the summer he usually wore a blue frock-coat, white duck trousers and straps, and the Waterloo medal, common to the Field Marshal and to the humblest private soldier who took part in, and survived, the last great struggle with Napoleon. I saw him on a memorable occasion, when the Emperor of Russia, the King of Saxony, and other great folk, were present at a grand review in Windsor Park. He had issued an order that no salute was to be fired when the Royal carriage arrived on the ground. Some unlucky Colonel, whose loyalty outran his discretion, ordered his men to fire when the procession approached. The Duke was furious, sent for the unfortunate officer, and stormed at him. I was told that the Queen herself interceded for the offender. His Grace could be uncomplimentary to subordinates who made a mistake; it mattered not what their rank was. When Crawfurd brought on the action on the Coa, the splendid results of his rashness did not save him from the merciless wigging of his chief.

We treated the old Duke rather badly in

some ways, seeing that we belaboured him with bad verses, and maundered woefully over his great enemy, whose setting sun at St. Helena was a trite theme for prose and verse as well. We were very lachrymose over Napoleon's embrace of the eagle at Fontainebleau. Examiners, too, were fond of setting as a subject, 'The Last Charge of Waterloo,' very considerately suggesting Livy as a model for our Latin prose. I remember one sentence '*Jam invesperascebat—Tum clamavit Wellingtonus—Surgite, satellites, et currite in eos!*' for '*Up, guards, and at them!*' Sometimes we adopted an arch familiarity with the hero; this passage was in a Greek sapphic,

εὖ κάρα τόδ' οἶδα τὸ καλλίνικον;

and in 'Pop,'* whenever, through ignorance, we avoided the immediate subject for debate, we glided off at a tangent to the 'Duke of Wellington's sun, setting in meridian glory on the plains of Waterloo,' supplementing this fustian observation with an expression of our firm belief in the purely mythical story about the Duke having declared 'that the battle of

* Our mimic Parliament.

Waterloo was won in the Eton playing-fields.' It is a matter of history that the Duke, when a boy at Eton, had a turn-up in 'Sixpenny Corner' with Bobus Smith; but what affinity have such mimic battles and affairs of honour with Quatre Bras and Waterloo? Eton boys are the most credulous of beings on all matters supposed to reflect distinction on the school. The Westminster boys, in 1837, gave us a handsome beating on the river; William IV. looked on at the race, and sulked at our defeat. He died a few days afterwards, and, as I have said before, it was currently reported at Eton, of a broken heart, because of the Westminster victory. Said Smith *major* to Brown *minimus:* 'I say, Brown, have you heard the news? The King is dead; he was so awfully cut up at our losing the race that it killed him.' Poor King William! Nelson's best man at his wedding with Widow Nesbitt in the West Indies, Nelson's royal mourner at St. Paul's on a certain historical day, when the memory of Trafalgar was fresh! Think of His Majesty reduced to dust by the agonies of the Eton eight catching a crab or two, and the Westminster crew winning by four lengths!

I regret to say that the chapel was once the scene of an ignoble wager. Not that betting was a popular vice or a plague-spot in the school, though the Ascot week was a passing excitement, and touters, with programmes in their hands, haunted the precincts of the College, bawling, 'Cards of the races—names, weights, and colours of the riders!' The students of these documents could be numbered on the fingers. A Hungarian Count and a few Yorkshire lads, pious believers in Charley Wise and his 'tips' for the Gold Cup, might have been amongst them. The return from Ascot of the coaches and four, crowded with weary gentlemen on the roof, wearing wooden dolls in their hats, was a mild kind of Carnival for us, and we used to range ourselves on the Long Wall and hurl pincushions and other harmless missiles at the racing men on their way back to Slough or London. A strawberry pottle, ballasted with an occasional egg, was the only mischievous form of artillery, and the enemy retaliated with the wooden dolls. The skirmish began opposite the Christopher, though once fairly on the Slough Road, after passing Weston's Yard, the tipsters were at peace. Gambling I take to be an hereditary instinct in some families. The rattle of the dice-box must have been familiar music to the ears of Charles Fox in his Eton days. I fear that Lord Holland sent him an occasional 'fiver' just to keep his hand in at the art of wagering. In later days there was a sporting youth who dominated his form, and must be always laying the odds on something or somebody. I assume him to have preferred the betting ring as the more obvious scene of his operations, but to use Eton Chapel as a race-course showed some originality and catholicity of mind. The competitors in these improvised races were caterpillars, detached from their homes on the lime-trees near the entrance-door of the chapel, trained on fragrant leaves, and innocent of the curious destiny which awaited them. Lest they should run wildly and deviate from the strict path of duty, a certain number of extemporary stewards was told off to fence in the race-course with Prayer-books and anthem-books on the benches of the College Chapel, where the boys were kneeling 'stern outwards' during the service. The chief race, *i.e.*, the Caterpillar Derby, took place during the Litany, when there was plenty of time for the pivot boys at the end of the form to turn the racers on their backward journey to the original starting-point. 'Expel Nature with a fork, yet she will always recur'; it is needless to add that the reckless sportsman who originated the insect handicap transferred his energies in after-life to Epsom, Doncaster, and elsewhere, with the usual results to his material progress. 'A horse is counted but a vain thing to save a man,' though it is said that an Oxford betting man, weak in dates and cunning in 'making a book,' got through his ' smalls ' by using the language of the betting-ring as a *memoria technica* for dates in Ecclesiastical History. When challenged by an examiner to give the dates of the call of Abraham and the existence of Malachi, young Rapid would be hopelessly at sea for an answer in numerals, unless he suddenly called to mind the state of the betting on the two events. It was nineteen to one (*i.e.*, 1921 B.C.) against the Patriarch, and forty-three to nothing (*i.e.*, 430 B.C.) upon the last of the Minor Prophets.

I once knew a Judge who studied the Racing Calendar and the law of the land with equal assiduity; he was impatient of every word from counsel that had no bearing upon the point at issue. In forming his own judgment of the favourites for any great race, he carefully read and as carefully distrusted the utterances of a racing seer in *Bell's Life*, who signed himself a 'Prophet'—in nine cases out of ten a false one. The Judge was trying a horse cause. Though rather hard of hearing, he caught faintly the words of a Mr. Stammers addressing the jury, 'As the great Prophet observes.' *The Judge:* 'Ah, Mr. Stammers, don't talk to me about them! I never knew the Prophets right yet' (meaning, of course, the *Bell's Life* Prophets). *Stammers:* 'But, my Lord, I am quoting Jeremiah.' 'Ah! your friend Mr. Meyer is just as wrong as the rest. I don't believe in Mr. Meyer!'

If the sight of the first soldier of the age in Eton Chapel remains indelibly impressed upon my memory, equally vivid is my recollection of the first Churchman of those days, Bishop Wilberforce. It may be that, intellectually, he was inferior to Thirlwall, but that illustrious Prelate reserved himself for great occasions; Wilberforce never spared himself. In his remote Welsh diocese Thirlwall was a great, but to a certain extent a hidden force; whereas Wilberforce, in his archdeacon days and in the earlier years of his episcopate, was ubiquitous. There were few English counties which he had not visited as a preacher, or as an advocate of the Church's interests. His fearless eloquence had attracted the sluggish admiration of the great Duke himself, who, on being pressed to reply off-hand to one of Wilberforce's attacks on the Minister for the time being, said that he 'would rather march unarmed against a battery of cannon,' or words to that effect. It was a good day for us when the Bishop of Oxford claimed the pastoral right of confirming Eton schoolboys, the Bishop of Lincoln still remaining visitor of Eton and King's College. Who can forget those confirmations? I pity any candidate amongst my contemporaries, if he be disloyal enough to listen for one moment to any depreciatory words respecting that Prelate. He was a real orator, and we saw him in his prime. It fell to my lot to be present at one of the last confirmations he ever held, about two months before his death. The old power flashed out again; it was a resuscitation of that light which I had seen as a boy, just as strong, just as searching.

He had a rare gift of adapting himself to any special class of hearers to whom he happened to be ministering, and of kindling the faintest spark of goodness in any who were brought under his influence. Boys are emotional, no doubt, and easily touched, though too often superficially, at the solemn time of confirmation. But I have seen stern, strong men dissolve under the spell of Bishop Wilberforce's oratory, and rough soldiers, too, on their being shown the way to become good centurions. He was an untiring worker, and having no time to prepare his addresses, he would drive straight from Slough station to the chapel door, where the head and the lower master received him. In the few moments that elapsed before the service began, the Bishop eagerly inquired of the two authorities if anything had recently occurred in the school which might form a topic for his extemporary address. On one of these occasions, and only three days before the day of confirmation, a boy of the name of Cotterell —a pupil of the lower master—had died, after a short illness. He had been keenly interested in his impending confirmation, and was altogether the hope and joy of his tutor. On this theme the young Bishop, who bore what he called 'the perilous heritage of the name of Wilberforce,' spake, and a malison be on us who heard him, if his words are forgotten! The echo of the preacher's voice is still audible; that one short half-hour placed my comrades and myself under a life-long obligation, of such a nature that no attacks on the Bishop's memory can shake my loyalty even for one moment.

'Ambitious,' 'time-serving,' 'insincere,'— such are the epithets thoughtlessly hurled at the name of a Prelate who was recognized by Tait as the great representative Churchman of his day. Let his enemies rave! No Bishop, before or since, made such a lasting impression on those who were brought before him for confirmation. In addressing us boys, he could terrify, but console and encourage as well, for he never lost sight of the wholesome words: '*Maxima debetur pueris reverentia;*' and we paid back the feeling with interest.

The next best sermons in Eton Chapel to those of Bishop Wilberforce were conveyed in song by two members of our borrowed choir.

John Foster, the unforgettable chorister boy, still lives, and the octogenarian Charles Lockey, *facile princeps* of English tenors in sacred music before Sims Reeves appeared, is an undoubted G. O. M. Lockey was a friend and contemporary of George Elvey, the Windsor organist, and a few years before Mendelssohn's 'Elijah' was written, took part in a sacred cantata which was originally called 'Elijah.' When Mendelssohn's great oratoria appeared, Elvey modestly re-baptized his cantata (which, I think, still remains in manuscript) 'The Prophets of Baal.' Lockey was the original tenor in Mendelssohn's 'Elijah,' which was brought out at the Birmingham Festival in 1846. His singing of 'Then shall the righteous' moved the composer to tears; we have his own testimony to the fact, which is recorded in one of his letters; further than that, he expressed in an autograph letter to Lockey his sense of gratitude for the eminent services rendered by the young English tenor. I have seen the original, carefully framed and preserved. Lockey's musicianship (he had studied for some years under Sir George Smart), his perfect intonation and style, made him indispensable as first tenor at the Exeter Hall oratorios and provincial festivals. Mendelssohn tested his powers of reading at sight, on a memorable occasion, at the same festival when 'Elijah' was first given. To the dismay of the committee, the band and vocal parts of one particular number in an anthem of Handel's were not forthcoming, and Mendelssohn, in the emergency, was forced to compose, there and then, a Recitative, by way of substitute for the missing number, and to score it for the orchestra. A copy of the vocal part was put into Lockey's hands, and every note was sung correctly at the concert, though, of course, unrehearsed. This slight incident, so honourable to an English singer, has never been forgotten at Birmingham, where it might well have been crowded out by all the glorious memories that attended the first production of 'Elijah.' At the time I speak of, Lockey was at his zenith, a finished artist, who satisfied people accustomed for years to Braham in sacred music. I believe he copied the famous Jew in his version of 'Comfort ye, My people'; the result, anyhow, left an indelible impression on us Eton lads, and no tenor since that time can obliterate the memory of Lockey in the stock oratorios.

His friend Elvey wrote for him tenor solos in anthems and cantatas, which it was my good fortune to hear performed for the first time at St. George's Chapel, or at Windsor concerts. The singer's fame soon spread beyond the limits of Eton and Windsor. It was a bad day for us all, when he migrated to St. Paul's Cathedral, and was succeeded by 'Moiety Mudge,' a singer who 'followed after,' but at an immeasurable distance, Sir George Smart's favourite pupil. Elvey was supremely fortunate in his four leading chorister boys—Foster, Schreiber, Winterbottom, and Thorburn. They had been admirably trained, and Foster was as good a reader at sight as Lockey himself. His voice and his delivery of certain Handelian solos seemed to make all other interpretations false and counterfeit. He was a born vocalist, was this leading 'canary.' That was our name for a chorister boy, and we were rude enough to accost him in that capacity. If there was a new importation in the choir, very young and barbaric, and given to concealing the birth of the aspirate, this sort of dialogue was heard on

Saturday or Sunday afternoons in the schoolyard: 'I say, canary, what's the anthem?' Answer: "'Oly, 'oly, 'oly, allelujah, 'Andel.' Sometimes the insulted bird would indulge in a gloomy and irreverent joke: 'What's the anthem? Why, The Lord is a ship of the line' (meaning thereby 'a man-of-war')!

It was my privilege to have a slight acquaintance with Josiah French, master of the chorister boys at Windsor. He had a true artistic instinct, bought good pictures, and possessed a valuable collection of autographs and portraits or engravings of all the celebrities whose letters and memoranda he had got together. At French's death, this rare collection, arranged and classified in chronological order, was sold and dispersed. In the Royalty volumes were letters from every King and Queen of England since Henry VII.'s time. I remember a long letter of Rubens in my favourite volume—that of the painters. French's collection of manuscripts rivalled that of the late Lord Houghton.

A not infrequent visitor to Windsor in those days was Turner, the famous painter. He was a friend of Stark (once a pupil in the

Norwich school), who in my time lived a quiet, unnoticed life at Windsor. I never heard his name mentioned by Evans or Nesfield, who worthily represented the fine arts at Eton, and were honourably noticed by Mr. Ruskin, whose art-criticisms were then fresh and oracular.

Three other characters in Windsor deserve a passing word — Silly Billy, alias William Leggett, Tucker, the verger, and Roach, the organ-blower at St. George's Chapel, whose quaint sayings were remembered by Sir George Elvey, and have been faithfully recorded by his widow. William Leggett could neither read nor write; he was a curious compound of reverence and cunning, thought and idiocy. His passion for the daily services in St. George's and in Eton College Chapel continued for about half a century. There was no holding Billy, if he heard the chapel bell; no weather, foul or fair, stopped him from running helter-skelter to his devotions. Billy was a strenuous but inelegant Defender of the Faith. He combined High Churchmanship with bargee language. Fourth-form boys would waylay him on his running expeditions to St. George's or our chapel, and sing out, 'I say, Billy, the Queen is the Head of the Church,' whereupon the angry man twiddled the end of his coat-tail, and spat furiously, like an Italian.

Though the Canons of St. George's were indulgent enough to provide a mat for him in cold weather to stand upon, he would never spare their feelings if they read the wrong lesson or the wrong collect. Billy would spring from his seat and cry, 'That's wrong!' One offender, hoping to escape obloquy and to propitiate Billy with gifts, or to secure his silence, addressed him thus: 'Oh, I've an old waistcoat, and if you'll come to my lodgings, I'll let you have it!' Billy went, secured the waistcoat, and then turned short upon the giver: 'You read the wrong collect last night.' His audible squeaks, his quiver and quake 'Amens' at the end of the collects or prayers, were very trying to Sir George Elvey and the lay clerks of Windsor.

A friend writes to me: 'I was in St. George's when the Dean gave out a chapter for the first lesson, "The 12th of Isaiah." Silly Billy said, "No, it ain't; it's the 13th." The Dean turned to him, said, "Thank you," and gave out the 13th.'

In early days Billy fell desperately in love with a young lady who lived near the Castle. His only way of making known his attachment was by serenading her at ten o'clock each night with Lord Mornington's chant and the 'Gloria Patri,' but his passion was not reciprocated; he lived and died a bachelor. A passing reference to the devil, in sermon or talk, would cause the old man to gnash his teeth, clasp his hands, and become excited. 'I see *him* perched on the organ,' said he; and he would occasionally ask of Sir George Elvey: 'You wouldn't like to meet *him* on the organ-loft stairs, would you?' Hearing of a murder, he would quietly console himself: 'Oh yes, the old un's bin at it. It's all *him!*' If a lay clerk had been away on a visit to any of our cathedrals, he would ask: 'Did they run *him* down where you've been?' The answer, 'Oh, yes, Billy; they always do it,' would delight him, and he would exclaim with joy: 'Then he *must* be guilty. He must be! He ha'n't got a leg to stand on.' But he looked upon *him* commercially as well, and said once to a dignitary of St. George's Chapel: 'You're always running *him* down; but he's the best friend you ever had. If't 'adn't bin for *him*, you'd have had nothing to do.' One afternoon, in hot weather, he became faint in chapel, and had to be taken out, and later on, one of the Military Knights sent him a glass of port-wine, which he swallowed at a draught. A lay clerk said to him in sympathy: 'I suppose it was the hot weather.' 'It's 'otter somewhere else, where *he* is!' Billy shouted. *He* also, according to Billy, was conversant with all that was going on, delighted in setting people by the ears, and, above all vices, took in the local papers every week.

Billy Leggett was unable to follow any trade, and in the old days helped his mother by turning her mangle. But directly the time for the Eton service approached, no more mangling for Billy. Persuasion was useless; he was off at once. He lived in Dean Hobart's time at Bier Lane, and the Eton and St. George's Chapel services following each other, the choristers at the first function could take part in the second. One of the singing men was blind and lame, yet could not be excused, and Billy was accustomed to conduct him to Eton, and then back to St. George's. Now and then, on the return journey, the ring of the chapel-bell was heard ere they had reached Windsor, and Billy, suddenly waxing furious, would let go his charge, and toddle off without mercy.

Anecdotes without number, in relation to his adventures and oddities, might be drawn from the dwellers in Windsor. At one time the wide road opposite the Castle, now leading from High Street to the Great Western station, was called George Street, and a colony of sweeps lived around the then borough gaol at its lower end. Houses were being built near the gaol. One day Billy was being enraged by the sweeps. Mr. Wagner, the private tutor to the second Duke of Wellington, happened to be riding along the High Street with other tutors, and at once dismounted, and chased the sweeps with his riding-whip towards the gaol. They slipped through the doorways of the half-finished houses, and in a moment were out of sight. Mr. Wagner was puzzled; they had taken refuge in the chimneys.

The Canons were kind in giving Billy cast-off clothing and similar articles, and he picked up trifles by using his wondrous memory for reminding many persons of their birthdays. From one Eton friend he had a pension of a penny a week, and Billy never omitted to call for the copper on the right day—Monday. A certain lady in Windsor possessed a number of sketches by French, one of the lay clerks who was clever with his pencil, and had a keen sense of fun. Most of them are on scraps of letter-paper. Two of them present us with Billy Leggett. On one we have only a sedate portrait, inscribed, with all honour to the reflected celebrity, 'Mr. Billy Leggett'; on another, he appears only as far as his collar; his pointed nose is thrown forward, his lips are apart, and we read on a faint line above: 'Billy singing King in C.'

One of his great desires was to see the devil, but on a chimney-pot, or somewhere at a distance, because he feared that once within his gaze he would be imprisoned for ever. He thought he might get away by pleading that he had not a clean shirt just at that moment, but then he was not sure. He was very fond of Luther's hymn, and prevailed upon Sir George Elvey one evening to hear him sing it in the choristers' singing-school. Billy's chief desire was to show off a remarkable shake, which one of the lay clerks was wont to introduce at the end; and after he had succeeded to his own full satisfaction, he requested further of Sir George that he would ask the Dean to let him sing the hymn in the chapel next day, saying off-hand: 'If you'll tell him my name is Leggett, he'll know all about me.' He one day succeeded in securing for himself a highly distinguished position for the time being. We give his own version of the story.

Once a year, the choristers belonging to Billy's two places of worship had what they called their Eton feast, and for that afternoon the service at St. George's was omitted. Billy was always an invited guest, and on one of the occasions, in the interval between the beef and the plum-pudding, the St. George's bell began to ring. No one could hold him back, and off he toddled to Windsor. The Dean and canons were then obliged to be on duty twenty-one days in succession, and either through inadvertence, or (as some have it) to secure himself from losing his residence, Dean Hobart had most unexpectedly arranged for the service. He read it himself, and his sole auditor was Billy, who made himself answerable for the responses and chants. The Dean, wanting apparently to shorten the service, omitted the

Magnificat, and was going on with the *Nunc Dimittis*. This was too much for Billy. He rushed up to the Dean in his stall, and exclaimed in something louder than a whisper: 'My soul doth magnify.' 'Oh, oh!' was the quiet reply, and Dean Hobart went back to the proper place. He was very kind to Billy's mother, and when she lay ill, sent her some jam. It was left untasted when she died, and Billy went forthwith to the Dean: 'Please, sir, mother's dead: may I eat the jam?'

He didn't like half the service; he liked all or none, he said. He was buried at the cost of the Dean and Canons of Windsor, who erected a tombstone in the cemetery, bearing the following inscription:

In Memory of
WILLIAM LEGGETT,
For upwards of 50 years a regular attendant at the
Daily Services of St. George's Chapel,
Died January 23rd, 1875.
Aged 73 years.

'Lord, I have loved the habitation of Thy house.'—PSALM xxvi. 8.
'The entrance of Thy word giveth light: it giveth understanding unto the simple.'—PSALM cxix. 130.*

---

* I derive my information from a pamphlet which was published in Windsor, shortly after Silly Billy's death.

If 'Silly Billy' is impressed on my memory, as a sort of gurgoyle which once belonged to St. George's Chapel, there were other eccentric characters, familiar to everyone who haunted the place. Many of us smarted under the rudeness of Tucker, the senior verger. He rattled a huge bunch of keys at his side, calling on everyone to be quiet, himself the incarnation of fuss, and 'full of sound and fury.' His odd boast was that he had held up to the light the mouldering head of Charles I. in 1814, when the Prince Regent and Sir Henry Halford, after unearthing the poor body, proceeded to cut off the hair and beard, and to divide the ghastly spoil. Whether Tucker romanced or not, I cannot say, but he talked of seeing the stitches connecting the head and trunk, and of a hole in the coffin, inflicted by the spear of an angry Cromwellian soldier. I wish the memory of the obsequies of the 'White King' were entirely free from incongruities or grotesque associations.

A stately scene is that depicted on the panels of the corridors of the House of Lords, where, following the snow-clad pall, Archbishop Juxon makes an impressive figure amongst the few mourners privileged, at their risk, to pay the last honours to their slaughtered Sovereign. We read in Whitelock that about twelve years afterwards, the Primate, on his retirement to Little Compton, in Gloucestershire, 'went to the dogs,' or (to drop the metaphor) kept a pack of harriers!

Juxon in the pigskin strikes me as a bathos, though it is pleasant to learn that 'a southerly wind and a cloudy sky' made him a genteel and courteous whipper-in. M.F.H.'s in our time can be unparliamentary in their language. 'I didn't come out here to be d——d,' said an imbecile curate, who persisted in riding over the hounds. 'Then go home and be d——d!' answered the Assheton Smiths and Sir Richard Suttons of our time. 'Orderly' is the epithet applied by Whitelock to Juxon in the management of his harriers and the field, and yet I cannot much relish the idea of the retired Prelate getting up from his study table, on the anniversary of the death of King Charles I., rising in his stirrups, and shouting 'Yoicks! Gone away!' as poor Wat is seen stealing away from his lair on the neighbouring hill. There have been Prelates much addicted to fishing and shooting; I believe Juxon is the last who went well to hounds. At no period of English history are the 'inferior clergy,' especially if of Irish extraction, so squeamish.

A reverend contemporary of mine was addressed by a friend, at the meet of the Atherstone Hounds, at Lord Howe's country seat in Leicestershire: 'Good-morning, parson; I saw you in the pulpit yesterday.' 'Yes,' was the reply; 'Gospel on Sunday, Gopsall on Monday.'

'Juxon delighted in hunting, and kept a pack of good hounds, so well ordered and hunted, chiefly by his own skill and direction, that they exceeded all the hounds in England for the pleasure and orderly handling of them. He was a person of great parts and temper, and had as much command of himself as of his hounds.' Such is the testimony of a biographer.

Dean Hook supplements his account of Juxon, in his huntsman's capacity, with two stories traditional in the neighbourhood of Little Compton. 'Juxon's hounds were running through a neighbouring churchyard, whilst certain Puritans were engaged in "seeking the Lord," and a deputation from the offended congregation was sent to lay a complaint of the affair before Oliver Cromwell. "Pray," said the Protector in reply, "do you think that the Bishop prevailed on the hare to run through your churchyard at that time?" "No," was the rejoinder; "and, please your Highness, we did not directly say he did; but through the churchyard the hare did go at that time." "Get you gone," replied the Protector, "and let me hear no such frivolous complaints. Whilst the Bishop continues not to give my government any offence, let him enjoy his diversion of hunting unmolested."'

The Bishop had conferred a great obligation on a gentleman in his neighbourhood, and refused to receive any kind of return. 'Give me leave,' said the gentleman, 'to add at least one stanch hound to your pack.' This was an offer which the Bishop could not resist; the dog was to be sent; it came; on its collar the name was engraved: 'Jowler.' Jowler was a silver drinking-cup, and the Bishop was evidently amused by the determined gratitude of his friend. It became the law of the house that every stranger should take off 'Jowler's' head at a draught.

'Silly Billy's' vagaries in St. George's Chapel

were ably seconded by Roach, the organ-blower and belfry-keeper. This official was in full blast when my old friend, Sir George Elvey, was appointed to the organistship, but he had not yet succeeded to the coveted post of belfry-keeper. After receiving that extra appointment, Elvey congratulated him, and Roach, highly elated, answered: 'I tell you what, young man, whenever you wants wind, you shall 'ave it.' He patronized and depreciated the young organist, as the humour took him. Said he: 'It's all very well for that young man to sit figuring there, but it'll take all the wind out of any man to blow the "Hallelujah Chorus," I don't care what country he comes from.' When the King died, Roach went off to the Deanery, to announce the fact to Dean Hobart. 'Well, Roach, what's the matter?' 'Billy be dead; be I to ring the bell?' 'What Billy?' 'The King, to be sure.' 'You may toll the bell.' Roach was a great stickler for adhering to the musical programme of anthems and services, when once it had been signed and settled by the proper authorities. On one occasion, when the service had been changed to please some visitors, Roach, highly offended, addressed

Elvey thus: 'You can play Rogers in D, if you like, but I shall blow Attwood in C.'

A contemporary of 'Moiety Mudge' was Robert Bridgewater, a bass singer, who migrated from York Minster to St. George's Chapel, where he did good solid work for many years. The Eton boys hated his singing, which at times was rather coarse and aggressive. We had a great deal of him in and out of chapel, for he was a capable musician, and an inexpensive item at concerts given in Eton and Windsor.

I have observed that, except in Russia and Austria, bass singers, gifted with abnormally low notes, are only popular with a few. It is well known that Herr Formes, the German *basso profondo*, was in such favour with our Royalties, that to the dismay of Costa and his Italian singers, his engagement at Covent Garden became, for a few seasons, an annual necessity. He was very terrible in oratorio at Exeter Hall, notably in the 'Creation' and 'Elijah.'

'I never troubled Israel's pease.
It is thou, Ähārb!'

'With long dimenshuns kreeps vith scenuous trace the vorm (worm).'

These were amongst his gems in Haydn's and Mendelssohn's music. Anyhow, Bridgewater, with all his coarseness, understood the Queen's English, and deserved a more elegant name than 'Thunderguts,' bestowed on him by Etonians of later date than mine.

Robert Bridges, a poet we are proud of, has written a Requiem in honour of old Thunder***s, the three stars being substituted for the monosyllable equivalent to 'entrails.' Rather misleading, rather squeamish! I take it that the '*Es brennt mein Eingeweide,*' in Goethe's famous lyric, exactly represents to the German mind the short English equivalent, though I also know that the unhappy word '*Eingeweide*' was a grievous trouble to Lord Tennyson, who never could repeat it without palpably wincing. Here is Robert Bridge's

EPITAPH ON A GENTLEMAN OF THE CHAPEL ROYAL.

'Old Thunder***s is dead, we weep for that,
He sings for aye his lowest note, B flat.
Unpursed his mouth, empty his mighty chest,
His run is o'er, and none may bar his rest.
We hope he is not d——d, for if he be,
He's on the wrong side of the middle sea.
Nay, we are sure, if weighed, he will not fail
Against the devil to run down the scale;

While e'en three-throated Cerberus must retreat
From that which bellows from his sixteen feet;
Or, should he meet with Peter at the door,
He'll seize the proper key as heretofore,
And by an easy turn he'll quickly come
From common time straight to *ad libitum*.
There in the equal temperament of Heaven,
Sharps, crotchets, accidentals, all forgiven,
He'll find his place directly, and perspire
Among the basses of the Elysian quire.
Fear, dwellers on the earth, this acquisition
To the divine ethereal ammunition;
A thunder is let loose, a very wonder
Of earthborn, pitiless, Titanic thunder;
We, who remain below and hear his roar,
Must kneel and tremble where we laughed before.'

One of the Queen's worst bargains was an old bass singer, of the name of Salmon, a choir-man in St. George's Chapel. He was not given to a mood of resignation, and held on to everything he had once got hold of, with tenacity, to the last. His voice in early days had been a fortune to him, and secured him freehold appointments in three or four London choirs, independently of that of St. George's Chapel. He was a square-built, powerful man, with a head large and ugly enough to have satisfied Fuseli, when he wanted a model for 'Giant Despair.' He was a son of the famous

Mrs. Salmon, unequalled, people say, as a Handelian singer; her very big son perpetrated very small jokes, which, as coming from such a Caliban, provoked the laughter of his friends and associates. 'Try that fine *celery*,'[*] said Hobart to him, at the annual dinner given to the choir by the Dean of St. George's; 'I raised it myself.' 'Now, did you, Mr. Dean? I wish you would raise mine.' Unquenchable laughter—as the retort came from old Salmon.

I used to watch the thirsty veteran on Election Mondays, dipping his enormous head into the gilt loving-cup, and taking a long draught of the contents. Before this ceremony, he used to mutter audibly: 'Man and boy sixty years,' meaning that he had been a member of the Eton and Windsor choirs for that period. Salmon and 'Hoppy' Batcheldor, who lived at Black Potts, were supposed to have consumed a haunch of venison between them.

The last of Sir George Elvey's Levites, and the *doyen* of bass singers, was Mitchell, who died quite recently. He had been a Windsor and Eton chorister boy in Mr. Gladstone's schooldays, and was proud to be reminded of the fact by the Minister himself.

[*] Pronounced *salary*, in the old-fashioned way.

CHAPTER VIII.

THE PLAYING-FIELDS.

I AM told that affairs of honour are no longer transacted in 'Sixpenny Corner,' which lives in Eton history as the classical arena of famous battles. A good stand-up fight, between big boys, was a treat to us little fellows, who, perched on the Playing-fields wall, looked down upon Hector and Achilles and applauded lustily our favourite champion, none of us knowing or caring to understand the rights or wrongs of the quarrel. Though unrecorded in *Bell's Life*, mighty men have pommelled one another in 'Sixpenny,' and washed their wounds at the college pump. There should have been a sacred poet, an eighteenth-century Pindar,* to record the particulars of each

* Hartley Coleridge called Pindar 'the Newmarket Poet.'

round between Arthur Wellesley and Bobus Smith. The story is that Bobus Smith was bathing, and that Wellesley threw a stone at him. Thereupon the outraged Bobus landed, had it out then and there in *puris naturalibus*, and got a licking. It is a pity that the Duke left no record of his first fight. To have damaged the historical nose, or tapped the Wellesley 'claret,' would have added lustre to the fame of Bobus, whose Lucretian verses were as good as Keate's, and twice as strong as 'Vinny Bourne's,' the assistant master, of whom Cowper says: 'I love the memory of Vinny Bourne. I think him a better Latin poet than Tibullus, Propertius Ausonius, or any of the writers in his own way, except Ovid, and not at all inferior to *him*.' I believe it was Sidney Walker who, when asked to classify his favourite *Latin* poets in their order, replied: 'Milton, Ovid, Bobus Smith, Virgil.' Poor Virgil! lag of his remove! Shakespeare's Bardolph speaks prophetically of 'Sixpenny Strikers.' Let me say in passing that 'Sixpenny' is rather a misleading term, seeing that the subscription to that club was a shilling; the unappropriated parts of the Playing-fields were occupied by 'Twopenny.' I stand up for the old names, though now and again 'the old order yieldeth to the new.' In the Playing-fields changes have been made in paths or roads; a path that used to run straight from Weston's Yard, between 'Sixpenny' and Lower College on the one side, and 'Aquatics' on the other, to Sheep's Bridge, has vanished; an improvement certainly.

I was told by a very old colleger that Lord Stratford de Redcliffe fought very gamely in 'Sixpenny,' and this I can well believe. He was not the 'Clemency Canning' of the Indian Mutiny, and when, to quote the language of *Bell's Life* and the ring, 'Round 1, Canning now stretched out his feeler,' I fancy he stretched it out to some purpose. Calthorp *v.* Forster was *the* battle of my time; it was very gallantly fought. Forster was terribly punished, and eventually threw up the sponge. Hawtrey, beetle-blind to the theatricals in Long Chamber, was deaf to the shouts in 'Sixpenny Corner.' The assistant masters wisely deserted the Playing-fields on fighting days, and the victor and the vanquished soon forgot their differences over a pot of 'half and half' at the Christopher.

'Sixpenny' became unexpectedly famous in the cricket annals of the school in the summer half of 1845. A tall, overgrown boy of the name of Abbott, backward in school, but precociously forward in games, presided over the Fourth-Form Club, where he was a 'Triton amongst the minnows.' The wicket-keeper of the school eleven, now a distinguished Chancery Judge, wisely indulged in cricket supervision visits in every part of the Playing-fields. He watched the play, whenever and wherever a game was going on, and reported to his captain the results of his observation. Nobody escaped him, not even the despised 'Aquatics,' who on rainy evenings, unfit for rowing, condescended to 'urge the flying ball,' and always in an upward direction.

This vigilance was well rewarded. 'Sixpenny' and 'Aquatics' furnished us, at different periods, with two really useful men in our matches at Lord's. Abbott's sudden elevation *per saltum*, from 'Sixpenny' to Upper Club, caused a great sensation; but he made a distinguished *début* in the Upper Shooting Fields, and scored over fifty in the Harrow match, thus more than justifying the wisdom of the future Judge, who had picked him out of the humblest club in the Playing fields.

The aquatic 'great by land and sea' in my time was my old friend Augustus Rivers Thompson,* now, or, until recently, a Judge in India. Thompson was one of the best oars in the eight, and though he just missed being in the eleven, acted as my deputy in the Winchester match of 1847. I have been informed quite recently, that I had, for a part of the match, a second deputy, Wiss, who, on Thompson's being called away from Lord's to row in the Westminster match, fielded out for the ubiquitous 'Bill.' It has taken about fifty years for me to recover from my disappointment and mortification at missing my share in that victory, for it was an *annus mirabilis* for Eton that year—we triumphed on land and water.

In modern days victory does not invariably sit on the Eton helm, so that I may look back with some justifiable pride on the one blessed year when we lowered the colours of Westminster, Harrow, and Winchester. I was detained by an examination in Election Chamber when the wickets were pitched at Lord's for

---

* Always called Bill Thompson at Eton.

the Winchester match, and had received an agonizing letter from my captain (now Lord Justice Chitty) to the effect that, if I could not appear at such and such an hour on the ground, Thompson must play for me. Almost immediately after the receipt of this agreeable announcement, the examiners renewed their tortures for two more hours; I had to write thirty bad iambics on a speech of Miltiades, and thus was too late to contribute to the defeat of Winchester. To compare small things with great, it was Sir Charles Colville fretting his life out at Hal, nine miles from Waterloo, and not allowed to fire a shot. I arrived in time to take my proper place in the Harrow match, when Blore and Aitken made terrible havoc with their deadly straight bowling, and Jem Aitken, in an innings which became historical, hit two consecutive balls for six and seven each. We got out the Harrow eleven in their first innings for 27 runs. It was a famous victory, but I grudged Will Thompson his share in the earlier match.

It is a curious thing that Marcon and H. W. Fellows, the two fastest Eton bowlers that I remember, should have been in the same eleven.

LORD JUSTICE CHITTY.

Marcon, when he was bowling in practice, broke a man's leg at Oxford, and old Lillywhite refused to go in at Lord's against Fellows. The veteran bowler was returned on the scoring-sheet, 'Lillywhite, absent 0.' I observe another and very curious record of a famous Etonian, C. G. Taylor, commonly called 'Charley Taylor.' This was in the 'Gentlemen and Players'' match in August, 1843 : 'C. G. Taylor, Esq., hat knocked on wicket—bowled Hillyer 89.'

The attachment of Eton cricketers to their bats is proverbial. Nor is the fetish worship of a wooden idol confined to amateurs, for I remember on the solitary occasion of Alfred Mynn's visit to Eton, when I had the honour of playing against him, that an inscription on his bat, as it lay majestically in the tent, was studied very conscientiously by every member of our side. The inscription, carved *à la Finmore*, beneath the handle ran thus : ' Presented to Alfred Mynn by his friend, Fuller Pilch, in commemoration of his innings on ' (date added). We were greatly impressed by this record of Pilch's devotion to the good-natured giant, who earned a more durable epitaph later on. Here it is, and old cricketers will be glad to see it again. The elegy first appeared in *Bell's Life,* November 10, 1861 :

'Jackson's pace is very fearful, Willsher's hand is very high ;
William Caffyn has good judgment, and an admirable eye ;
Jemmy Grundy's cool and clever, almost always on the spot ;
Tinley's slows are often telling, though they sometimes catch it hot ;
But however good their trundling—pitch or pace, or break or spin—
Still the monarch of all bowlers, to my mind, was Alfred Mynn.

'Richard Daft is cool and cautious, with his safe and graceful play ;
If George Griffith gets a loose one, he can send it far away.
You may bowl your best at Hayward, and whatever style you try
Will be vanquished by the master's steady hand and certain eye.
But whatever fame and glory these and other bats may win,
Still the monarch of hard hitters, to my mind, was Alfred Mynn.

'When the great old Kent eleven, full of pluck and hope, began
The grand battle with all England, single-handed, man to man ;

How the hopmen watched their hero, massive, muscular, and tall,
As he mingled with the players, like a King among them all;
Till to some old Kent enthusiasts it would almost seem a sin
To doubt their county's triumph when led on by Alfred Mynn.

'Though Sir Frederick and "the Veteran" bowled straight and sure and well,
Though Box behind the wicket only Lockyer can excel,
Though Jemmy Dean as longstop would but seldom grant a bye,
Though no novices in batting were George Parr and Joseph Guy—
Said the fine old Kentish farmers, with a fine old Kentish grin,
"Why, there ain't a man among them as can match our Alfred Mynn."

'And whatever was the issue of the frank and friendly fray
(Aye, and often has his bowling turned the fortune of the day),
Still the Kentish men fought bravely, never losing hope or heart,
Every man of the eleven glad and proud to play his part;
And with five such mighty cricketers 'twas but natural to win—
As Felix, Wenman, Hillyer, Fuller Pilch, and Alfred Mynn.

'With his tall and stately presence, with his nobly moulded form,
His broad hand was ever open, his brave heart was ever warm.

All were proud of him, all loved him . . . as the changing
　　seasons pass,
As our champion lies a-sleeping underneath the Kentish
　　grass.
Proudly, sadly we will name him, to forget him were a sin ;
Lightly lie the turf upon thee, kind and manly Alfred
　　Mynn.

　　　　　　　　　　'W. J. PROWSE,
　　　　　　　　　　　　'Tottenham.'

Why should not bats be christened as well as ships? Hardy, a famous cricketer at Eton, called his bat 'Mrs. Keate,' and that graceful lady was pleased with what ordinary dames would have thought a wooden compliment. Theobald, K.S., who was one of the last tenants of Long Chamber, called his three bats: 1. 'Jehu,' 'for it driveth furiously'; 2. 'Nimshi,' because it had been 'Jehu's' predecessor; and 3. 'Sheep,' 'for it lammeth.' This dreary joke needs a glossary. To 'lam' or 'lamb' was in my day an equivalent for swiping, driving, hitting hard. The owner of these three instruments was one of the few collegers of my time who entered the army; he went into the 18th Royal Irish regiment and died young of cholera in India. I am assured that some years after my time there were three Tugs in the Guards!

In my first year at Eton, the Mitchell of the period was Emilius Bayley (the present Sir Emilius Laurie), whose praise is in many churches, as well as in cricketing annals. His father, Sir John Bayley, for many years Clerk of Assize on the Northern Circuit, and an old Wykehamist, was a good lawyer and an ardent sportsman, though he never owned a race-horse nor made a bet. In the year 1823, when he was hoping for a son and heir, the Derby was won by a horse called 'Emilius,' after which the child was named. He narrowly missed being called 'Tancred,' or 'Cephalus,' for those animals came in second and third after the winner. There was a myth to the effect that he ought to have been 'Lollipop.' 'Lollipop,' out of 'Sweetmeat,' would have been a very trying name for an Eton boy. Think of the ignominious shout from Lord's pavilion : 'Run it out, Lollipop !' 'Chuck it up, Lollipop !' or, 'Now then, Bull's-eye !' for there are many shades and variations in a boy's vocabulary, when a name is suggestive of variation, or metaphorical language.* Sir Emilius

* I remember Frank Blomfield's name for Ronconi, the singer, was 'Misguided Rabbit' (*i.e.*, wrong coney), and for

himself says: 'I was called "Derby" before I was born, as I have been ever since by my relatives. It was assumed that I should be a boy, and that Emilius would win.'

Bayley's innings of 153 against Harrow was a fine performance. He had the rare distinction of beating our opponents in a single innings off his own bat, for the Harrow score in the two innings fell short of Bayley's in one. Strange to say, we had been beaten hollow by our Winchester opponents prior to the match with Harrow that same year, and nothing shows the 'glorious uncertainty of cricket' more than the fact that each of the three schools scored a complete victory, and each suffered a humiliating defeat.

The Lord's matches in those days were, I take leave to think, far more sporting occasions than in these degenerate days. Three thousand spectators was reckoned a large 'gallery.' I hear of 20,000 people at the Harrow match, and wonder how many, attending the luxurious

---

Tullibardine, 'Cicero in prison' (*i.e.*, Tulley barred in). Poor wit enough! but pundits and learned historians have been known to play with names and words. See Professor Freeman's letters *passim*.

picnic, care about the game, or enjoy the play. Does one lady in five hundred understand the alphabet of cricket, any more than she does the points of a racehorse on the Cup day at Ascot? Few have Dr. Arnold's honesty, as represented by Tom Brown, when he overhears the doctor's confession, whilst looking on at a Rugby cricket match : 'I don't understand cricket, so I don't enjoy those fine draws which you tell me are the best play, though, when you and Raggles hit a ball away for six, I am as delighted as ever.'

For four consecutive years we never lost a match at Lord's, and I invite the present generation at Eton to take note of that chain of victory, broken only by the historical tie with Winchester in 1845. J. C. Patteson was our captain on that memorable occasion. A bad accident to his hand had deprived us of his services, except as adviser and controller of the match, and many of us attributed our misfortune to the fact of his being unable to play; but candid people must admit that Blore's bowling was a great compensation for the loss, seeing that Blore, as first choice out of the eleven, played for Patteson, temporarily disabled. We were never good at an uphill game, and Dewar, the Winchester change bowler, as nearly as possible secured the victory for his school. I never remember, before or since, to have heard of an actual tie in a Public School match. One of the two bowlers, Blore and Holland, ran the other out, when the winning run was wanted. Whenever in after years the victims met, they reopened the question as to whose fault it was. My friend S. Deacon (*clarum et venerabile nomen* amongst Eton cricketers) still condemns them both, and is very bitter about it. I myself was accused of running out Barnett in a Harrow match, and smarted under the reproof of Jem Aitkin, who girded at me when he reached the wicket: 'Now, Arthur, don't run me out!' I felt savage, but had the felicity to make the winning cut of the match without sacrificing the satirical Jem by my overeagerness.

We always had a great respect and liking for our Winchester opponents, whereas, for the space of two days every year, we cordially detested the very name of Harrow. The sympathy existing between the two old colleges of Eton and Winchester (*esto perpetua*) is as old as the hills (including St. Catharine's and Salt Hill); but the want of cordiality in our feeling for Harrow is rather unaccountable. Anyhow, we shouted for Winchester in their match with Harrow, and Winchester, to a man, went with us in our battle against the common enemy.

The Winchester cricketing costume in those days and their sporting lingo were peculiar. The eleven always appeared at Lord's wearing tall white beaver hats—a curious contrast to the Eton straw, which in my earliest cricketing days was *de rigueur* our head-gear, and for which to this day I have an amiable weakness.

What splendid leg-hitters those Winchester fellows were! I remember being put on, as a change bowler, in 1848, and I happened, by the merest fluke, to disturb Ridding's middle stump. Ridding was the Winchester captain, and my ball was a half volley, which I expected to see sent flying into space, instead of flooring the sticks. As the gentleman returned crest-fallen to the pavilion, he was heard by a friend of mine to observe: 'Catch me hitting again at young Coleridge's barters!'*

* Barter, a Winchester synonym for half-volley.

There was plenty of good-humoured chaff from the on-lookers and partisans of Eton and Harrow, and an annual battle between Picky Powell and Billy Warner, two tipsy cads, hailing from the two schools, who championed their respective teams.

I recently read in the 'Autobiography of Sir William Gregory,' a distinguished Harrovian, that as far back as 1831 there was not a field within miles of Harrow in which he had not poached by day, or a pond he had not dragged by night, with a celebrated loose character, Billy Warner by name. Old schoolfellows plied these thirsty souls with bitter beer *ad lib.* during the day of the match, and towards evening Picky Powell and Billy Warner began to square at one another. Picky, our man, had been a notable cricketer in his youth, and when sober could tell us many yarns about Lord Frederick Beauclerk, Ward, and other ancient heroes of the cricket-field. Billy Warner had nothing to recommend him, save his devotion to Harrow, and his pluck in annually standing up to Picky, who was much the bigger man of the two. 'All the good I sees in 'Arrow,' said Picky, 'is, that you can

PICKY POWELL.

see Eton from it, if ye go up into the churchyard.' This insult to the memory of John Lyon was too much for Billy, who squared at his enemy at once, and was generally pounded into a jelly. The fight was so much a matter of course, that we players hardly noticed the brawl, or the excitement of the strangers looking on, who used to inquire what it was all about. 'Oh, it's only Picky and Billy Warner fighting,' was the invariable answer.

I remember a very amusing episode in one of the Winchester matches. Our opponents were playing an uphill game with conspicuous success, and their captain scored so fast, that the easy victory we had reckoned upon in the earlier stage of the proceedings seemed likely enough to end in defeat. At last, and not without great difficulty, Ridding (a brother of the Ridding who played in my time) was bowled, and the last man in the eleven, Jones Bateman, came in to get thirty and odd runs, if his side was to win. Our longslip, McNiven, commonly called 'Snivey,' was a great character, and not given to ceremony or overpoliteness. When Jones Bateman timidly advanced to the wicket, 'Snivey' roared out:

'Hullo, 'ere comes Jones Bateman, to get thirty runs; I knows I shall catch him out, as 'ow his brother boards at Mrs. Ward's.' The argument was peculiar: 'Because Jones Bateman, *minor*, boards at my dame's house at Eton, therefore, Providence means that I shall compass the destruction of his brother, a boy at Winchester.' However unsound 'Snivey's' logic, poor trembling J. B. fulfilled 'Snivey's' prophecy to the letter, for a moment or two after it was uttered, he sent the ball up aloft and straight into 'Snivey's' large brown hands, and exit J. B. 'Told you so!' roared 'Snivey,' as he caught and chucked up the ball simultaneously, and ran with his rejoicing companions to the pavilion.

'Snivey's' exploits have been recorded in the pages of the late Sir John Astley, whose words I quote and heartily endorse: 'One of the most remarkable boys at Eton with me was McNiven, *minor;* he was a real wonder. He was in the upper sixth, in the football team, in the cricket eleven, and in the eight, and upon my life I don't know in which of the three games he most excelled. He was a brilliant football-player, but a terribly untidy fellow; and his shoes were always down at heel, so much so, indeed, that I have often seen his shoe fly after turning the ball, or when he made a kick. I once saw him catch and eat a cockchafer for a bet of one shilling. I hope he liked it. Poor old fellow! he came to a sad end. He was staying with his brothers in the Isle of Wight, and was driving a dogcart to some place where he was going to shoot, and his dog was tied behind the cart; he turned round to encourage the animal, which was quite a new purchase, and somehow he lost his balance, fell over the back of the dogcart on to his head in the road, and broke his neck. So ended poor old "Snivey," as we used to call him.'

Such were Sir J. Astley's recollections of 'Snivey'; I wish to supplement them with a few of my own, and some which have been sent to me by my contemporaries, one of whom says:

'I always think of "Snivey" as sitting down in the middle of the football-field, putting on a fresh pair of boots which he had just fagged Bill Atcherley to fetch from his dame's, with a circle of admiring boys round him; no doubt the boots he had begun the game in had suddenly collapsed.'

There is an allusion to another member of the family in the old Montem Ode:

> 'The elder McNiven, to whom has been given
> A skin not so white as the snow that's called driven.'

It should be remembered to 'Snivey's' credit that he could appreciate and pride himself on his intimacy with his friend and contemporary, J. C. Patteson. Their relations were superior to those of the ordinary *camaraderie* founded on cricket, fives, and football distinctions, for the future Bishop and martyr, though he excelled in games, was nothing to speak of as an aquatic, and very inferior in physique to the robust and sinewy 'Snivey.' They were strongly contrasted. With nothing of the fop about him, Patteson was always neatly dressed. 'Snivey,' unless disguised in clean flannels on a match day, was a notorious sloven. His turn-out on Speech-days was remarkable. A large moss-rose in the button-hole failed to atone for the greasy, dilapidated dress-coat, and the pumps, always down at heel, as his ordinary shoes were, were patched with lumps of red sealing-wax, borrowed for the occasion from the bureau of some lower boy at Mrs.

Ward's. Thus accoutred, 'Snivey' stepped valiantly into the arena of the Upper School, and declaimed 'Ajax' or 'Agamemnon' to the Provost and Fellows, battered pumps, moss-rose, sealing-wax and all, in full evidence, before his admiring schoolfellows. Nothing came amiss to 'Snivey,' scholar as well as athlete. He could be very troublesome in the headmaster's division, for to sit still was torture to him.

One day at eleven o'clock school, 'Snivey' put a shocking bad hat *en évidence* upon Hawtrey's table :

E. C. H. : ' What a dithgratheful hat !'

Next day 'Snivey' puts a suspiciously shining one on the same spot :

E. C. H. : ' Glad to see you have got a new hat.'

'SNIVEY': ''Taint a new one—old 'un done up.'

The retort was meant to be double-edged, implying that the hat was the veteran complained of, and that E. C. H. (' the old un ') had been taken in.

I have been furnished with another dialogue between E. C. H. and 'Snivey,' though I am doubtful as to the authenticity of the story :

E. C. H.: 'McNiven, why are you so late?'

'SNIVEY': 'Please, sir, I wasn't called till a quarter to eight.'

E. C. H.: '*I* can get up in a quarter of an hour.'

'SNIVEY': 'But *I* wash.'

One summer morning, a large brimstone butterfly flew into the 'Library,' as we called the room of the headmaster's division; it took the direction of the bench where the 'Liberty' collegers sat. 'Snivey' roared out: 'Catch her! catch her! Jack Day!' The escape of the insect vexed the soul of 'Snivey,' whose mania was for reducing everything he came across into possession. 'Snivey's' superb cricket made him very famous at Cambridge, but the University had small attractions for him after the happy life at Eton. I remember his terse but sorrowful letter to Coley after a few weeks' experience of Trinity College, Cambridge:

'DEAR PATTY,

'This place and I b'ant (are not) mates.

'Yours ever,

'SNIVEY.'

A TOWN AND GOWN ROW.

In these days he was commemorated as 'Fitzwiggins' in an Ode printed in *Punch* April 11, 1846. I have to thank Messrs. Bradbury and Evans for allowing me to copy Richard Doyle's illustration of the Town and Gown Row in which 'Snivey' was a protagonist. The title of the Ode was: 'The Fight of the Crescent: A Lay of Modern Cambridge.'

He died prematurely. With all his wildness and oddity, he had succeeded in winning the affectionate regard of the noblest Etonian of those times.

As an old cricketer, I have a special tenderness for the memory of E. H. Pickering, an assistant master in my time, whose fairness of mind, quiet consistency of life, and serenity of temper, secured for him the affection of his pupils, and the goodwill of everybody who came in contact with him. He was one of a cricketing family, and, to my thinking, the best of the lot. In Upper Club, his advice (sparingly and cautiously given) was highly prized, for he understood the game thoroughly, and abstained from all interference, unless the captain of a side threatened some hopelessly wrong policy, in a critical moment of the match. Pickering was the hero of a remarkable exploit at Lord's, in the year 1843. His professional duties at Eton had for many years stopped him from all but an occasional practice of the favourite game, in which he had so distinguished himself at school and college. But we boys, proud of his reputation, used to watch his beautiful play, when he practised on Saturday afternoons, and envy the neatness and correctness of his batting. His defence was nearly perfect; he was not a hard hitter, but no leg ball ever escaped him.

A contemporary of mine, Sir Charles Oakeley, writes: 'I was longstop in my tutor's house, and used often to be taken up to longstop for Pickering and Dupuis, when they practised in Upper Club, being rewarded with strawberries after I had performed well.' When our French master, Mr. Tarver, brought out his dictionary, we were highly delighted with his compliment to our deservedly popular assistant. Under the word 'batting' the compiler added: 'Pickering batted excellently.' '*Pickering a bien manié le battoir.*'

One of the Gentlemen selected to meet the Players in the great annual match at Lord's failed at the last moment, and a messenger was sent to Eton to secure, if possible, Pickering's services in the emergency. Hawtrey was not the man to throw any obstacle in his assistant's way. Time being precious, Pickering, 'clothed in customary suit of solemn black,' and seemingly most imperfectly equipped for taking part in the historical cricket match of the year, hurried off to London, and was welcomed with eagerness at Lord's Cricket Ground by both Gentlemen and Players. He never had an enemy, least of all amongst the cricketing fraternity, professional or otherwise. Hillyer and Lillywhite bowled for the Players, and soon found out that in the clerically-dressed gentleman they had an awkward customer to deal with. As a rule, they were deadly straight on the wicket, but an occasional ball on the leg stump, or an inch to the left of it, meant a certain score for the gentleman in black. I remember watching with joy and pride the embarrassment of the Players, who kept on shifting their field, and eventually placed three men on the leg side. Though the Gentlemen were defeated, Pickering scored 19 in the first, and 20 in his second innings, and in those days of rough grounds and small scores, the double achievement of such numbers by an amateur cricketer, in the first match of the year, was a triumph. Eton boys talked for many a day of Pickering's performance, which very likely lives in some forgotten strains, composed by an admiring pupil.

For three or four summers, dating from 1845, or thereabouts, we 'Upper Club' boys did suit and service to a very old Etonian, W. H. Trant, of whose antecedents we were profoundly ignorant. He came to Windsor to end his days there, and to be near Eton, his first and unforgotten love from boyhood. He had been a pupil of Goodall, and a contemporary of Lord Metcalfe, both at Eton and in India. These facts alone would have given him, or anyone else educated at Eton, the freedom of the Playing-fields, but a padded Polonius, aged eighty, batting and bowling, is a sorry sight. 'Plum-tree gum and very weak hams' are more honoured when distilled and exercised in the pavilion, but old Trant practised cricket in his second childhood, and expected us to admire his performances.

Some of us, I fear, treated him with scant respect, and we were annoyed at his being called upon at an Election dinner to return

OLD TRANT.

thanks for the toast of 'The Old Etonians present on the occasion.' This stirred me to look up the Trant antecedents, and I found that he and W. Butterworth Bayley had been associated with Charles Metcalfe in the office of the Governor-General of India, who was no less a person than the Marquis Wellesley himself. The lads in that office, out of admiration for another Etonian, had formed themselves into a sort of club or association in Calcutta, and called themselves 'Howe Boys,' in honour of the famous Admiral. Trant served chiefly in the financial department, and on his return to England he was sent to Parliament by the electors of Dover. At one time, when Metcalfe's policy was assailed by the India House, Trant, who had worked beside him in Lord Wellesley's office, stood up with affectionate enthusiasm to do honour to the noble character of his old comrade. I copy a note in Kaye's 'Life of Lord Metcalfe,' for it is in every way creditable to an old gentleman, whose feeble cricket irritated us youngsters, and made us disrespectful and cynical towards him. Some passages of Mr. Trant's speech are worthy of quotation:

'His gallant friend (Sir John Doyle) had

said that Sir Charles Metcalfe was more fitted to be resident in Bedlam than in Hyderabad. Now, he need not remind the honourable and gallant officer of what an illustrious person had said, when he was told that General Wolfe was mad. "If he is mad," said that illustrious individual, "I wish he would bite some other Generals. . . ." He would say it, and he wished it most sincerely, if Sir Charles Metcalfe was mad, that the Company had a great many more such mad servants. He congratulated the Company on having such a useful madman in their employ, and he should not be sorry if he bit a few of their civil servants. The gallant General had informed them that he was acquainted with the Marquis of Hastings during a period of forty years' duration. He (Mr. Trant) must look back to a date, which would not make him appear a very young man, when he called to his recollection his first acquaintance with Sir Charles Metcalfe. They were children together; they were at school together under the same tutor, Dr. Goodall; and Sir Charles Metcalfe went out to India about the same period. They there pursued their studies for some time together. . . . The Company's

SPANKIE.

servants were often placed in very delicate situations, where duty and feeling were opposed to each other. He congratulated the Court on having amongst their servants a man so entirely devoted to the discharge of his duties—a man whom threats could not intimidate, nor promises mislead—a man who realized the picture drawn by Horace.' Trant's apogee was the India House, his aphelion the Upper Shooting Fields at Eton.

On match days in Upper Club, 'Spankie,' historical purveyor of 'sock,' did a brisk business with his tarts, cakes, sweets and fruit. Some scorer wrote the following line on him, when the cricket was getting slow:

'*Totaque Tartiferis Spancheia fervet ahenis*,'

a Virgilian touch, which has a pathos for former debtors of that illustrious man at the Long Wall, who held such heavy mortgages on the school in general, and new fourth-form boys in particular. A great and mysterious character was Spankie, the acknowledged head of sock providers, and a fixture at the wall, his daily haunt from morning to 'lock-up' at all seasons, except in the summer, when he did a roaring trade with strawberries and cherries in the Playing-fields. We supposed him to be a son of a General le Marchant, and in a playful mood addressed him as 'Mr. le Marchant,' though he was as silent on the subject of his parentage as Webber, the College cook, on his supposed flight from the battle of Waterloo.

Spankie's affectionate notice of every new boy was a distinct danger to the innocent and unsuspecting neophyte, for the tarts, cakes, and sweets piled up in his portable bronzed can were purchased on tick every day of the week, and if not paid for on Monday, 'allowance day,' became an unendurably heavy mortgage at the end of the half. Spankie was a sort of Melchizedek. We knew nothing about his father or mother, but he knew accurately everything about ours, and he cross-examined us on our return from home on any event incidental to the family history. His curious and accurate knowledge was constantly tested, when strings of Royal carriages passed through Eton, and Spankie called out the names of the occupants to his admiring clients. If the officer commanding the Queen's escort was a former debtor of Spankie's, he gave him a friendly nod of recognition in passing—in fact, we all liked him, mercilessly as he fleeced us, especially in the matter of bigaroon cherries, which, barring the three or four at the top of the pottle, were fraudulent, and sour, and naughty throughout. He habitually addressed the sons of Prime Ministers, Bishops, Judges, or Chancellors by their fathers' names. This was the sort of thing on Monday afternoon:

'My Lord Cottenham, I should like to see that three-and-six.' 'Have you got the *pec*,* Sir Robert?' 'You've not forgotten the half-crown, my Lord of Cuddesden?' etc. These reminders were interspersed with painful allusions to events best forgotten. 'I hear, my Lord Monboddo, that you couldn't stand the first cut last Wednesday, and called out to the Doctor: "Oh, dear! oh, dear! Don't flog me; you know my mother at home, sir!"'

If Spankie made an ample fortune out of us boys, with that fraudulent tin of his, he now and then astonished the world by heading a church subscription with £50. He was trusted by the headmaster, on more than one occasion, to reclaim and trace a fugitive from school. I

---

* 'Pec,' *i.e.*, pecunia—money.

also remember a young contemporary of my own, who died in Spankie's lodgings, where he was faithfully nursed and tended. So Spankie had his merits, the least of them being that inseparable tin of tarts, cakes, and sweets, which had so fatal an attraction for impecunious, sweet-toothed boys. When he retired from business, an Eton poetaster thus alluded to him in his 'Vale':

> 'No more shall Spankie's cherries
>   My pockets fill again;
> For we have both left Eton,
>   Which has caused us both much pain.'

There was a pathetic incident in Spankie's career. He went mad just when he was about to retire to his estate. 'The parting from that bronze tin unhinged poor Spankie's mind,' said a friend; 'some men should die in harness; Spankie's was rather mouldy.' I agree. When Spankie turned his face to the wall it should have been the Long Wall. He died in the Isle of Wight.

The Queen's peace in Eton proper, and the immediate neighbourhood, was sedulously watched by two old superannuated soldiers—Bott and Macallion. Both of them were greatly respected in Eton. Though well stricken in years, they were no Dogberry and Verges, but able and trustworthy officers. Bott had fought at Albuera, and, as one of the 1,800 who survived that battle, was an object of interest to two old comrades in the great days of the Peninsular War, who spent their declining years at or in the neighbourhood of Eton. These were Major Brine and Major Bent; the one lived at Eton, and the other at Wexham Lodge, close to Stoke Poges; both sent their sons into College.

I must say a few words about Major Bent, an old friend of my family, and a proverb with us for loyalty to his county of Devon, and all who belonged to it. He had served with great distinction in Picton's 'Fighting Division' in the Peninsular War, and was highly appreciated by that officer. About the year 1824 his regiment was on duty in the West Indies, and to the joy of two of my relatives, Bishop Coleridge and Henry Nelson Coleridge, his cousin, they were greeted by their old friend with all the geniality they had known in former days. I am quoting from 'Six Months in the West Indies,' a little book written by my uncle Henry, shortly after he had left Cambridge. 'On landing at Dominica with the Bishop, I met my hearty, smiling, gallant friend John Bent, with left hand arched upon his cap's brow, and his right drooping his Peninsular sword to the sand that was unworthy of it. Days, months, years have passed since I was in the fifth form at Eton; what time, John Bent, I used to give thee breakfast in my room at Bristowe's, and thou wert wont in return to do thy worst to make me and the minor tipsy at the mess-room, Captain Bent! I am the most changed of the two since then. Thou art married, it is true, and art most happy with a wife and child in twelve feet by six, but thou wert then a man, a veteran soldier, a practical liver on God's earth, and mirthful to boot,' etc. I have good reasons for remembering Major Bent, for I was interested in an old soldier at Ottery St. Mary—Samuel Hall, by name—who had served in the Peninsular War, and complained to me that the Waterloo men had medals, and he had nothing to show for his services in Spain. I wrote at length to Major Bent, who had recruited the man himself, and well remembered marching off with him from Exeter, proud of annexing a real Devonian. The Major took infinite pains to put Hall's case before the Duke of Richmond; medals were eventually sent to the veteran, who bequeathed them to me in his last will. But the episode I remember with the greatest pleasure in connection with Major Bent was an incident of which he was naturally proud. A few days before Sir Thomas Picton started for the Waterloo campaign, a number of Peninsular officers, who had served under him, entertained him at a farewell dinner; and Sir Thomas, in proposing the health of his entertainers, singled out Captain Bent to respond to the toast in words highly eulogistic of his rare usefulness in the great days of the Peninsular War. To a later generation, another John Bent, son of Picton's favourite officer, will be a familiar name and a welcome sound. We old Tugs challenge all Bishops to find us a better parish priest than J. B., and who but Sydney Smith or Mansell made better puns or said better things? In his curate's days at Woolwich, a stranger asked to be shown over the church; J. B. did the duty of showman with his well-known courtesy and kindness. On taking leave of his benefactor at the church door, the stranger, on shaking hands, said: 'I assume that I am speaking to the incumbent?' J. B.: 'No, sir, plain Bent without the income.' Eton men will enjoy the account of a scene that occurred at the table of Dr. Jeune, when he was head of Pembroke College. J. B. was one of the undergraduate guests. After dinner, the master spoke of the reprehensible practice of buying rats at sixpence ahead for the dogs to worry. Turning to Bent he said, 'I suppose, Mr. Bent, *you* have nothing to do with things of this kind?' 'Oh no, Master; I wouldn't do such a thing for the world. Mine is only a very little dog, and I never give more than threepence for my rats!'

So few collegers in my time could afford to enter the army, that I gladly record the names of any who served their country as soldiers. Years ago an old Tug wrote to me: 'Long Chamber was to me the abode of a hero, such as I have never known since—Andrew Gram Brine. Pacing up and down those grimy boards in Long Chamber with him the last half-hour, 10.30 to 11 p.m., night after night, I had my myopic mind lifted by his pure enthusiasm. Is he still alive, I wonder? I remember with all my heart my last talk with him, on the Man-

BOTT, 'THE HAPPY WARRIOR.'

chester-Liverpool rails, whilst he was waiting for the signal to get into the train with his regiment (the Lucknow regiment) on the way to Dublin. His brother subalterns, not being provided with pea-shooters, amused themselves by calling out to him " Philosopher," which avenged me on his habit of calling me " Socrates."' (The writer of this extract was wont to say that Bott was his ideal of 'the Happy Warrior.') ' Bott asked me to come and take leave of him on his deathbed at Eton Wick. I believe he was as good and happy a warrior as ever lived. I wish I had known him better ; he is far above St. George and St. Maurice in my hagiology.' I should like to have been present at their conversations, for the old colleger who wrote these words was a profound student of military and naval history. He could have cross-examined Sir William Napier himself.

My earliest recollection of Macallion is with reference to Tawell, the notorious murderer, who was tried, convicted, and executed at Aylesbury, in 1841. Tawell was the first victim captured by means of a telegraphic message. He was apprehended in the Jerusalem Coffeehouse in London, and for one night detained at Eton, on his way to Aylesbury gaol, where he was ultimately locked up before the trial. Macallion, as police officer at Eton, had the custodianship of this infamous Quaker, who poisoned his mistress.

The murder took place during the Eton holidays, and Macallion, on the return of the boys to school, found himself famous. He submitted to the closest questionings from excited fourth-form boys. 'I say, Macallion, how did Tawell look? Did he look in a funk? Do show us how you tied him to your bedpost!' It was currently reported and believed that such was our policeman's method of restraint. The more fatal knot was tied by Calcraft a few weeks afterwards, and very effectively, at Aylesbury, Sir Fitzroy Kelly's 'apple-pip' defence having been torn to shreds by Baron Parke, the presiding Judge.

About the same period, a much less conspicuous felon, Towers by name, a tradesman in High Street, Eton, was also tried and convicted at the Aylesbury Assizes. Though the school had suffered depredations at his hands, the plundered boys rather enjoyed their losses than otherwise, for the four-in-hand coach, filled inside and out with Eton witnesses, and starting from Keate's Lane for the Aylesbury Assizes, was an object of envy and admiration to the whole school. The start of 'the witnesses' was a very exciting moment. They received a parting ovation, and were much envied; many of us were very sorry we had not been robbed of our property. Towers lived in a shop just beyond Barnes' Pool Bridge, and 'after four' we were admitted to his garden, to practise with crossbows. These instruments were made by Towers at the same cost as that of a new cricket-ball—viz., 7s. 6d., and for a short time were very popular, especially with Pickering's pupils. Whether that eminent batsman's practice with a catapult, instead of a bowler, gave his pupils an odd taste for missiles, I cannot say, but the young gentlemen who were shamefully robbed by the artful proprietor, whilst practising with his crossbows, were, as a matter of fact, mostly Pickering's pupils.

The 'witnesses' came off very well at the trial, and the thief was sent to Botany Bay for seven years. The return of the coach to Eton with the exulting boys was made the subject of a fresh triumph. Shooting with crossbows, besides being rather an expensive diversion, was discredited from henceforth; but the Robin Hoods had had their picnic to Aylesbury, and the 'distant Towers' was transported and forgotten.

Two other sports had a very short innings, though a lively one. I rather blush to own that for two halves the school went mad on the subject of tops. The school-yard, before lessons began at eleven o'clock of a morning, was humming all over with peg-tops, and he who could split his comrade's plaything into two halves at the first fling was voted an expert. The top mania, like the crossbow fever, had its little day of popularity, and then vanished into limbo.

Leaping-poles seemed at one time likely to ripen into an institution, but when a boy of the name of Dimsdale fell from the top of a high bank, and nearly impaled himself on the top of his pole, an unpopular fiat was issued by Hawtrey, and leaping-poles were condemned to death. We grumbled, but obeyed. Like the crossbow, a seven-foot pole was an expensive article, and had the whole school been seized with a vaulting ambition, the question of storage would have become serious.

Hockey flourished for a few years; I regret it is out of fashion. A mistaken notion prevailed that it was a subterfuge for boys too careful of their shins at football. Well played, it was a far more artistic game than 'the wall,' and the legs of the players were plentifully battered by the sticks, instead of the football shoes of their opponents. To an impartial observer, the wounds received at hockey were equally honourable, if a little less savage, than the maiming and disabling in the football matches.

There was a curious game in vogue at Eton from the year 1805 to 1812; it was called 'The Devil on Two Sticks,' and was played with a sort of double cone of wood balanced, tossed, caught, and made to run along a string attached to two sticks held in the two hands of the players.

Fishing as a science was imperfectly understood, though we had an occasional professor in the art who despised bleak and gudgeon, and aspired to pike and barbel. The rows of fourth-form boys 'dropping their caddised hooks' at Perch Hole or Fellows' Pond were looked on as loafers, who shirked their cricket. They, in their turn, had a silent contempt for the barbel fisher, hurling a lob-worm half across the Thames, and catching nothing but weed. The barbel fisher, with a long rod, forty yards of line, and a noisy reel, required such a large area for his performances, that he was rather a nuisance, as well as an object of envy.

I remember two distinguished performers in the big fish way—a colleger and an oppidan. Both were passionate Waltonians, neither of them vainglorious; but any suppression or reticence on the subject of a captured pike, or barbel, would have defrauded the whole school, and I can see the colleger on a hot summer's day, running to 'absence' with a huge barbel, suspended by straws, on the back of his serge gown, and plentifully scaling the same. 'Here, sir!' shouted the triumphant Tobit, marching off with his spoil to the College cook, or his deputy, old Webber, cunning at soups and stews, and making 'kabobs' out of the sempiternal mutton in hall.

I don't know what foundation there was for

the story, but Webber was said, '*relictâ non bene parmulâ*,' to have run away from the Battle of Waterloo. The second item to his discredit was that his master, General L——, did the same thing. These wild legends were piously believed in, and Sunday after Sunday, when the child of Ephraim carved for us in hall, the agreeable message reached his ears: 'Pass up to old Webber that we want to see his Waterloo medal.' I expect this purely mythical cowardice was attributed to him because he made the birches, and it became necessary to retaliate on anyone who, by trading with instruments of torture, aided and abetted in the ignominy of corporal punishment. Webber, if the deserter we supposed him uncharitably to be, would never have figured as a College servant to any Provost of Eton that I ever heard of.

The oppidan fisherman was, and is, my old friend 'Peter' N——. I accentuate the 'Peter' because his real name was Charles. Fishing-rod in hand, N—— was making for the Playing-fields one summer morning, when some boy accosted him : 'I say, N——, where are you going to?' Answer : 'I go a-fishing.' The scriptural reply stuck to him for ever, and he was called 'Peter.' He bears an honoured and historical surname, but in the Etonian vocabulary, 'Peter,' not 'Charles,' is the invariable prefix.

A nickname, if derogatory, was a refined cruelty, for it stuck to the victim sometimes for life. To ensure its sticking, verses were occasionally written to enshrine the joke for all time. Collegers of my day will remember Bungar Young. This rather awkward *prænomen* is commemorated in the following couplet:

> '*Bungar sum, Bungarque fui, Bungarque manebo,*
> *Dum cælo stabunt sidera, Bungar ero.*'

A few boys (not more than six or ten in my time), with a real turn for entomology, exchanged an 'after twelve' of a summer's day in the Playing-fields for the pursuit of butterflies in Windsor Park. A cricketer, armed with a blistered bat, and on his way to 'Sixpenny' or 'Upper Club,' would look contemptuously on his comrades, waving a gauze butterfly net, and making for Windsor Park, intent on 'bug-hunting,' as the pursuit was called by the uninitiated.

The bug-hunting fraternity was limited and special; it was a mutual admiration society which, if outsiders hissed, applauded itself at home. Two of the best scholars in College were the recognized leaders of the company, and under their ægis I managed to catch and impale butterflies, without damaging my chances of ultimately succeeding to a place in the eleven. We insect-hunters were prone to exaggerate one another's captures and exploits, which, for some unexplained reason, were nearly always supposed to have come off in the holiday time. My friend D—— spent £5 on two beautifully-illustrated volumes on moths and butterflies. These books were interleaved for the purpose of recording the capture of rare insects in various parts of England. My brilliant, but credulous friend too hastily made a short written note of any achievement vouched for on the moment by the mischief-lovers, with whom all schools (Eton included) abound. When the evidence came to be tested subsequently, and the imposture was detected, the record had to be effaced. Take these entries for an example:

'Last August, Calmady (Durnford's pupil) caught a splendid specimen of the Queen of

Spain (a rare fritillary butterfly) at Sidmouth, in Devonshire.'

'In the following September, Fred Coleridge caught a death's-head moth, and two Purple Emperor butterflies, at Budleigh Salterton, in the same county.'

But when Calmady and Fred Coleridge broke down helplessly under cross-examination, a melancholy appendix exposed the purely imaginary history of these exploits. It ran thus: 'This information has subsequently turned out to be erroneous.'

I knew of two instances where Eton and Cambridge 'bug-hunting' led to solid results. The present Lord Walsingham, whose collection of moths and butterflies, in all stages of their existence and in their final apotheosis, is a glory of the South Kensington Museum, was a butterfly-hunter from his youth upwards. My short-lived enthusiasm was fanned by a colleger friend, whose knowledge of entomology constituted one of his many claims to the respect of all who knew him. He enticed me one summer's day to Windsor Park, promising me a sight of a locality for the marble-white butterfly. Sure enough, the information in this instance was the reverse of erroneous. To the left of the Long Walk, about a mile from George III.'s statue, we came upon a patch of ground some twenty yards in length, over which were hovering scores of these delicate creatures. Some special attraction seemed to fix them to the spot, for they took no further flight beyond, and we caught with ease as many specimens as we pleased. I have seen the same thing with a colony of fritillaries in a Devonshire wood, near Ottery St. Mary.

With the view of encouraging my taste, my friend, in his scholar's days at King's, sent me a number of swallow-tail chrysalises, reared in the Cambridge fens. Their arrival at my dame's caused a sensation; several developed into the full-grown butterfly, and were distributed amongst the elect.

'Bug-hunters' at Eton pride themselves on some forbears whose love of entomology, so far from hindering their progress in severer studies, would seem to have given their scholarship a wider range, as bearing upon and illustrating their particular hobby. Cotton, whose name appears high up on the list of the Newcastle scholars, was from boyhood an ardent bee-fancier, with so delicate a touch and such a fine sense of hearing that he could distinguish a drone by the sound it made when flying, and, blindfold, put his hand into a beehive and extract the idle one from amongst the workers. Some of us who had stared pretty often at the head-roll of Newcastle scholars and medallists, with their names recorded in golden letters on the wall of 'Library,' were given to repeating the list to one another with abbreviations and curtailments; the apocopated forms made the task an easier one. The juxtaposition in three successive years of the names of Creasy, Cotton, Wickens, seemed to justify us in snuffing out the last half of the name of the future Vice-Chancellor, and altering the C. into a G. in that of the author of the 'Fifteen Decisive Battles of the World.' The transformation into 'greasy cotton wick' was not meant as an insult to the distinguished triad. I am told that Harrovians of the present day are much addicted to shortened forms of speech, and that they talk of travelling to Padder (*i.e.*, Paddington), or an invitation to 'brekker,' *i.e.*, breakfast. A young Etonian assured me that he heard a voice from a crowd of lookers-on at a football-match, addressing itself to a friend amongst the players who had recently won a place in a distinguished eleven, 'Heaps of congratters upon the Internatters!' in common parlance, 'I congratulate you on getting into the International eleven.'

The Cotton brothers, genuine working-bees, not drones, improved each shining hour both at Eton and at the University. The elder of the two seems to have been more interesting to his contemporaries than the future Lord Justice, for his singular and absorbing devotion to his pets was sure to attract a small circle of admirers, and possibly some few imitators. Cotton *major* traversed Tony Lumpkins' contemptuous utterance, 'It's all Buzz'; there was no music so sweet to his ears as that of a bee-hive. His motto was that of the old Greek philosopher:

Θεῖόν τι τὸ γένος τὸ τῶν Μελιττᾶν.

Where the bee sucked, there lurked Cotton *major*. History is silent as to the whereabouts of the sacred hives in Eton or Windsor; they may have been in Trotman's garden, Trotman, of course, having a considerable lien upon the honey and the honey-comb; but it is certain—for I have his and my tutor's word for it—that Cotton in the summer time had free access to his favourites, and would take the best-behaved out for an airing, or, more strictly speaking, a stifling, for the poor insect was harboured for a time in the pocket of his white waistcoat, and duly emancipated for the gratification of his tutor and the family. Some people thought that Cotton had permanently 'a bee in his bonnet,' but the creature was more frequently lower down in his dress, where it could be conveniently stroked and fingered; for the owner handled him so dexterously and coaxingly that he seldom, if ever, felt the stings of insect ingratitude.

We have Cotton's own account of the formation of his early taste, which had been stimulated to action by a translation of the fourth Georgic of Virgil, which was read aloud to him by his father. The boy determined then and there to carry out to the letter the instructions of that ancient bee-fancier. These, it will be remembered, were of the rough-and-ready order in the primitive days of Roman husbandry. First of all, catch your bees or hatch them. But how? Begin by tramping to death a poor cow; then stop up the nose-holes, allowing 'the warm humour to ferment inside the soft bones of the carcase until there appear creatures, footless at first, but which soon, getting unto themselves wings, mingle together and buzz about, joying more and more in their airy life.' Cotton remembered Samson's spirited performance of cracking a young lion in two, and being rewarded for his sporting act by the discovery of a swarm of bees and plenty of honey inside the carcase of his victim.

'I had no pity for the poor cow—no, not I—when a swarm of bees was to be the glorious result. She would surely, I thought, be happy in her death, as she would give life to so many glorious creatures. But I was not quite sure that I should be able to act the part of Guy, Earl of Warwick, the cow-killer, however much I might resemble him in spirit. I mistrusted my infant strength, and doubted much whether I could stop up her nose-holes without assistance; so I straightway let the farming man into my counsels, promising him what I considered an irresistible bribe not to tell—a very small taste of my first honey. He, however, to my astonishment, did not enter into my views; my cow-killing propensities were divulged abroad, and the matter was compromised, and the cow's life spared, by the gift of a stock of bees. If any excuse were wanted for my infant credulity, I would refer to an extract from the work of a full-grown man, who declares that Virgil's experiment was in his time repeated with success in Cornwall.'

This bee-worship was no passing fad or whim with the Newcastle scholar, for his pets, or their immediate descendants, followed him to Oxford, and after his University career to New Zealand, whither he had migrated under the auspices of the apostolic Bishop, George Selwyn. Sir Francis Doyle (Cotton's distinguished Eton contemporary at Christ Church) tells an amusing story of the bee-worshipper in his Oxford days. Dean Gaisford in person complained to him that a gentleman commoner had one summer's day been stung in Tom Quad. This was mere Bumbledom to the entomologist.

'Mr. Dean,' said he, 'I assure you that you are doing us a great injustice. I know that bee well. He is not mine at all, but belongs to Mr. Bigg, of Merton.'

There was some humour in the assumption that every member of the 'House' would feel aggrieved by the Dean's frivolous accusation, but the gentlemanly character and inoffensiveness of Cotton's favourites must be made known and vindicated. Could a Christ Church bee with an Eton pedigree, trained within the sacred precincts of the 'House,' so far forget his noble origin as to sting a well-affected Tuft? Perish the thought! Whereas the stinging proclivities of Bigg's bees was a matter of common knowledge to Cotton and his friends.

We were told at Eton that the sailors who accompanied the Bishop and the missionary to New Zealand were not over-civil to the bees on their transportation voyage, and that they would have shipped the hives overboard, queens and all, had they known how to catch the inhabitants without sharing the fate of the indignant gentleman commoner of Christ Church.

The pets of scholars and poets are delightful to me. I have seen the room at Olney where Cowper's hares gambolled; I hope some day to see the common where Thirlwall's favourite geese cackled and gobbled. Sir Samuel Romilly's two leeches, Cline and Hone, were distinguished ornaments of their blood-sucking profession. Cotton's books should have been ornamented, as the Pompadour's were, with golden bees stamped on the cover.

Stag-beetles abounded at Eton and in the neighbourhood; their activity and sonority were conspicuous at evening prayer-time in Lower Chamber. Carried to vespers in the pocket of a colleger's gown, the insects were quiet, respectful, and torpid; all their energies revived under the combined influence of Hawtrey's voice and the blaze of candles. The buzzing and flitting were sore trials to the officiating headmaster, who thus remonstrated after prayers were over: 'Somebody has been letting off chafers!'

Nobody pleaded guilty, so it passed for a miraculous swarm, which had migrated from the lime-trees facing Upper School to Lower Chamber, by way of diversion and change of air.

Snake-worship was fortunately uncommon. Had the taste prevailed, we should have had heavy consignments of creeping things forwarded by Frank Buckland from the New Forest, for that mighty *chasseur* was ever bent on making converts to python-worship. I fagged for a master who was partial to reptiles, and seeing my horror, which he thought affectation, he set to work to cure me of my antipathy. 'If you don't take up that snake at once, and carry it to Coleridge's field, you'll find it in your bed to-night,' said he. I smuggled the brute into a red pocket-handkerchief and carried it to my tutor's field, where I liberated my soul, and the creeping thing also. My blind obedience did me no good; I hate snakes, even wooden ones; and when the genii, in the 'Flauto Magico' of Mozart, prod the wriggling beast successfully, I wish I had imitated them, and avenged myself for an act of oppression. I might have been less squeamish had I known of Alfred Tennyson's snake, which he harboured and comforted at Trinity in Cambridge days, to the horror and vexation of his bed-maker.

I began this chapter with recollections incidental to the Playing-fields, through which, on Montem-day, we marched in procession, on the morning of the pageant, and where we answered to our names at 'absence,' on the evening of that appalling festival. My friend and contemporary, G. Green, who has a strong and accurate memory for facts, allows me to reprint from a magazine his account of Montem. It is, in its chief features, as true and reliable as Miss Edgeworth's is fictitious and unreal. Twice in my Eton life I took part in the ceremony, but the details both of Thring's and D.'s Montem are fast fading from my mind. I remember, however, quite enough to vouch for the accuracy of my friend's account.

Maxwell Lyte has put upon record a curious defence of Montem, raised by a Protestant Fellow. He gives no name, but an Eton colleger has no difficulty in spotting the author of the truly grotesque plea for the continuance of a public nuisance. The old gentleman had got an idea into his head that the triennial procession to Salt Hill had taken the place of a pilgrimage to a shrine of the Virgin, and he desired that the ceremony, happily free from superstition, should be retained as a symbol of the Reformation, and a standing protest against Popery.'

'ETON MONTEM: A MEMORY OF THE PAST.

'Eton! Dear old Eton! The thoughts of all your sons, and even of all who read the newspapers, have been forcibly called to your glories, past and present, by what has lately appeared in the various journals recording the celebration of the four hundred and fiftieth anniversary of the foundation of Eton College. One of the greatest attractions on that day was an exhibition in the Upper School of dresses worn at Eton Montem, and other mementoes connected with that once famous event.

'Eton Montem! How many are there in the present day who had before this ever even heard of the existence of such a thing? How many of those who have heard of it have the least idea of what it was like? And of these I wonder how many now living have been present at, and taken part in, one or more of these gorgeous pageants which for so many years shone alone and unrivalled for splendour in the annals of school-boy life? As I look over my old Eton lists of those years so long gone by, and see how many there are that to my own certain knowledge have passed away, I cannot but fancy that soon very few will be left who, like myself, have shared in these glories or follies—which shall we say?—of long ago; for I suppose they will be counted glories or follies according to the view that is taken of them by the wise and highly enlightened men and women of the present generation. At any rate, as people, whether they think such things follies or not, generally like to learn all the little particulars about any manners or customs which happened before their own time, I think it may be interesting to many to give an Eton boy's account of the two Montems in which he took part; which, moreover, were the last Montems that ever took place. To all Etonians, both past and present, I am sure such memories will prove attractive; and, if I mistake not the hereditary nature of the old Eton feeling, they will have a charm for our children and grandchildren for some time to come.

'Although Eton Montem lasted for so many years, and attracted such large crowds to see it, including many of our sovereigns, it is a remarkable thing that no very detailed account of it exists, so far as I am aware, further than that given by Mr. Maxwell Lyte, in one chapter of his "History of Eton," which, although it is fairly correct as far as it goes, does not give a reader the impression of having been written by an eye-witness of the scene; and also that given by the Rev. W. Lucas Collins in his work "Etoniana," which first appeared in this Magazine in 1865, and in which are delineated the leading features of the Montem. There is a story called "Eton Montem" to be found in that old book which we used to read in our childish days, Miss Edgeworth's "Parent's Assistant"; but this gives such an erroneous idea of it that it is worse than useless; and the only other allusion to it in any well-known book that I am aware of is the very little that is said about it in Lord Beaconsfield's "Coningsby," which, though a perfectly correct picture of what might have happened at any Montem, is not a full enough description of it to bring it before the mind of anyone except an Etonian who had taken part in it.

'My first reminiscence of anything connected with Montem dates from my very early childhood. On the top-shelf of my mother's wardrobe there used to repose, in grand state, a plume of feathers which had been worn by one of my uncles at a Montem long before. This plume we children used to be allowed to take down and wear when we were "dressing up," as we called it—that is, putting on all the fantastic finery that we could get together to surprise and amuse our parents on some grand evening in the drawing-room after dinner. We used to imagine that the uncle who had had the privilege of wearing that plume must have been a hero at least equal to the conqueror at Waterloo. And although we did not know that at the time, that plume must have been exactly similar to that worn by the Duke, for it was a regular field-marshal's plume of red and white feathers worn on a cocked hat. My father and other uncles must have had such plumes, as they had all been at Montems; but this was the only one that had been kept. I never thought at that time of the day to come when I should wear such an one myself. Nor, I am sure, did my parents think of a day to come when a Montem plume should be as extinct as a dodo or the great auk.

'It is now, in the year of grace 1891, just forty-seven years since the last Montem took place, and fifty years since Thring's Montem, which we considered at that time to be probably the gayest and most magnificent that had ever been seen. Both of these were graced with the presence of our young Queen and her handsome husband; and at the latter another sovereign, who was before long to lose his kingdom, Louis Philippe,* the King of the French, was present. Montem happened at intervals of three years for the last seventy years of its existence. In its earlier days it used to happen every year. I do not intend to enter into any discussion about the probable origin of Montem. People in the present day will, I think, be much more interested to read a description of what it was, than to speculate about its origin and meaning; and those who do want to investigate this can find all that has been said about it in that excellent book, Mr. Maxwell Lyte's "History of Eton College," to which I have already alluded. We find records of its existence in some form in

* This is an error. Louis Philippe's visit to Eton was in the autumn; Tzar Nicholas came in the summer.

the early years of the reign of Elizabeth; but from the beginning of the eighteenth century it existed in very much the same form that it wore to the last, except that it took place in the last week in January till the year 1758, when the date of holding it was altered to Whitsun-Tuesday, and so it continued to be held ever afterwards to the end.

'And now, what *was* Montem? What did it appear to be to the eyes of an outsider, who saw it for the first time? The quaint assemblage of fancy dresses would have suggested that a fancy-dress ball was about to be enacted in the daytime; but the order and the predominance of the two colours, scarlet and blue, looked more like a military procession, and this was borne out by the two military bands that were present, and the flag that was carried in state, like regimental colours. This procession consisted, on the occasions in which I took part in it, of schoolboys numbering more than six hundred, varying in age from nineteen to ten or less: and to describe how these boys were dressed, how they were arranged, and what they did on this momentous day, will be my endeavour in the following pages. But before we start on any description of the day itself, it will be necessary, in order to make it fully intelligible to our readers, to say something of what had been done beforehand in preparation for it.

'The spectacle itself was such a gorgeous one, and it was associated with so many old memories and associations of the past, that all old Etonians throughout the country, and all the friends and relatives of Etonians from far and near, strove to be present on that day, and curiosity drew immense numbers besides, who were perfect strangers, so that a greater crowd assembled at Eton on that day than has probably ever assembled there since its discontinuance, and every single person who was present was asked to contribute something, large or small, according to his means, and all the money so collected was given to the lucky boy who happened to hold the proud position of captain of Montem. How this money was collected, what it was called, and the expenses that were defrayed out of it, I shall state further on. The first thing to make clear is the rule by which one particular boy became captain of Montem.

'At Eton the head colleger—that is, the boy who is first on the list of collegers, or King's scholars—is called the captain of the school. And so whoever was captain of the school on the Whitsun-Tuesday in a Montem year, was by that fact captain of Montem. But who would be captain of the school could not be known for certain till within twenty days of the eventful Whitsun-Tuesday.

'All King's scholars, or collegers as they were called, were allowed, if they succeeded in passing their examinations every year at the end of July—Election trials, as they were called—to remain in the school a twelvemonth after passing the last examination, which must be passed before their nineteenth birthday. If by that time they had not gone to King's College, Cambridge, they were superannuated, and had to leave the school. At the examination at the end of every July, those boys who had passed their eighteenth birthday were placed in school in order of merit, and were called from thence to Cambridge at any time of the year, whenever—through death, marriage, or any cause—a vacancy occurred in the number of the seventy members of King's

College. King Henry VI. founded his school at Eton of seventy scholars, as a nursery to keep constantly supplied his other foundation of seventy members, scholars and fellows, at King's College, Cambridge. Now, as of late years Montem only happened every third year, of course it was only possible that a boy who was born in such a year that he would have passed his eighteenth birthday on the July previous to a Montem could ever become captain of Montem. From the time of my birth it was clear that neither I nor my brother could ever have been captain of Montem, even if Montem had lasted beyond our time. . . .

'As I said before, all the money that was collected on Montem-day was given to the head colleger, the captain of Montem. And now let us see how this money was collected. This was done by certain of the boys, chosen according to their position in the school. The chief collectors were two, who were called salt-bearers, and these were assisted by twelve collegers, who were near the end of the sixth form, or at the top of the upper division of the fifth. These were called runners, and all of these were dressed in fancy dresses, chosen by themselves, those of the two salt-bearers being especially gorgeous. They all carried satin money-bags and painted staves with mushroom-shaped tops, on which were inscribed appropriate Latin or Greek quotations. Now, why were the chief of these collectors called salt-bearers?

'It appears that at first they used to carry a large bag of salt with them, and give a pinch of salt to each person from whom they collected money, as a kind of receipt to show that they had paid their footing for the day. But after a time they adopted the more business-like plan of giving tickets, rather than salt, in exchange for contributions, and then the money itself that was given was called salt, and the cry of these young tax-gatherers for "Salt! Salt!" was almost perforce responded to by opening the purse. Montem has passed away, but the mound to which the procession was made, and which gave it its name, as being a procession "ad Montem," still remains; and this mound and the place where it stands still bear the name of Salt Hill, because of the money or *salt* that for so many years was collected there, although probably very few of the young sportsmen who resort there now year after year to meet the Royal Staghounds have any idea whence the place derives its name, or associate it in their minds with the festival that for so many years made it almost a sacred spot to all Eton boys.

'The two salt-bearers were the second captain of the collegers and the captain of the oppidans. It was their province to collect the money in the college itself—from the college authorities and the guests of the Provost, including personages of the highest importance. The twelve runners were all collegers, and they were generally posted as follows: Two at Maidenhead Bridge; two at Windsor Bridge; two at Datchet Bridge; two at Colenorton, or Fifteen-arch Bridge, as it was called; one at Iver; one at Gerrard's Cross; one at Slough, and one at Salt Hill. These were each of them accompanied by a hired attendant, who was always armed with pistols if the station was at any distance from the college—a very necessary precaution to protect these young adventurers, who might very possibly in the course of the day have some hundreds of pounds under their care; and, of course, for the distant stations they were also provided with a horse and conveyance of some kind. They started early in the morning for their respective stations, and were generally entertained at breakfast at country houses in the neighbourhood. Those who had the more distant stations appointed to them missed all the festivities of the early part of the day in college ; and whoever had the long run, as Gerrard's Cross was called, was absent nearly the whole day. But they generally had some adventures of their own to enliven the proceedings for them, and to give a spice of variety to their narrative as they recounted their doings to their companions on their return. Of course, the sums collected at different Montems varied in amount, but a fair average collection at the last few Montems was about £1,000, or perhaps rather more, and this was all given to the captain of Montem ; so now let us see what he had to pay out of it. He had to provide a breakfast in the college hall for the first hundred boys in the school ; he had to pay for the dinner for the whole school at the hotels at Salt Hill, and here it was that an opportunity was given of testing the popularity of the captain. It was very easy for the boys to increase his expenses by contriving a large breakage of plates and glasses; and also during the after-dinner promenade in the gardens of the inn, where there were many valuable shrubs, a reckless use of the swords which these young heroes were carrying would soon do enough damage to swell the landlord's bill considerably. Besides this, the captain had to pay the salt-bearers, runners, and other officials for the trouble they had taken on his behalf, and there were a number of minor items to diminish the profits, so that it was very often anything but a large proportion of the sum collected on the day which found its way into the captain's pocket.

'And now to describe the formation of the procession and the dresses worn. The senior colleger being captain, and the second colleger being salt-bearer, the next sixth-form collegers ranked as marshal, ensign, lieutenant, sergeant-major, and steward, and any other sixth-form collegers who were not runners were sergeants. The captain of the oppidans was always a salt-bearer, and the next to him on the school list was colonel. The other sixth-form oppidans ranked as sergeants. All the fifth-form oppidans ranked as corporals, but with a dress very different in many particulars from that of a corporal in any regiment in the army, for, while they had a red tail-coat with gilt buttons and white trousers, they had also a crimson sash tied loose round their waist, a black-leather sword-belt with gilt buckles, and a sword hanging at their side, and a cocked hat and plume of feathers exactly like that worn by a field-marshal. The fifth-form collegers' dress was like that of the fifth-form oppidans, as far as sash, sword, and cocked hat and plume went; but the coat was blue, with gilt buttons instead of red, so that it resembled very much the uniform of a lieutenant in the royal navy. The coats of the sixth form, both collegers and oppidans, had the distinctive details of uniform that denoted the rank which they bore, and could be at once distinguished from the fifth-form corporals by their epaulets and greater prevalence of gilt. The steward wore the ordinary full dress of the period. The lower boys wore blue coats with gilt buttons, white waistcoats and trousers, silk stockings and pumps, and carried long white poles, from which they derived the name of polemen. A limited number of lower boys, whose parents were rich and willing to pay for a costly dress, were selected to act as servants or pages to the sixth form, and these wore fancy dresses, selected according to the taste of the sixth-form boy whom they were to follow, all the followers of the same master wearing the same dress. The order of procession was generally as follows : Marshal, followed by six servants ; band ; captain, followed by eight servants ; sergeant-major, followed by two servants ; twelve sergeants, two and two, each followed by a servant ; colonel, followed by six servants and four polemen ; corporals, two and two, followed by two polemen apiece ; second band ; ensign with flag, followed by six servants and four polemen ; corporals, two and two, followed by one or two polemen apiece ; lieutenant, followed by four servants ; salt-bearers, runners, and steward to bring up the rear, followed by a poleman.

'And now imagine a lovely June morning, as was the case at both the Montems in which I took part, and suppose the writer to be either a poleman filled with curiosity and awe at this his first experience of Montem, or a small corporal exulting in his first wearing of a scarlet tail-coat, sash, sword, and cocked hat and feathers, for each of those positions were occupied by him at one or the other of the two Montems; on both occasions he sets forth from the doors of his father's house round the cloisters to find out and take up his proper place in the procession as it is formed in the school-yard. My father being a Fellow of Eton, and having a house in the cloisters, I was allowed, during my earlier years at Eton, to board at home when he was in residence, and, of course, on these two occasions of Montem, he *was* in residence. So it was that I made my first start from his house to join the festivities. Both eye and ear must have been very ready to receive impressions, for I can recollect to this day, as if it was only yesterday that I had seen it, the vivid impression made upon me by the first dress that caught my eye as I entered the school-yard. It was that of a Greek, with white tunic, scarlet jacket and scarlet cap, both abundantly trimmed with gold lace. If I mistake not, the wearer of that lovely dress was afterwards one of our heroes that fell in the Crimea. And then, as I was looking about at my assembling schoolfellows, there clashed upon my ear from the band of the Blues the sounds of a military march, which I then heard for the first time and never forgot; but I did not find out the name of it for many years, not until after I had left Eton. I used to hum the tune, and call it the Montem tune, but did not learn its name until, during a visit to Eton, I heard two young ladies play as a duet upon the piano this very march which I had heard at my first Montem, but had never heard since; and then I found that it was called the "Warrior's Joy," but who the composer was I have forgotten. I saw more fancy dresses moving about, more Greeks, some Robin Hood's men in green with bows and arrows, Highlanders with kilt and tartan and claymore, and the school-yard was gradually filling. And now "absence" was called—that is, we all had to answer our names to the roll-call. The captain, and those who had been his guests at breakfast, appeared on the scene, and the masters began gradually to marshal us into our places to form the procession. This could not be done very quickly, but as soon as it was accomplished, we began our march somewhat slowly round the school-yard. Three times round this we marched, and when in the third round the ensign arrived in front of the clock-tower, a pause was made by all, and he waved the great flag energetically, amidst the most enthusiastic cheers from the assembled multitudes. The Royalties and grandest personages were assembled in the Provost's Lodge to look down upon this scene from the great bow-window in this said clock-tower. And then, before we resumed our march, the polemen were required to hold out their poles horizontally, and the corporals drew their swords and cut them asunder. And here I will relate an incident that happened to myself to which I can look back with amusement now, but which, I am sure, caused me great distress for a few minutes at the time. It was at the second of the Montems, when I was a corporal, in all the glory of a red coat and sword.

'At the age of fourteen I was not by any means of great size, and as we all chose our own swords according to our fancy, I had chosen rather a small one, as more suited to my appearance. I did not apprehend that I should find any difficulty in cutting through my poleman's pole when I was called upon to do so, and had not practised my powers of cutting and slashing beforehand. But when we drew our swords to commence this operation, I found that I was standing immediately under the window where all the grandees were assembled, and it seemed as if all their eyes were directed full upon me. I began to feel nervous. Down came the stroke. Oh, horror! I had not cut the pole at all. Again and again I slashed, but I could not cut through it. The staves were hewn asunder at the gate leading into cloisters; we went through cloisters into the Playing-fields, and so to Salt Hill. I thought myself a special object of public derision, but this was entirely my imagination, for all the spectators were laughing at the general effect of this onslaught of such puny warriors rather than singling out the prowess of any individual; but I know that, when I found I could not properly cut through the pole in the time allowed me, I felt so mortified and ashamed of myself that at the moment I would gladly have slunk out of sight altogether, and lost all the enjoyment that was to come afterwards. Whether any other corporal at that Montem or any other ever found himself in a similar predicament to myself I do not know. I know that polemen who were tall and strong often chose particularly strong poles on purpose, so that if they found themselves assigned to a rather small or weak swordsman, they might give him some trouble in carrying out his task of cutting the pole asunder. However, this mortification, bitter as it was for the moment, was soon forgotten when we had resumed our march, and I found that my nearest companions had not noticed my failure. Our journey was now continued through Weston's yard and the Playing-fields, the bands playing up merrily. A long line we formed, as may be easily imagined, being over 600 strong. And so we streamed out into the Slough road on our march for Salt Hill. And the procession was swelled all along its route by the thousands of visitors from all parts of England, on horseback, on foot, in every kind of conveyance, ladies in their gayest dresses, all combining to make such a picture as will never be seen again.

'On arriving at Salt Hill, the ensign waved the flag a second time at the top of the mount, the boys all clustering round like a swarm of bees, and giving such cheers as Eton boys know so well how to give. "Absence" was called in the middle of the day, and then we all adjourned to the hotels to eat the dinner which had been ordered for us, and for which each had a ticket, assigning him his own table and his proper place at the table. After dinner we wandered for a time, according to our pleasure, in the beautiful gardens belonging to the hotel; and then it was that the swordsmen had the opportunity of doing such a vast amount of mischief, if the captain was unpopular. Later in the afternoon the procession returned to Eton in something of the same order, but more irregularly kept. Many got a lift in the carriages of some of their friends. All that was required was that they should be back in time to answer to their names when "absence" was called. There was no particular programme for spending the evening. The boys were chiefly with their friends—those who had any present—and were to be seen wandering about the grounds or the neighbourhood, presenting a very bright picture in their quaint and varied dresses. Before my time, I believe the chief resort for both the boys and the visitors used to be the terrace at Windsor Castle, but at the two last Montems at which I was present there were very few that went there, most of us having had quite enough walking about, and preferring to loiter about and rest on the benches in the playing-fields, which, after all, was perhaps as enjoyable a way of spending the time as any that could be devised.

'Of the two beautiful water-colour paintings of Montem that were drawn by that delightful artist, the late William Evans, the prints from which are probably well known to many old Etonians, the one that is certainly most pleasing is that which represents the scene in the evening in the Playing-fields; although the other, which shows the procession beginning its march round the schoolyard, may, perhaps, be more strictly characteristic of Montem. These pictures represent Thring's Montem in 1841. There are paintings of the Montem of 1820 in the possession of the Rev. John Wilder, who is now the venerable Vice-Provost of Eton, and who was captain of Montem in that year. But I do not think that any engravings were ever made from these.*

* This is an error; Evans's pictures were engraved.— A. D. C.

'I will now mention some of the most striking of the fancy dresses that I can recollect as worn at the two Montems at which I was present. In the Montem of 1841 there were four brothers of the name of Smyth Pigott at Eton. The eldest of these was at that time the captain of the oppidans, and so was entitled to be one of the two salt-bearers. He wore the dress of a Spanish officer of long ago, something in the style of that drawn by Rembrandt in the well-known picture of the Spanish officer in the Fitz-William Museum at Cambridge. The large slouch hat, with an enormous plume; large boots of the Cavalier kind; a magnificent broad scarf across his chest, which was blazing with jewels, which it was always said included family diamonds, and that no attempt was made by any of the swell-mob to purloin them because it was thought that no one would dare to wear real diamonds so ostentatiously, and so they must be paste. Be this as it may, this was the story that was always most stoutly maintained all the time that I was at Eton. He was a very handsome fellow, and I should doubt if there was ever a more beautiful and suitable dress seen at any Montem.

'The second brother was in the sixth form, and so wore a sergeant's dress—scarlet coat, cocked hat and feather, epaulets, and abundance of gold lace. The two younger brothers were both lower boys, and were servants to their elder brother. They were dressed as pages in the time of Edward VI. White satin doublet, abundantly slashed with silver, and white silk hose; white satin mantle, trimmed with silver, and white satin cap, with long white plume hanging over it. A more perfect picture than that which these two boys presented could hardly be conceived. A dress that was worn by Arthur Browning, who was a runner at the same Montem, was very much admired as being particularly well chosen. It was that of Captain Macheath, the highwayman, in the "Beggar's Opera." These fancy costumes were generally hired from London for the day; but Browning bought his for his own, and wore it on subsequent occasions at fancy-dress balls.

'Another dress that I recollect very well was that which was worn by Charlie Brine, a runner at Drake's Montem, the dress of the Earl of Rochester in the time of Charles II. Then there were Turks and Persians and every variety of costume, but those which I have mentioned are those of which I retain the most vivid impression; and enough has been said now to enable the reader to form some idea of the *coup d'œil* presented.

'The red coats of the fifth form were worn by the boys throughout the remainder of the summer term, and made them very conspicuous objects in the Playing fields, or wherever they might be. After that they were put away. Some had them dyed. My own reposes in all its pristine splendour at the present day on the top shelf of my wardrobe, and serves occasionally to remind me how much smaller I must have been than I thought myself at that time.

'And now Montem has entirely passed away, and is quite forgotten by all except old—very old—Etonians. What brought about its total extinction? Well, many causes had been working for some time towards this end. The spirit of the advancing age was calling out more and more loudly that it caused a great waste of money, and a great waste of time. But the factor which did the most towards making it at last absolutely impossible to keep it up was the opening of the Great Western Railway, which brought down a promiscuous horde of sightseers, and opened the way for evils in such an assemblage that it might be found impossible to control.

'But the abolition of such a time-honoured festival was not brought about without much heart-burning and resistance for awhile, and not until there had been much discussion and weighing of all arguments for and against it by the authorities. I was still at Eton at this time, and I recollect well what bitter things were said, what party spirit was displayed, and what a burning question it was at first among the boys. And yet, after all this, it has always seemed astonishing to me how quietly, when the actual day came, the festival seemed to have died a natural death before anyone was aware of it, and Montem to be accepted at once by all as one of the things of the remote past. It speaks very well for the discipline and good feeling of the school at the time to have accepted such a great change so patiently and cheerfully, and it especially shows what confidence they had in the judgment of those who were set over them.

'Montem, as I have said already, has passed away. If it had not passed away exactly when it did, it must inevitably have passed away long before the present day. It could no more exist in the midst of the present ideas of the English people about schools, education, and economy, than could falconry, as it was carried on by our forefathers, exist in the enclosed districts which a higher state of cultivation has spread over nearly the whole of our country. Modern improvements have made such things impossible. Is it to be regretted? I would not venture to throw such a slight upon the advantages of our progress as to assert that it is. But still, allowing that such a pageant did open the way for great abuses, I think that it had its bright side, and to show that bright side has been my endeavour in these pages. I am sure that no such gorgeous and fascinating spectacle in connection with school-life can ever be presented again; and I firmly believe that to ninety-nine at least out of every hundred of those who have ever taken part in it the memory of Eton Montem will be sweet.

'G. C. GREEN.'

CHAPTER IX.

THE PROVOST—HEADMASTER—UNDER-MASTER.

PROVOST HODGSON had just received his appointment when I first went to Eton. Lonsdale, the successful candidate, had been actually elected by the college, but when it became known that the Queen favoured Hodgson's candidature, the Provost of twenty-four hours' standing withdrew, rather than involve the college in a serious contention with the Crown as to the right of appointment. Hodgson himself had been a pupil of Keate, the famous headmaster, and he laudably refused to stand for the provostship of Eton until he had been assured that his old tutor, then a Canon of Windsor, had no wish for further change or promotion. The new Provost's antecedents were all in his favour, but we boys, rightly or wrongly, sus-

DR. KEATE.

'But times are changed, and we are changed,
And Keate has passed away.'

pected that the College authorities, who were to a man for Lonsdale, gave a doubtfully cordial welcome to one who was not, in the first instance, of their own choosing.

Hodgson's career, as a man of letters, seemed in his early days full of promise ; but if Walter Scott turned to prose-writing from the conviction that Byron's star made all lesser lights look pale in the poetical firmament, the mediocre bards of those days might be justifiably coy about publishing original verse. Hodgson's translation of Juvenal was warmly praised by Byron. 'The man,' says he, 'who in this translation displays unquestionable genius, may well be expected to excel in original composition.' He appeals to Hodgson, too, to vouch for his 'excellent memory' in college days. 'I had an excellent memory — ask Hodgson, the poet, a good judge, for he has an astonishing one.' In the 'English Bards and Scotch Reviewers' Byron satirizes Cambridge :

> 'Oh ! dark asylum of a Vandal race !
> At once the boast of learning and disgrace !'

and glorifies his friend :

> 'So lost to Phœbus, that not Hodgson's verse
> Can make thee better, nor poor Hewson's, worse !'

With all his violent inconsistencies, Byron's loyalty to Hodgson was no mere profession. I fancy that nothing but strong personal attachment to the poet could have made the Newstead orgies tolerable to a man like our Provost, who at school and College was known as a quiet student and scholar, though surrounded by every temptation to let 'ambition expire in indolence.' I doubt if Scrope Davies, Charles Skinner Matthews, or any of Byron's circle, had the wholesome influence over the poet which was exercised by Hodgson, the least distinguished of the group; and no reader of the biographies of the two men can fail to see that the poet's nearest and dearest relatives cheerfully acknowledged their indebtedness to the future Provost of Eton for his judicious conduct in many crises of the poet's life.

I have often heard Sir John Patteson talk of his scholar's days at King's, when Hodgson was tutor and lecturer. Mysterious packets of manuscripts from Italy arrived at King's, and were opened with eagerness by the friend of Byron. 'After lecture, Patteson, we will go,' said he, 'to the inn at Trumpington, order eggs and bacon for lunch, and then we will read the new canto of " Don Juan " which Byron has sent me.' The mutual confidences exchanged between the poet and his Cambridge friend were well bestowed. Hodgson's loyalty and devotion never failed, and he was one of the few and select mourners at the dreary funeral in Hucknall Torkard churchyard. I remember the pathetic tones of my old friend's voice, when he showed me the marble bust of Byron which stood in the Provost's Lodge. The Provost formally introduced me to the bust with the words, 'My lamented but mistaken friend, Lord Byron.'

Hodgson, in early manhood, had lived on terms of intimacy with brilliant men ; Gifford, Dean Ireland, Bland, Harry Drury, Lord Denman had corresponded with and befriended him. As Archdeacon of Derby and Vicar of Bakewell, he had been a Churchman of the high and dry type, without a spark of sympathy for the Oxford Movement, which he deprecated, not only as tending to Latium, but as possibly threatening the strong Protestantism in the Eton cloisters. Rightly or wrongly, we boys believed that more than once he had put a curb on one of the assistant-masters, who championed the Tractarians with perhaps a trifle more vehemence than discretion. To Hodgson and Plumptre 'Tract 90' was a red rag, and when the mural paintings on the walls of the chapel were discovered in 1847, and the subjects found to be representations of legends of the Blessed Virgin, they were covered up by the Provost's orders, and very effectually *Nehushtaned*,* though no less a person than Prince Albert had entreated the College to leave them in such a position that, though hid from the congregation at the time of service, they might still be accessible to painters and copyists.

I have been told on good authority, that as regards the abolition of Montem, more credit has been given to Hawtrey and less to Hodgson than is due. When it was ascertained that the Queen and Prince Albert were against the abolition, Hawtrey, who had been willing to face the opposition of old Etonians, flinched, and the Provost found it difficult to keep him to the sticking point. This is quite consistent with Hawtrey's courtly character, though he would take quite as much trouble to make

* See 2 Kings xviii. 4.

himself agreeable to a schoolboy or an undergraduate as to Guizot or Rémusat.

Hodgson, in the pulpit, was audible and dull, though happily his preaching was free from the eccentricities which made some of the Fellows so truly comical in 'the wood.' He would occasionally drag George III. into his discourses, and presuming on our well-known ignorance of modern history, explain to us that the king alluded to was 'the grandfather of her present Majesty.' However little we knew, we were up to that interesting fact, and voted the explanation gratuitous. If Hodgson happened to have started the thrilling announcement on the first stroke of twelve, he waited until the College clock had had its innings, and then finished the interrupted sentence. This habit was quaint rather than impressive, for the silence in the pulpit was succeeded by the measured tones of the clock, and the loud expectorations of old Gray, the clerk, who chafed at any innovation in the chapel.

We were out-and-out loyalists, and had a good word for everything and everybody connected with 'Farmer George.' The green rugs, spread like fresh horse-cloths over the beds in Long Chamber at Electiontide, were first given by that old scoundrel, the Duke of Cumberland, 'Butcher William.' We blessed and venerated him accordingly. Eton tears are rather cheap driblets: they flow with uncommon freedom, and wash, at intervals, some rather sooty memories.

When the Duke of York died, his military prowess was the theme of many bad verses, and I remember we believed in George IV. as the first wine-taster in his dominions, because on one occasion he pronounced Dr. Keate's sherry to be the finest he had ever tasted. That was enough for us to found our unanimous resolution upon. It is recorded that, a member of the Royal Family dying in the middle of the summer half, the captain of the boats and the captain of the eleven enjoined a partial abstention from rowing and cricket. It was a time of chastened grief. For a day or so, there was silence at Surley Hall, on the Brocas, and in the Playing-fields. The sculler abstained from his 'lock-up,' and either locked himself up, or exchanged civilities with a very loud-mouthed lady on the Brocas, Mother Tolliday, whose language was thus commemorated by a boating-man:

'*Tollidiana furens inquit—tua lumina damna,*'

the cricketer contenting himself with oiling his old blistered bat and rubbing it with sandpaper at home.

We were from early times the slaves of custom, and custom once threatened, the Deluge was predicted by the authorities. The ram, provided annually by the College butcher, to be beaten to death by the school, armed with clubs of torture (the said instruments to be charged and paid for by the unwilling parents of the young ruffians), died in every sense of the word a lingering death. It took many years to abolish the poor beast, for even the ram died hard. The 'Ram Club' appears in a bill of extras in 1687. In 1730 the Duke of Cumberland took his first lesson in cruelty by striking the first blow at the wretched animal, and the hateful custom was not finally abolished until 1747. Are not these things written in Maxwell Lyte? After that, the College cook, with a fine sense of poetry, served up a ram pasty at the Election Monday dinner. I hope the Fellows liked it. I expect that the funeral fire, kindled in commemoration of Thomas à Becket, was more honoured in the breach than the observance. I am very glad that 'leaving books' survived into my time; the abolition of that pathetic custom must have wounded Ingalton and Williams. The bestowal of these parting gifts was wild and irregular; a popular sixth-form boy found himself suddenly possessed of 'Bell on the Hand,' or some other elaborate Bridgwater treatise. This selection of a present was made, in nine cases out of ten, without the faintest reference to the tastes or the intended profession of the receiver; enough that the lad was popular, and that his fags, friends, and henchmen must do all they could to assist him in 'getting the score'—*i.e.*, of making up a larger number of 'leaving books' than any of his contemporaries about to quit school for College, the army, or India.

Once in my lifetime, I remember a Cambridge scholar, under pressure of debt, selling his library, which consisted of 'leaving books,' full of pathetic inscriptions, and numbers of prizes, emblazoned with the college arms. The auction, I am glad to think, was only attended by outsiders, one of whom was thus accosted by an angry Etonian: 'I advise you to go to the auction; you will find my "leaving books" going cheap.' The sale was not popular. A real Eton man sticks to his 'leaving books' as loyally as Mrs. Micawber to the partner of her bosom: 'No, no; I never will desert Mr. Micawber.'

But in my ramblings I have forgotten Provost Hodgson, who took very kindly notice of me after I had the good-luck to be 'sent up for play,' and was awarded a Latin declamation prize. He stopped me on one occasion in the Playing-fields, and quoted Statius's lines on 'Sleep'; I rather think he had published an English version of them. My last speech in the Upper School was Horace's 'Ibam forte viâ Sacrâ,' and on the afternoon of that day I went to the Provost's lodge to be 'ripped.' The 'resignation man' from King's had brought the good news of the vacancy at King's the day before the speeches, and I was in a high state of exaltation and self-importance. Before the 'ripping' process, I was sent for by C——y, and found him raging at one of his boys in the pupil room. He addressed me thus: 'You are captain of the school. I want you to take and lick that boy within an inch of his life'—pointing to the delinquent. 'He has told me a lie, and he was to have been confirmed by the Bishop next week.' My plea was obvious. I was no longer a schoolboy, and whatever was to be done in the way of executioner's duty must be done by my successor. It was a merciful escape for me. I think I should have appealed to Hawtrey, and besought him to take the case out of my hands. I have since heard from a pupil of C——y's, that he had no objection whatever to administer personal chastisement to his own pupils, and that he could be very free with the 'doctor,' as he called the cane which he kept for enforcing, or rather trying to enforce, discipline in his house. For some reason or other, he attempted to thrust on me the odious function of punishing a boy for an unexplained offence, and I thought him grievously mistaken in his method of expiation. My leave-taking of that master was a singular one. I never had much sympathy with him, and with all his brilliancy and originality, he failed to win the affection of the school, which was cheerfully conceded to most of the assistant masters, who were far less intellectually gifted than himself.

C——y was a man of uncertain temper; he would act on the impulse of the moment, threatening a punishment and then withdrawing it, just as the humour happened to take him.

In School.

C——y (to Victim): 'Write out and translate your lesson for kicking Jones *mi.*'

Victim: 'Please, sir, I didn't.'

After School.

Victim: 'Please, sir, I really didn't kick Jones *mi*. I only pushed him off the form.'

C——y: 'Makes no difference; do the punishment.'

Victim: 'Please, sir, but he's such a beast.'

C——y: 'So he is; you needn't do the punishment.'

Another time a delinquent was not so lucky.

C——y: 'I have a very great mind to complain of you'—(long pause)—'and upon *second* thoughts, I will.'

Boys with red hair were sure to be reminded of their infirmity. He would address a youthful poet in this way: 'Here comes the rising sun!' And watching a row of shivering boys in a punt, awaiting their turn to swim the distance for 'a pass,' he would call out to some Rufus amongst them: ' Now let that red-haired fellow go in; he'll make the water warm for the next boy!'

He had a great aversion to Germans; the very name of Schweizerhausen was too much for him. 'I can't pronounce it,' said he; 'it's something between two spits and a cough!' He thought that Scott had done the lion's share of the work at the new dictionary. 'Now, secretary,' he would say to the Præpostor, 'where's my *Scott* and Liddell?' His own derivations were peculiar. 'Gylippus—now you know the Greeks were fond of compounding with ἵππος—you get *Melanippus*, black horse; *Leucippus*, white horse. Now I take it that *Gylippus* means *red* horse—*Gules*, you know!'

Sometimes he would apostrophize the two giants of his form. 'When those two Light Infantry gentlemen have taken their seats, I'll begin the lesson.'

His son Gustavus ('Gussy') was the smallest boy I ever remember at Eton, though Frank Tarver, who was five years old when he entered the school and could not jump over his hat, must have been a good second for the pigmy prize. He inherited much of his father's humour and audacity, even to the extent of imitating Bethell's voice at Speeches in the presence of the Bursar himself. The speech was Mercutio's on Queen Mab, and 'Gussy' amused the school by voicing old Bethell at the words:

> 'And sometimes comes she with a tithe pig's tail,
> Tickling a parson's nose as a' lies asleep;
> Then dreams he of another benefice,' etc.

After escaping the heated atmosphere of C——y's pupil room, and the vicarious doctoring of the poor lad, who, I suspect, was as much 'sinned against as sinning,' I adjourned to the cloisters, and the Provost's Lodge, where I was duly, not 'untimely ripped.' It was the last ceremony at Eton, incidental to a colleger on the eve of leaving the school for King's. This mystery must be explained to the uninitiated. The two folds of the colleger's serge gown were sewn together in front, and the Provost 'ripped' them asunder, pronouncing, I think, some Latin formula. Then he congratulated the embryo scholar of King's, and gave him good advice, after the manner of

Polonius. Hodgson's parting words are well remembered by me. After some kind expressions about my speech in the Upper School, he ended with a solemn warning: 'Don't let your histrionic power be a snare to you in after life.' Good old man! he knew my weakness and had heard of my ghastly performances in 'Cato' (of all plays in the world!), in 'Julius Cæsar,' and 'The Midsummer Night's Dream,' and my appearance as a low comedian in 'His Last Legs,' 'Box and Cox,' and 'Bombastes Furioso.' The caution was fully deserved. Should I blush or boast in the confession that I might have sung, and most probably have failed miserably, as a tenor on the Italian stage, not many years after that valedictory scene in the Eton cloisters?

Without saying that Provost Hodgson was a commanding personality, or that he left at Eton a name or record comparable in any way to those of his predecessor, Goodall, I maintain that we old collegers, whose *status* was so vastly improved under his reign, should hold him always in respectful and affectionate remembrance. I owe him one single grudge, and that was for the bad policy of refusing to endorse Hawtrey's proposal to offer assistant-masterships to two of the most brilliant oppidans of my time—Goldwin Smith and Henry James Coleridge. Had these obviously first-rate appointments been made, the 'Canadian Jeremiah'—a Latinist second only to Munro and Conington—might have conferred untold benefits on his old school, and my dear relative might possibly have escaped captivity at the hands of those ' who usurped the well.' It was a hardship on the school in general, to miss the services of such gifted and distinguished men, and doubly hard on those boys who were intended for an Oxford training, and would have profited by the teaching of men so highly honoured in their University. The limitation of the appointment of assistant-masterships to Fellows of King's has at times been disastrous indeed. Bethell's very slender classical accomplishments were well known, and Keate writhed under his assistant's incompetency; yet Fate ordained that this worthy man and blundering scholar should become the classical trainer and informer of Shelley, the poet.

The portrait of Edward Craven Hawtrey has been masterfully drawn, once and for all time, by one of his 'humble yoke-fellows,' who was the last boy, I believe, to receive a prize from the hands of Keate, and was destined in after-years to pass the remnant of his school-days, and the larger term of his assistant-mastership, under Hawtrey's command.

For the benefit of some who are not the happy owners of Maxwell Lyte's volume, I quote the few last paragraphs of that brilliant summary of the educational reforms accomplished under Hawtrey's rule, and the *résumé* of the headmaster's services to a school with which he and his family had been connected for a great number of years: 'Meanwhile, in spite of his own precarious tenure of Attic scholarship, and the disloyalty of many of his colleagues to the old Eton traditions, year after year Hawtrey's beloved young men went to the Universities better read and better trained than their predecessors, even if not so well read or well trained as many representatives of less fashionable schools. To put the case broadly, he lived to see (if he had eyes to see it) whole tribes of Eton men seasoned with the accurate philology which he had never himself acquired—men who knew his defects, and

DR. HAWTREY.

'Quàm delectabat pariter, pariterque monebat!
Quàm piger ad pœnas, munera promptus erat!'

were, notwithstanding, indebted to him, and consciously grateful to him for their better schooling. For although he had not improved the school-books materially, and had only unintentionally relaxed the grammatical discipline, he had made it possible for his assistants to teach in a leisurely and tranquil manner. He practically added theme-writing to verse-writing, as an exercise of some importance; he greatly improved "trials" by the introduction of printed examination-papers; he added new examinations from time to time; and, above all, he established a standard of attainment and a kernel of industry in that part of the school which, before his time, was the least satisfactory —the King's scholars or collegers.

'To state the case in another way, for there are more ways than one of elucidating even so slight a thing as the history of schooling, Hawtrey may be said to have done by encouraging what Keate tried to do by threatening. If there is any proof in that melancholy caricature by which Keate is known to most men—if his battle-cry really was "I'll flog you"—it is no less true, though it is by no means well known, that Hawtrey's characteristic utterance was " Very well; very good exercise," said with a gracious emphasis which never lost its charm. Keate's mission was to keep down mannishness and swagger; Hawtrey delighted to give boys the sweet pride of authorship. Men have almost grown old who still feel thankful that they once lived with a man who, though quite at home in the most brilliant circles, did, as truly as Lacordaire, " love young people." When he was at the height of prosperity, he said publicly : " Living here, I cannot feel the sadness of growing old, for this place supplies me with an unfailing succession of young friends." Other men have been more kind, more charitable, more tender: but he had a poetical enthusiasm which burnt through vanities and feeblenesses, and fell in light and warmth on shy boys, on proud and ungainly lads, on homely and ordinary teachers, not less than on brilliant and noble students.

'A school cannot be managed by sympathy with boys alone. It must be shown how Dr. Hawtrey's singular generosity told on the government of Eton. He was better supplied with assistants than Keate had been, though his field of choice was strictly limited to King's

College. But when he had selected a man, there were two ways of dealing with him. One was the way of repression, the other was that of encouragement. Hawtrey adopted the latter. To a very young man he was as respectful as to a man of mature age, bearing with those crudities and eccentricities by which young men often estrange themselves from their superiors. Therefore his colleagues worked for him, though not in his own groove, as the Marquis Wellesley's young men had worked for him at Calcutta—nay, there were some among them who were to him what young warriors had been to King David and to Admiral Nelson.

'Besides this universal generosity, bearing on all varieties of character, Dr. Hawtrey displayed a special liberality in dealing with that which of all things most shapes the character—religion. He was not a theologian, though he could deliver short sermons that were at once orthodox and eloquent. He could no more fathom the controversies of the age in which men were swayed by Newman or by Arnold, than he could take the measure of the new philosophies growing up by the side of the new theologies. Had he been suspicious, narrow-minded, or cold-hearted, he would certainly have quarrelled with three or four of the best of his assistants in the first ten years of his government. As it was, he became the faithful friend and moderate supporter of several Anglo-Catholic colleagues. Had he set his authority against them, had he even let them be thwarted, more than they were thwarted, by the alarmed Protestantism of Eton College, he would have lost the services of men who could not be replaced. But it must be understood that nothing could be further from his mind than a cool calculation of such results. He obeyed his good heart. He knew by a heavenly instinct when he had a truly good man at his side; he was sagacious enough to perceive that certain tastes might lead to Rome, but he was not to be scared by such a danger. He stuck to his friend, he backed up his colleague, because he knew and cherished goodness.

'Such was the man; not an accurate scholar, though versed in many tongues; not thoroughly well informed, though he had spent £30,000 on books; not able to estimate correctly the intellectual development of younger men, though he corresponded with the leaders of England and France; not qualified to train schoolboys in competition with a Vaughan or a Kennedy, possessing the advanced knowledge of a later generation, for he had never been a University man, only a Kingsman; not one that could be said to organize well, for from first to last he dealt in make-shift and patchwork; yet for all that a hero among schoolmasters, for he was beyond his fellows candid, fearless, and bountiful: passionate in his indignation against cruelty, ardent in admiring all virtue and all show of genius; so forgiving, that for fifty years he seized every chance of doing kindness to a man who had tormented him at school; and so ingenuous, that when he had misunderstood a boy's character, and then found himself wrong, he suddenly grasped his hand, and owned his error magnanimously. Many men have laughed at his rhetoric, and made themselves a reputation for wit by telling stories of his behaviour. Such men have probably never read the second part of Don Quixote. The knight was, after all, a true gentleman of fine mind, and his death was pathetic. Our headmaster was worthy of a high-souled poetical nation in its best age;

and old men who had been his compeers in society wept at his funeral with younger men who had been only his humble yoke-fellows.'

Yet during his lifetime it was difficult to take him quite seriously. 'He was so delightfully "rococo,"' one of his assistants said; and certainly his pineapple-shaped head, his curiously grotesque face and action, combined with his fine-gentleman ways, and much that belonged to the character of a Church dignitary, made a very strange *ensemble*.

Hawtrey used to talk with great veneration of Dr. Foster, a former headmaster of Eton, a relative of his on his mother's side, and a scholar of real mark. Foster was one of the many instances of headmasters whose classical attainments were no sort of makeweight or compensation for their utter inability to govern a school. What Wordsworth in our time was to Harrow, Dr. Foster was in old days to Eton, and when the number of boys had dwindled to 230, the unhappy man, at the age of 41, resigned in favour of Dr. Jonathan Davies. This failure of Dr. Foster, though recognized, as to administration, by Hawtrey, was atoned for, in his judgment, by the uprightness of his relative's character and the soundness of his scholarship. It was a misfortune for any man to succeed Barnard, Dr. Johnson's friend, whose popularity, as headmaster, was never exceeded. Barnard seems to have had many points in common with Hawtrey; neither of them was a profound scholar, though both were voracious readers and men of fastidious taste in the literature of their day.

It is a mistake to suppose that every headmaster in old days was so wedded to the ordinary *curriculum* of Eton studies as to ignore modern languages and contemporary literature. It is a fact not generally known that Hawtrey ascribed his early love of modern languages to Goodall, who, in teaching the sixth-form, expected the most studious members of it to answer questions relative to the best French and German authors. This early taste was so assiduously and successfully cultivated by our headmaster that he published a little volume, 'Il Trifoglio,' consisting of original poems in French, German and Italian. Of more importance than this achievement was his eager championship of an offer made by Prince Albert, to found an annual prize for modern languages. In construing Homer at the sixth-form lessons, we were always on the look-out for the headmaster's scraps of German. These were received with broad smiles and vague incredulity. 'The modern Germans,' said he, 'have borrowed from Homer's ἰφθίμη ἄλοχος—*eine wackere Frau.*' Inextinguishable laughter.

Hawtrey: 'What on airth is there to laugh about?'

Hawtrey's classical teaching was rather more picturesque than useful, but the time when Eton honestly prided herself on our headmaster's accomplishments was on such rare occasions as the visits of Soult, Guizot, or the King of the French. Then '*nitidissimus* Hawtrey' shone with peculiar lustre. His good French and glib German were safety-valves for the Provost and Fellows, who, but for their representative man, must have done the honours of the College pretty much in dumb show. He had an odd weakness for fine clothes, perfumes, and gold chains; one of the school beliefs was that 'Hawtrey stood up in £700,' the stiff figure at which we assessed his studs, sleeve-links, watch and chains, gold pencil and rings. His velvet collars were a costly item in the general get-up. We laughed at and caricatured and imitated him remorselessly, but we loved him well. I saw more practical jokes played before Hawtrey than before all the subordinate masters put together.

The high time for jinks was during the Windsor fair, when a sixth-form boy or a boy in 'Liberty' would cram his pocket full of toys, wooden animals, notably frogs, cunningly constructed, so as to jump two feet in the air at an unexpected moment. On one occasion, a perfect menagerie was successfully planted on the table before Hawtrey's very nose, and all the punishment we got for our tomfoolery was his withering remark, 'Babies!' Another favourite joke was to ring Hawtrey's bell furiously and summon Finmore. Then a dialogue would ensue. *Hawtrey:* 'I didn't ring for you.' *Finmore:* 'Yes, you did, sir.' *Hawtrey:* 'I tell you I did not—go away.' Lapse of ten minutes, and the same process repeated with the same result. I think McNiven was the first inventor of this silly device for worrying one of the best and kindest of men.

Our headmaster used Keate's famous desk and rostrum as a tribune from which he harangued us on state occasions, or read aloud to our patient comrades our 'sent up' exercises. These were invariably rewarded with the stereotyped form of commendation, 'Very well; very good exercise,' though now and then they were not only slipshod, but incorrect. Accents were imperfectly distributed by more than one of the assistant-masters, and I remember Hawtrey pausing over an Iambic which began thus: θύμω πέφηνε πάντα. This was intended to mean 'All things have appeared to my mind,' *i.e.*, 'I foresaw all that has now happened'—a poor sentiment, badly expressed in dog Greek, and the word θυμός wrongly accented, meaning, as it stood, a vegetable. Hawtrey paused after reading the passage, and when he had discovered the blunder, ejaculated, 'What on airth do you mean? All things have appeared to an onion!' Answer: 'Please, sir, my tutor looked over the exercise.' Discreet silence. The gold pencil was produced, and after a scrawl or two, the proper accent laid on; θύμος lost its vegetable quality and became a prophetic instinct.

Hawtrey's harangues to the school in the penultimate years of his reign were, now and then, highly comic. The bust of William IV. in Upper School had been scored with pencil marks, either recording the names of the writers, or a playful reflection, such as 'Good old Billy—our Sailor King.' We were summoned and harangued : ' My servant informs me that you have been writing with your filthy pencils your st*oo*pid names on the bust of our late revered Monarch.' These portentous announcements were almost always *bruta fulmina*, ending in smoke ; the real culprits too often escaped under a censure, which was supposed to reflect upon the general lack of order and discipline.

I remember our being summoned to hear our headmaster give out the subject of a holiday task :

E. C. H. : 'The subject will be the " Colitheum," " Amphitheatrum Flavianum," where amongst other animals, exhibited only to be slain, was that beautiful creature, the camēlŏpard.' (Roars of laughter.)

E. C. H. : 'This laughter is highly indecorous !' (Renewed guffaws.)

I have had some difficulty in unearthing the fragments of a poem [?] supposed to have been dictated in Chambers by Hawtrey to his assistants, before November 5, an anxious day with the authorities:

> 'You, Coleridge, be sure to look out;
> Never mind any meeting; keep running about.
>   (Wilder, Cookesley, Pickering *desunt*.)

> 'And now, old long-nosed, long-legged Harry Dupuis,
> You're famous for sneaking, so hide in a tree,
> And whomsoever by this means you see,
> Take hold of his collar, and bring him to me.'
>   GOODFORD *deest*.
> 'You, A——m, act up to the patriarch's name;
> Though you cannot see straight, you can run all the same.
> You, Carter and Durnford, you go in a pair,
> As you did t'other day at the last Windsor fair.'

In Chambers, after the event:

E. C. H.: 'Oh! well done, I commend your pains.'
           MASTERS.
> 'Through water we waded, through mud and through lanes,
> And though some did us outstrip,
> Yet two stragglers* from the flock
> In our clutches safe we lock,' etc.

A friend of mine sends me his version of two scenes in the late days of Hawtrey's head-

---

* Farmer and Spottiswoode.

mastership, adding that as they are those of a lower boy, they need to be balanced by the more generous recollections of those whom he admitted to his intimacy. 'He was calling "absence," and two big fellows, Follett and Metcalfe, both now dead, engaged in fierce conflict on the outskirts of the ring, not twenty yards from his nose. But it was beneath his dignity to interfere personally in a vulgar "mill." Accordingly he appeared to be quite unconscious of the row; but just before he left his platform, he beckoned me from the ring. "Lower boy," he said, "lower boy, go and call Mr. Marriott to stop that fight!" Marriott rushed out, and flung himself between the combatants, but not before Metcalfe had been severely mauled by his antagonist. Years afterwards Metcalfe came to live near me, and I asked him if he remembered his fight with Follett. He had good reason to remember it, and the satisfaction he felt when Marriott delivered him from his awkward situation. Of course he had no notion that he was indebted to me for his happy rescue. What the old man practised, that he preached. Fights and dogs, and the like of these, he could only condescend to touch with a pair of tongs. So when he held forth to us on the Rich Man and Lazarus, he warned us against the danger of faring sumptuously *every day;* and excited the opposite feelings to what he intended for Lazarus, by representing his condition as such as to excite 'the compassion of those animals that naturally attack beggars with instinctive suspicion.'

I suspect that dear old Hawtrey was made Provost none too soon. His leave-taking, I was told by a boy who heard it, was dignified and pathetic. He began with: 'This is the saddest day in my life,' and I believe he spoke the sober truth, when he exchanged the incessant activities of the headmastership for the quiet retirement in the cloisters. He had been *adscriptus glebæ* since childhood, and with the exception of three years at Cambridge, and the vacation intervals, had remained a permanent fixture at Eton. Generous and open-handed to a fault, it was said that he was always *magnas inter opes inops*, and the dispersion of one-half of his costly library, at a fearful loss, must have given him a pang. To this day, if I detect a dainty volume on a London bookstall, and see on the title-page 'E. C. H.,' the initials of the original owner, I feel humiliated, and not over-tolerant of the reckless expenditure which was the fashion in my time at Eton. But generosity is a splendid fault, and Hawtrey lived and died in the affections of all Eton men who knew him best, and could appreciate his fine taste and true nobility of character.

I have reasons for knowing that Matthew Arnold's expressed admiration of Hawtrey's English versions from Homer and Callinus gave him, as an old man, the genuine pleasure of being appreciated by such a critic. These translations should be more widely known.

Our lower master, Richard Okes, though he took precedence over all the assistants, and was invariably consulted by the headmaster in any crisis affecting the school, had no perceptible influence, out of his own house and pupil-room, on the Upper School, which he had served for fifteen years as an assistant. Remembering his great popularity as an Eton tutor—for at one time he had as many as ninety private pupils—perhaps I should qualify my statement as to the lower master's negative influence on the school in general. Without saying that those ninety boys—forming a large fraction of the school, when it stood at a lesser number than in our present time—would leaven the whole of the rest of the lump, they certainly would constitute an important factor, and very considerably affect the tone and character of the school. My belief is that Okes' integrity and righteous life, his good scholarship, consistency, and honesty, inspired numbers of parents with just confidence in his supervision, and were the main elements of his popularity. These qualities will always tell in the long-run; and in my school time, when all my experience of Okes was an impressive personality in chapel, and the fact that I, now and then, 'snatched a fearful joy' in shirking him successfully when out of bounds, I had an unqualified respect for his character.

The sons of his earliest pupils in 1823 were entrusted to him in the penultimate years of his service as lower master; he told me himself that he never remembered his house without a 'Miles' in it. I have strong reasons for knowing that the members of his household and pupil-room were devotedly attached to him. At first, they were awed into submission

by his solemn injunction to every new-comer:
'You must be particular in observing the
customary obeisances,' which was his round-
about way of cautioning the youngster to take
off his hat to the authorities; but boys of the
right sort soon forgot the drill-sergeant, and
paid homage to the kind and loyal-hearted
tutor.

I knew something about Okes from the
letters of my uncle, Henry Nelson Coleridge,
his contemporary at school and College. These
letters are part of my family archives, and I
argued correctly from these, that Okes, in
dubious times at King's, was *integer vitæ
scelerisque purus*, as well as a reading man,
who was regarded as a formidable competitor
for the University scholarships. He told me
that he remembered Porson's visit to his
father's house in Cambridge. I have seen a
copy of the famous 'Hecuba,' which the
Professor presented to Richard Okes when he
was a very small boy; the book bears a neat
inscription in Porson's own handwriting.

The name of 'Mr. Okes,' the late Provost's
father, appears in the list of those who attended
at Porson's funeral in Trinity Chapel. The

Provost's library was sold after his death. If the lucky purchaser of that 'Hecuba' volume would act magnanimously, might I suggest that the proper place for it would be in King's College Library?

From 1850 to 1888, the late Provost of King's was my stanch, loyal, and intimate friend. I was in constant correspondence with him up to the last, and treasure the many written proofs which I possess of his attachment and confidence. A short biography, the work of my friend Oscar Browning, appeared in the *Cambridge Review* immediately after the Provost's death. It is a valuable and truthful summary of a good man's life, and I thankfully reproduce it in these pages, and vouch for its truth and accuracy:

'Born in 1797, the son of a Cambridge medical man, he went to Eton at an early age, and in 1817 was admitted as a scholar to King's College. The college of those days stood on the north side of the chapel, in the space now occupied by the buildings of the University library. The late Provost was one of the few survivors of that ancient society, and had many stories to tell of the quaint names and usages which hung about the old buildings until they were destroyed. The King's men of that day, and of many years later, were debarred from the ordinary University competitions. Okes carried off the prize for the Greek and Latin epigrams two years in succession,* showing his innate tendency to a certain smartness of Attic wit, which never deserted him. In 1823 he went as a master to Eton, where he joined his old friend George John Dupuis, the late Vice-Provost of Eton, to be joined in his turn by Chapman, Bishop of Colombo, and John Wilder, the next Vice-Provost. At this time Goodall was Provost of Eton, and Keate headmaster. Whatever was the state of education in the school, there was much promise of literary excellence. *The Etonian*, the flower of school magazines, had been running its course during Okes' sojourn at Cambridge. The early years of his mastership saw the publication of the *Eton Miscellany*, with Gladstone, Selwyn, Rogers, and Arthur Hallam among its contributors, and of the

* W. Green, of King's, enjoys the distinction of having gained it *three* years in succession.

first literary efforts of Lord Lyttelton and Sir Francis Doyle. Mr. Okes had at one time as many as ninety pupils, and he has been heard to say that he could only get through his work by sitting up the whole of one night in the week. In 1838 he was appointed Lower master, Dr. Hawtrey having become headmaster four years before. The present writer saw him for the first time some seven years later, when, as a boy of eight years old, he was inscribed on the roll of the lower school. He impressed upon the new-comer, with much elaboration of phrase, the necessity of inscribing his name in the Lower master's book with the surname first, the contrary order to that which I had seen followed just before in the headmaster's book; but the expressions he used had to be interpreted by a friendly mentor before they could be understood by a small boy. In 1850 he was elected Provost of King's in succession to Provost Thackeray. At that time the college consisted of not more than ten or fifteen scholars, who became Fellows on the third anniversary of their admission, and who, by a special composition with the University, received their degrees without having passed the usual examinations. The first step taken by Provost Okes was to abolish this untoward privilege.

'King's had been rightly stigmatized as the grave of talent. Gifted students, on arriving from Eton, found little inducement or stimulus to work, and were, by the arrangements of the College, cut off from the main currents of University life. This reform soon showed its results. The College was able to claim a third classic in 1853, a second classic in 1855, and a senior classic in 1860, although its Senior Wrangler did not arrive until twenty-five years later. In these years the Provost was the tutor of the College, and the teaching of the undergraduates was committed mainly to strangers. A still further change was made by the statutes of 1861, by which the exclusive connection of the College with Eton was broken through, and students were admitted from all quarters. Thus, by degrees, during the last five-and-twenty years, the College has grown until it has come to occupy no undistinguished position amongst its sisters. Provost Okes was a strong conservative; he had a deep-seated reverence for the past, and a distrust of change.

He once said in a speech at Eton that the position of a drag was a very useful and honourable one. It might have been feared that a ruler with such opinions would have regarded the development of the College with dislike, and would have met it either with a factious opposition or with cynical indifference. But his deep love for the College which he governed, and his inherent magnanimity of character, saved him from such courses. Those who for many years have attended meetings in which old privileges were being abolished, old landmarks swept away, and courses of temerity inaugurated, could not but admire the dignity, fairness, and self-reliance with which the Provost presided over deliberations in which, if he had voted at all, he must have voted with the minority. His acuteness and observation were never at fault. He never took an unfair advantage, nor failed to recognize loyally an accomplished fact. Many who disagreed with him rose from a heated debate with the consciousness that the Provost had spoken wiser words than anyone else. Most conspicuous was his abiding sense of the dignity of the College. He asserted it on all occasions with a firmness and an emphasis which makes his loss very bitter to those who served under him, and renders it very difficult to supply his place. Till within a very short time of his death, he took the keenest interest in every detail of College life. He complained sometimes that he did not hear enough, never that he heard too much, of what was going on. He presided over all College meetings, large and small, at times when his doing so must have been an heroic struggle against physical weakness. He had hoped to take the chair at the annual congregation of the year of his death, on November 27. His last act was to sign the notice-paper of the business for that congregation. He attended service in the College chapel far into the same year, and presided as long as health allowed him at the College feast.

'Next to his love for King's came his love for Eton. He frequently visited his brother Provost, although he no longer drove into Weston's yard in a stately yellow coach, and greeted his good brother of Eton with a ceremonious embrace. He kept up a lively memory of his old pupils, and continued to correspond with many of them. His memory of old times was very keen, and many traditions die with him which it will be difficult to recover.

'He was a scholar of the old type. His principal contribution to literature is the edition of the "Musæ Etonenses," the high-water mark of that original verse composition which was once the glory of Eton. Perhaps the sense that scholarship had moved into other fields checked him when he would have published more. His wit was never at fault. His epigrams on passing occurrences will live in the annals of University life. His thirty-eight years' rule marks a momentous epoch in the history of King's. It is probable that for some little time after its foundation King's held the first place among Cambridge Colleges, a supremacy which passed first to St. John's and then to Trinity. With the development of Eton, under William III. and Anne, the College was called upon more frequently than before to supply masters to that institution. During the eighteenth and first half of the present century, the College of the white rose gave the best of its life-blood to the school of the white lily. It has now risen to an independent position. Four-fifths of its undergraduates, and more than a third of its fellows, are non-Etonians. The death of the Provost closes a period. It will never be forgotten how the head, who presided over this transition so wisely and so well, subordinated private feelings and opinions, which must have been very strong, to the wider interests which appealed to a keen sympathy with every educational advance, and a deeper reverence for the founder's will and design.'

In youth, manhood and age, Okes was really remarkable for his peculiar wit—wit, apart from gaiety and humour. He was more than the successful epigram writer at Cambridge, and it is no negative praise of a man with a quick temper, to say that his wit never pained nor left a wound. As a boy, I had the good fortune to be present at the opening of the Fives Courts, at Eton, 1847. It was felt on all sides to be an occasion worthy of record. Greek, Latin, French, German, Italian verses, the effusions of different masters, were strung together and printed; but Okes's Latin speech, admirably delivered, 'took the cake.' I remember Cookesley, on his way to Trotman's garden, soliloquizing, 'I hear Okes is going to make a Latin speech; the air will be redolent of puns.' So it was, or rather of paronomasia, which were caught up and cheered lustily. The oration has been found too long for insertion in these pages; it was full of good-natured chaff, and we boys were informed, for the first time in our lives, that '*nitidissimus*' Hawtrey had been a good fives player in his early days. The poems, contributed chiefly by the assistant-masters, were, I think, taken as read; but an epigram by the Rev. Edward Balston was thought very neat and appropriate :

>Τέσσαρες ἦσαν ἀγῶνες ἀν' Ἑλλάδα, τοῖς δ'ἀπ' Ἐτώνης,
>μὴ μέμψῃ παριών, πέμπτος ὅδ' ἐστὶν ἀγών.

The allusion to dear old Hawtrey's early fame as a fives player made a sensation; we did not believe in our headmaster as a sportsman, for he seldom hazarded a criticism at a cricket-match, and sat rather uncomfortably in a punt, watching the swimming and diving contests, or a boat race of a summer evening.

I remember a sentence in *Bell's Life*, the great sporting paper of the time : '" Upper Sixes" were rowed last Tuesday. Buller's crew won. Dr. Hawtrey witnessed the finish, and expressed himself well satisfied with the style of rowing.' He was perturbed at the introduction of outriggers, and the gradual disappearance of tubs, barring the old 'ten-oar.' Looking from Windsor Bridge, on a sculler whose hair was said to be parted in the middle lest the boat should upset, Hawtrey murmured to his friend: 'I really think the time is coming when Eton boys will go up to Surley on a stick.'

Our headmaster was no craven except by name; he had plenty of pluck, as the following incident will show. His one single feat of horsemanship is a historical fact. It was a favourite story with him, as illustrating his conviction that a strong and determined will may prevail against any amount of physical difficulty.

'I was staying, in the winter holidays, with an old pupil of mine, a great sportsman and a fine rider. To my consternation, he said one morning at breakfast: "Doctor, the hounds meet near us to-morrow, and I insist on your following them." I answered: "It's very kind of you, but I have never been on horseback in my life." "Oh, that be hanged! I have a fine Irish mare for you, and she will carry you over everything." Seeing there was no help for it, I screwed my courage to the sticking-point, and my body to the saddle. Camilla flew like a thunderbolt—the "free and exulting animal" hopped merrily over hedges and ditches, bringing me in triumphant and un-scathed at the death of the wily animal, sly "Reynolds." They gave me the brush—there it is,' and the headmaster, γέρων πρίνινος, used to point to his well-earned trophy. Well-bred Almack dandies fought stoutly, and bit the dust at Waterloo. I glory in the fact that the '*nitidissimus*' was applauded and laurelled by an Assheton Smith of the period. Sir J. Coleridge told me the story. Hawtrey enjoyed the mischievous pupil's admiration of his old tutor's fine courage ; no honest compliment was lost upon him, though he was singularly modest and habitually reticent on the subject of self. An old friend wrote to me:

'The last time I ever spoke to E. C. H., I told him, to his manifest comfort, that Matthew Arnold had just printed in his " Lectures on Homer " a very strong compliment to E. C. H.'s

English hexameters—the translation of Helen on the Walls.'

ILIAD, BOOK III., vv. 234-244.

Helen from the Walls of Troy, looking for her brothers.

'Clearly the rest I behold of the dark-ey'd Sons of Achaia,
Known to me well are the Faces of all; their names I remember;
Two—two only remain, whom I see not among the Commanders,
Kastor, fleet in the Car—Polideukes, brave with the Cestus—
Own dear brethren of mine—one Parent lov'd us as infants.
Are they not here in the Host, from the shores of lov'd Lakedaimon,
Or, if they came with the Rest in Ships that bound thro' the Waters,
Dare they not enter the fight, or stand in the Council of Heroes,
All for fear of the Shame and Taunts my crime has awaken'd?'
  So said she; long since they in Earth's soft Arms were reposing,
There, in their own dear Land, their Father-Land, Lakedaimon.

ILIAD, BOOK VI., vv. 394-502.

The parting of Hector and Andromache.

There came hast'ning to meet him his Consort, the fair and the wealthy,
She, that Andromache hight, stout-hearted Eëtion's Daughter,

Daughter of him who dwelt under Placus, the forest-becrownèd,
O'er Hypoplacian Thebes and Cilician warriors reigning.
His was the Daughter whom Hector, the brazen-crested, had chosen:
She was the Wife who met him, her Handmaid pacing beside her,
Holding a Babe at her Breast, that tender, delicate Infant,
Hector's only belov'd, who shone like a Star in its Brightness.
Hector had named the boy Scamandrius, Astyanax all beside Hector.
Then did he smile, as he gaz'd on the Child in affectionate silence.
Near him Andromache stood, and the tears stream'd fast from her Eyelids:
Then did she cling to his Hand, and with words such as these she address'd him:
'Hector, my brave one, but oh, too brave to be safe, or to pity
This, thine infant Child, or me, the unhappy—thy Widow
Soon to be called; for soon the Grecian Warriors will slay thee,
Rushing together on One; but for me far happier were it—
Were I bereav'd of thee—to sink in the grave; for what other
Hope of comfort have I, when Fate thy career shall have ended—
What, but to grieve? They are gone, both the father and mother who bare me;
For my father was slain by the Hand of the mighty Achilles,
Then, when he took by Storm the Cilicians' populous City,

Thebes, with her high raised gates, and Eëtion slew in the capture,
Slew, but spoil'd him not; for a sense of religion restrain'd him.
Him did he burn on the pile with his arms in their brightness around him;
Then on his ashes a tomb did he raise; but the nymphs of the mountain
Planted an elm-grove around—the Ægis-arm'd Jupiter's daughters.
Then too the seven brave Youths, the brothers that dwelt in our palace,
They in a day went down to the darksome Mansion of Hades.
All were in one day slain by the swift-footed mighty Achilles,
While they were tending the white-fleeced sheep and the slow-footed oxen.
But for my mother, who reigned under Placus the forest-becrownèd,
Her he had taken away with the rest of the spoils of the conquer'd,
Then did he let her go free for a ransom of infinite value,
So by Diana's shafts she died in the hall of my father.
Hector, to me thou art all and enough for Father and Mother,
Aye, and for Brothers too — my brave — my beautiful husband!
Oh, then pity me now, and stay where thou art on the Ramparts!
Make not thy child here an orphan, thy wife too a desolate widow.
Bid the men halt by the fig-tree-grove, where approach to the city

Seems to invite the foe and to give a clear path to the
   onset.
Thrice already the bravest have that way tried to assail us;
Ajax, the swift and the bold, and the far-famed King of the
   Cretans.
One must have told them the way, well skill'd in the art of
   divining,
Or their own spirit has urged them, prophetic of victory,
   onwards.'
  Then to her answer made the great helm-quivering
   Hector:
'I too have thought of all this, dear wife, but I fear the
   reproaches
Both of the Trojan youths and the long-rob'd maidens of
   Troja,
If like a cowardly churl I should keep me aloof from the
   combat;
Nor would my spirit permit; for well have I learnt to be
   valiant,
Fighting aye among the first of the Trojans marshall'd in
   battle,
Striving to keep the renown of my Sire and my own un-
   attainted.
Well, too well, do I know—both my mind and my spirit
   agreeing—
That there will be a day when sacred Troja will perish.
Priam will perish too, and the people of Priam, spear-
   armèd.
Still, I have not such care for the Trojans doom'd to
   destruction,
No, nor for Hecuba's self, nor for Priam the monarch, my
   father,
Nor for my brothers' fate, who, though they be many and
   valiant,

All in the dust may lie low by the hostile spears of Achaia,
As for thee, when some youth of the brazen-mailèd Achæans
Weeping shall bear thee away, and bereave thee for ever of freedom.
Then for another perchance thou'lt handle the shuttle in Argos
Slave-like, or water bear from Messeis or else Hypereä,
Sorely against thy will, for force will weigh heavily on thee.
Someone perchance will say, while he looks at thee bitterly weeping,
" Lo, this is Hector's wife, who once was first in the battle
'Mong the Dardanian host, when they fought for the safety of Ilion."
So will the stranger say ; and thine will be bitterer anguish,
Widow'd of husband so brave, who might have kept off the enslaver.
Oh! may the earth o'erspread first cover me deep in her bosom,
Ere I can hear thy wail, when they drag thee from Troy as a captive.'
 Thus said Hector, and stretch'd his arms to encircle his infant ;
Then did the child on the breast of the deep-zon'd handmaid in terror,
Screaming shrilly, recline, all alarm'd at the look of his father,
Dreading the brass and the crest that fearfully nodded with horsehair,
While he beheld it shake from the glittering cone of the helmet.
Oh, then his father laugh'd out, and so did his beautiful mother !

Quickly did Hector take down from his head that quivering helmet,
And on the ground where he stood, all glittering laid it before him,
But when he kiss'd his boy, and fondling gently carest him,
Loud then pray'd he to Jove and the other gods of Olympus:
'Jove and ye other gods, oh grant that this child may be honour'd
E'en as I honour'd have been among all the Dardanian heroes,
Brave like me in the fight, and to rule over Ilion with valour!
So shall some Gazer exclaim, "Far braver is he than his father,"
When he returns from the fight with blood-stain'd trophies adornèd,
Freshly ta'en off from the slain, while the heart of his mother rejoices.'
  So said the chief, and replac'd his child in the arms of his consort
Gently, but she then at once on her fragrant bosom receiv'd him,
Smiling amidst her tears, and her husband pitied her weeping,
Soothing her grief in his arms, and thus consoling address'd her:
'Dearest, do not much afflict thy spirit with sorrow.
None can in spite of the fates send me to the mansion of Hades;
Yet what they have decreed no man has the power of escaping,
Coward or brave tho' he be, from the hour when he first was created

Go then, go to thine House, where duties befitting await thee
There by the distaff and loom; and order thy handmaids about thee
All to their daily employ. For men is the care of the battle,
Most of them all, for me among native heroes of Ilion.'
  Such, then, were Hector's words, and he raised his helm at departing,
Crested on high—but his wife was now on her way to the palace,
Turning again and again, while tears flowed fast from her eyelids.
Soon did she reach the abode of Hector, the hero-destroyer,
Fair to behold; and there did she find her numerous handmaids
All in attendance within; and their grief was arous'd at her coming.
Sorely for Hector they griev'd, yet alive in his palace at Ilion.
'Never,' they said, 'will he come back from the din of the battle
Safe to his home from the hands of the Grecians in fury assailing.'

I add to Hawtrey's versions from Homer the 'War Song of Callinus':

War-Song of Callinus.

Bright and glorious it is, that soldier's fate, who in armour
  Stands for his children and home, stands for the wife of his heart,

Bravely oppos'd to the foe. So death may come on when he listeth,
   And life's thread's at an end. Then let him on to the field,
Holding on high the spear, and pressing his heart to the buckler
   Firmly, when Ares first calls us amain to the fray.
Think not fate will allow for a man to live always unharmèd,
   Great though he be, though he boast sires of the race of the gods.
What tho' the coward pass thro' the rattle of lances and arrows,
   Safe to his home he may flee—Death will assail him at home.
But then think not he dies lamented, lov'd by the people,
   While both the high and the low weep by the tomb of the brave.
Yes; with a nation's tears, where'er he may die we bewail him;
   And, if he live, he is hail'd all but a Mars upon earth.
Strong as a tower of defence in the fight do we gaze on our hero:
   His are deeds of an host—ay, and he does them alone.

These episodes anent Hawtrey's horsemanship and his poetical gifts have made me wander from the subject of the Provost of King's.

Manner is something to everybody and everything to some. In the early days of his

Provostship, Okes was conscious of a difficulty in divesting himself of a schoolmaster manner; this weakness was thrown in his teeth with some shade of truth, but less of generosity, by more than one of the Fellows of King's. He said magnanimously of himself: 'I put on buckram early in life, and I could not take it off afterwards.'

It has been said that taste is a commodity sold rather dear at Eton; hats, supplied by Saunders with remarkable liberality, were equally dear. I have seen a bill with items of seven hats charged for in one half; these were not all worn out in 'customary obeisances, for they had served as temporary wickets at stump and ball, or had been used, accidentally, as cushions in chapel. Lower boys, in my time, were not surfeited with kindness and delicate attentions from their superiors in age; their new hats shone only for a space, and were often discrowned and smashed in by bigger boys on the prowl for mischief. I have heard of a cautious and frugal lower boy purchasing two hats, one for morning and the other for evening school; the latter he called 'my five o'clock louser.' In summer, if rain was plentiful, Saunders did a roaring trade, for three hats, at twelve yards apart, made delightful wickets for stump and ball in the cloisters or school-yard.

A straw hat worn outside the Playing-fields, or off the river, was an abomination to Richard Okes, and he impounded it, then and there, remorselessly. This embargo on illicit head-gear was a craze with the Lower master. It was currently believed that he had a large depot of straw hats; many were unquestionably forfeited. I was furnished with some curious testimony, a few years since, as to these piratical habits of Richard Okes. I had written to a friend for his recollections of the ways and doings of the assistant masters in our time. This was his answer respecting the future Provost of King's: 'All I know of Dicky Okes is, that he bagged my straw hat.'

Okes succeeded to the Provostship of King's in the second year of my scholarship. I have a very vivid memory of the election, and the excitement in the college at the time. The votes were pretty well known beforehand; H. Dupuis, Barrett, and Goldney had no real chance in the contest, and Okes was a certainty, if the Fellows stuck loyally to their promises.

Harry Dupuis, an upright Christian gentleman, 'took his licking' with imperturbable good temper and equanimity. Our College statutes empower the Fellows to elect one of their own body, as a '*discretus et fidelis socius*,' to carry the news of the result of the election to the chosen candidate, and Harry Dupuis was told off for the duty.

To outsiders this may seem to have been rather a refined piece of cruelty; but the two men were friends of long standing, and I am certain that the messenger's congratulations were cordial and sincere.

Harry Dupuis had been popular with us in old Eton days, though as a determined disciplinarian he lives embalmed in a very uncomplimentary couplet, composed, I assume, by way of *revanche*:

> 'Long-nosed, long-legged Harry Dupuis,
> So famous for hiding up high in a tree.'

From this point of vantage Harry unquestionably had an unfair bird's-eye view of three fellows emerging, I think, from Botham's at

Salt Hill on a Sunday. One of the unfortunates became Colonel of the 1st Dragoon Guards; he never forgot Harry's Zaccheus performance.

At the inaugural banquet in King's Hall, when the College welcomed the new Provost, we feasted off a huge turtle, presented by the defeated candidate. The animal was inspected before the day of sacrifice in the College kitchen, and our best Latin scholar at the time quoted from Martial, '*Inclytus hæret adeps lateri,*' as he licked his lips in anticipation of the unwonted soup. The Provost alluded to the handsome present in his speech: 'We are indebted to my old friend, Harry Dupuis, for an onslaught on his *testudo.*'

We were told that H. Dupuis had canvassed old Hunt, our Senior Fellow, and met with a doubtful reception from that old gentleman:

'Get out of my room, you lousy son of a sea-cook! If you don't I'll call you hard names. None of your d———d French blood in the College!'

Old Hunt hated Frenchmen as vehemently as Lord Nelson did, and in imitation of that great seaman, kept his coffin in his bedroom.

This curious effort at discipline (strange in a man whose wild and dissipated life had, long years before, served Simeon for an object-lesson in admonishing his young disciples) failed to modify Counsellor Hunt's unparliamentary language.

On the eventful morning of the election, we were all of us assembled in chapel, where, for the first time for many years, old Hunt appeared, swathed in flannel and coats, under a short and ill-fitting surplice. It was a strange apparition, but Hunt was bent on recording, if possible, his vote for Okes as against the supposed Frenchman.

I think the service had only proceeded as far as the *Venite* when old Hunt was seen to be fumbling for his stick and fidgeting, obviously with the view of getting away from the scene of action. To our great amusement, the old gentleman slowly and deliberately walked down nearly the whole length of the chapel (for he had ensconced himself in the very last seat on the north side), so that his movements were in full evidence before the whole College, and the exit from chapel was quite a public performance.

The Fellows remained in chapel, after the

fashion of the Cardinals at an election of the Pope, and we scholars withdrew when the service was over. I addressed old Hunt sympathetically, for I knew he was for my man:

'Why, sir, couldn't you stay and vote for Okes?'

'Couldn't stand it, sir; the organ made such a d —— d row.'

Poor old Billy Hunt! Amongst the countless good deeds of Harvey Goodwin, then the Vicar of St. Edward's, it must not be forgotten that he attracted Hunt to his church as a regular worshipper. The old gentleman shared the admiration we undergraduates felt for Harvey Goodwin's earnestness and his great preaching, and though Hunt would stop in the quadrangle on a wet day, and apostrophize a worm on the lawn—'You haven't got me yet, sir'—the speech was not prefaced with the familiar 'D—n,' and he treated the creeping thing with civility.

Without saying that old Hunt died in the odour of sanctity, his last years were creditable to him, and I bless the memory of Harvey Goodwin for the part he took in working the happy change.

In his early College days, Okes and a friend agreed to have a tour in Wales together during the summer vacation. At some wayside hostelry, Jones, the landlord, piled up the bill with extravagant charges for very ordinary fare. The friend deputed Okes to remonstrate, and the landlord was sent for and cross-examined on the particulars of the reckoning. In defence of his 'increased charges,' the landlord pleaded *high-priced times*. Okes murmured a quotation from the Eton Greek Grammar: '*Iones in auctis temporibus geminatione uti solent.*'

At the Founder's Day dinner next after the unveiling of the west window and the dedication of the fountain, the Provost was unluckily absent, but he sent a message to the company through Oscar Browning:

'" O Fons splendidior vitro "—so think not I.'

One winter term, at a congregation held in the Provost's Lodge, there had been some warm discussion over College matters, and Nixon, one of our Fellows, took an active share in the debate. A heavy fall of snow had taken place during the proceedings. The Provost, after the breaking up of the assembly, stood at the window looking out on the whitened lawn in front. 'Well,' said he, 'indoors as well as out of doors we have had plenty of Nix—on.'

One of his raciest impromptus was uttered at an election dinner in the College hall at Eton. The weather was insufferably hot, the speeches were deadly dull. The late Lord Overstone, the famous banker, had got off the line of Eton topics in his speech, and wandered into a dreary dissertation on monetary matters. The audience was considerably bored, and Okes, who was the next in order to speak, began thus : 'I think it's high time for a run upon the bank,' a sentiment received with shouts of applause by the guests, who were longing for the Playing-fields and the riverside.

At a feast-day in Trinity a swan was served up at the high table. The Provost could not resist a joke. 'O-lor!' said he, whereupon the Hon. George Denman got the better of him by observing : 'Oh, Mr. Provost, don't sicken us' (cycnus)!

When Chandos Pole, familiarly known as 'Fat Pole,' was nearly run over by an omnibus,

Okes, his tutor, addressed him: 'You had a very narrow escape.

> '" . . . . . *rotundum*
> *Percurrisse polum, morituro*."'
> (Horace, Od. I., xxviii.)

Watching the headmaster as he drank a glass of champagne at Surley on June 4, Okes quoted from the first book of the Æneid:

> '" . . . . *Hauris*
> *Spumantem pateram, et pleno te proluis auro*."'

I have, amongst my letters from the Provost, some that show an extraordinary memory for faces, and for the humblest details bearing on Eton and Windsor life and associations. He shared my prejudice in favour of the old brown Windsor soap, and wrote me a small essay on the history of its origin, kept for years and years as a secret, and never divulged by the family of the original makers. The names of the traders in the genuine article were duly recorded, and I am satisfied that the Provost was accurate in the pedigree, and knew to a nicety when the fraudulent imitations were first introduced in the market.

From time to time he sent me Greek and

Latin verses; once, and once only, a few English stanzas in the shape of a version from the Latin. These were intended as a consolation to me in the summer of 1869. I had had a bad attack of ophthalmia during the Leeds assizes in that year, and on my return to London, I was laid up in bed for several days. I was very sorry for myself; my wife and family were in Switzerland, and there was no likelihood of my being able to join them for some considerable time. Fortunately for me, I enjoyed at that time an intimate friendship with Madame Goldschmidt, the Jenny Lind of former days. She knew of my solitude, and came to nurse and look after me—a kindness never to be forgotten.

Naturally, I boasted of my good luck in letters to the Provost, and he answered me in the Latin verses given here:

'LUSCINIA AMICUM ÆGROTANTEM VISIT.'

ELEGIA.

' Pœne oculis captus magnâ cubat " Arthur " in urbe,
 Distantesque dolet se " Miniam " que suam.
 Anxius Helvetiæ niveas desiderat Alpes :
  Acris iter morbi vis Medicusque vetant.

> Quid faciet tenebris et tanquam carcere clausus
>   Londini "strepitus inter, et inter opes?"*
> Flebilis incassum sublime per aera ferri
>   Optat, et in longas protinus ire plagas.
> Tanquam germanas audit Philomela querelas:
>   Audit, et ingenuas solvitur in lacrymas.
> Advolat ægroto meditans solamen amico,
>   Et minuens tenebras assidet ægra toro.
> Ipsa, velut cœli demissa à sedibus adsit,
>   Humanam illustrat lætificatque domum.
> Æger, paullatim lenitus voce, dolorem
>   Non meminit, votumque deposuitque fugæ.
> Felix officio vere, Philomela, benigno,
>   Vive ministerio, vive beata tuo.
> Parce querelarum, paullisper parce, tuarum
>   Inter divinum nunc meminisse melos.
> Ede aliquid fervens et non "miserabile carmen."†
>   Ægrotum è stratis erige voce suis;
> Aufer in Helveticas renovato pectore rupes
>   Languentem ingratâ nocte morâque virum
> Ipse resurgentes numerorum sentiat æstus,
>   Et te vocalem vim revocasse suam:
> Et, quando e tenebris sibi rursum exire licebit,
>   Officium referet voce animoque tuum.
>
> '*August*, 1869.'   'R. O.

I have been told of a learned Canon of Durham Cathedral who, when bored, or wilfully deaf to the sermons of his colleagues, would amuse himself by turning anthems and collects into Greek and Latin verses. A Rowland Hill,

---

* Hor., Od. III., xxviii.   † Virg., Georg. IV.

with a lynx eye for an irreverent listener, would soon have detected the profanity, and launched his thunderbolt from the pulpit at a scholar practising his old arts in the wrong place. Okes did his verse translations out of chapel, in his study, and I used to receive them as postscripts and additions to an ordinary letter. Here is a specimen:

'K. C.
'*December* 7, 1860.

'MY DEAR COLERIDGE,

'I was last Sunday reading some hymns of Prudentius, and fancied the words of our * favourite anthem would run well into his Dimeters. The enclosed is the result of my attempt, which, if nothing else, is literal.

'Yours very truly,
'RICHD. OKES.

> 'Sleepers, awake! a voice is calling;
> It is the watchman on the walls,
> Thou city of Jerusalem!
> For lo! the Bridegroom comes.
> Awake, and take your lamps—
> Hallelujah!
> Awake! His kingdom is at hand;
> Go forth to meet your Lord!'

---

* The Provost alludes to the magnificent chorale in Mendelssohn's oratorio 'St. Paul': 'Sleepers, awake! a voice is calling,' etc.

Idem Latinè redditum.

> 'Vigilate, dormientium,
>   Vigilate, turba, vox sonat:
>   In mœnibus custos vocat,
>   O civitas Jerusalem!
>   Jam Sponsus en! adest, adest!
>   Exsurgite, O exsurgite,
>   Et lampadas sustollite!
>   Una canentes " Laus Deo!"
>   Vigilate, nam sponsi prope
>   Est regnum! In adventum Deo
>   Exite vos vestro obviam!'

Occasionally a distinguished correspondent would ask the Provost's leave to print the Greek or Latin verses sent from the Lodge, in acknowledgment of a present, or in answer to questions on business. Wordsworth, the Bishop of Lincoln, would from time to time interchange a copy of verses with Dr. Okes. The Visitor of the College was in frequent communication with him, and opportunities occurred for varying the monotony of business, affecting the College, by a supplement in verse on subjects entirely disconnected from it. Here is an average specimen, which seems to have fairly satisfied the writer, who sent a copy to my uncle, Sir John Coleridge, and his son, the late Lord Chief Justice, who at that time held the office of Attorney-General:

'Præsuli eruditissimo et omni reverentiâ dignissimo
Christophoro
Dei gratiâ Episcopo Lincolniensi
S. P. D.
Ricardvs Okes
Collegii Regalis apud Cantabrigienses præpositus.

Ut prius, accepi, Præsul venerande, Camœnæ
   Dona et amicitiæ signa verenda tuæ;
Nec mihi deest amimus tanto pro munere gratus,
   Nec calamo tibi quem posse referre velim.
Quæ mihi misisti nuper tua carmina legi,
   Et caluit sacro pectus amore meum:
Ad vetera historiæ facilis mens sæcla recurrit,
   Et tecum antiquos finxit adesse viros,
Quos vera agnovit pro Vero Ecclesia Christi
   Non timidos stimulum mortis in igne pati,
Qua sibi doctores hodie Constantia cœtu
   Colligit insignes ingenuosque fide;
Et secum cupiit te, constantissime Præsul,
   Corde pio verum quærere et ore loqui;
Et memini quales accenderit Anglia flammas,
   Et quos indigno torserit igne viros;
Nuper enim cautus me sanum Octobribus horis
   Præstare officio Granticolisque meis,
Sum consanguineos inter collesque moratus
   Et petere, ut solitus cultor, in æde Deum,
Qua primum egressus nostras Latimerus in auras
   Morte sua parvum signat honore locum.*
Saxa recens pietas ornata exstruxit amore
   Insigni insignem testificata virum.
His actus, monituque tuo per carmina lecto,
   Prisca recordanti tempore mente sequor,

---

* Thurcaston *in agro Leicestriensi*.

Et miror quanto possit sævire tumultu
    Religio, quantis arma movere minis,
Atque rogo, "Tantæne animis mortalibus iræ,
    Nectere quos uno fœdere debet amor?"
Ah miseri! exclamo, quos iste fefellerit error,
    Ut sua præ Vero somnia ferre velint!
Me regat ingenua Veri Sanctissimus aura
    Spiritus, unde Fides unica, solus Amor!

Magne, vale, Præsul, mitique hos aspice vultu
    Et lege versiculos quo prius ore meos;
Nec minus hæc grato quæ sunt ex corde profecta
    Accipe successus vota precata tuos.

Thurcastoniæ, xiv. Calendas Octobres.'

'MY DEAR COLERIDGE,

    'The accompanying verses were printed at the wish of the Bishop of Lincoln, to whom they are addressed. They otherwise tell their own tale. . . .

        'Kind regards,
           'Yours ever,
              'R. O.

'*October* 8, 1873.

'P.S.—The Attorney and his patriarchal father have approved.'

I remember a ludicrous incident which occurred in chapel one Sunday after the election to the Provostship. My friend and contemporary, Mathias, happened to be the scholar whose turn it was to read the first lesson in the afternoon service. He had been a pupil of Harry Dupuis, and naturally was in favour of his old tutor's election to the Provostship. The lesson was from the first chapter of Isaiah, and at verse twenty-nine occur the words, 'They shall be ashamed of the oaks which ye have desired.' The reader gave out the warning with unction and some emphasis. Dear fellow! he lived to see and own that the College had chosen wisely and well. We never were 'ashamed of our Okes' at any time, and those who knew and loved him will glory in his memory.

A pathetic interest attaches to the memory of the Provost's ninetieth birthday, which was greatly honoured at Cambridge on December 15, 1887. The interest was by no means confined to the residents in College, for Cambridge, where he was born and bred, knew the worth and honoured the life of its 'oldest inhabitant.' Conspicuous amongst the gifts were four handsomely bound volumes of Clarke's 'History of Cambridge,' presented by the Vice-Provost and

Fellows, with the following inscription and verses:

> 'Præposito suo
> Ricardo Okes, S.T.P.
> Annum Nonagesimum Primum Ineunti
> S. P. D.
> Collegii Regalis Socii
> XV^{mo} Die Decembris MDCCCLXXXVII.

> Alter adest annus septem post lustra, Sorori
>   Ex quo Præpositum tristis Etona dedit;
> Excipit, exceptumque fovet Soror usque magistrum,
>   Haud alio tantum rege vigoris habet.
> At tu, iam decies nonos emense Decembres,
>   Cui placet et cordi est laus utriusque domus,
> Accipe quem dedimus, natalia munera, librum,
>   Fida cohors læto iuncta sodalicio.
> Annorum series quanquam tibi plena peracta est,
>   Vivis, inexpleto cinctus amore, Pater.'

> 'A little flock we were in Henry's hall,
>   Few were the subjects of your early sway;
>   Hardly the circle widened, till one day
> The guarded gate swung open wide to all.
>   Many and mighty are they now that call
>   The saintly King their Founder, when they pay
>   Their fuller reverence in the ancient way,
> And with fresh numbers keep the festival.
>   Three generations of the lives of men,
>   Of scholars' generations three times ten—
> And still your hand lifts high the golden flame
>   Of sacred knowledge, till to-day you hear
> Our birthday homage to our Provost's name,
>   With ninefold honour for your ninetieth year.'

The Provost's answer was sent immediately; it is characteristic of one of the best men I have ever known:

> 'Vice Præposito cœterisque Sociis
> Collegii Regalis Cantabrigiæ
> Quatuor Voluminum
> Splendidis Teguminibus Vestitorum
> Datoribus
> Ricardus Okes, S.T.P.
> Collegii ejusdem Præpositus
> S. P. D.
> Et gratias agit maximas—

Decimo quinto die Decembris, 1887.

> 'Juvenes Senesque, qui salutastis meum
>   Nomen benigni laudibus,
> Si quid, piorum Regis Henrici memor
>   Nobis avisque munerum,
> Feci, quod olim profuit Collegio,
>   Id omne votis debui
> Scriptis in ipso Principis sancti libro
>   Sacrisque genti posteræ.
> Vobis supersit omen instantis boni
>   Et vita sit felicitas.
>   'R. O.'

ALFRED MYNN.

CHAPTER X.

MORE ABOUT CRICKET AND MORE ABOUT FIREPLACE —ETON MASTERS FIFTY YEARS AGO.

SINCE writing my reminiscences of cricket in connection with the public-school matches, I have come across a number of the *Daily Graphic* giving the score of Kent *v*. England in 1842, and here the name of Emilius Bayley appears as a man of Kent. Subjoined is the score :

KENT *v*. ENGLAND FIFTY YEARS AGO.

On Monday, August 1, 1842, the grand return match, Kent *v*. England, commenced, and continued for three days in splendid weather. The following is the score :

KENT.

Adams, c Ponsonby, b Barker	12	c Lillywhite, b Dean	7
W. Mynn, Esq., c Box, b Dean	21	b Dean	0
Hillier, st Box, b Lillywhite	3	c Fenner, b Lillywhite	8
Pilch, c Dean, b Lillywhite	98	c Box, b Dean	0
N. Felix, Esq., c Box, b Good	74	c Dean, b Lillywhite	0
A. Mynn, Esq., c Fenner, b Dean	27	c Hawkins, b Lillywhite	3
Wenman, c Fenner, b Dean	0	c Fenner, b Lillywhite	0
Dorrington, b Lillywhite	15	c Lillywhite, b Dean	0
C. J. Whittaker, Esq., c Dean, b Lillywhite	3	c Fenner, b Lillywhite	2
E. Bayley, Esq., not out	5	not out	17
W. De C. Baker, Esq., b Lillywhite	3	c Ponsonby, b Lillywhite	3
Byes, etc.	17	Byes, etc.	4
Total	278	Total	44

ENGLAND.

Barker, st Wenman, b Hillier	58	Sewell, c Dorrington, b Hillier	19
Fenner, b Hillier	1	Hon. F. Ponsonby, b Hillier	26
Box, c A. Mynn, b Adams	22	Lillywhite, run out	1
Guy, b Hillier	80	Dean, not out	0
Good, b Mynn	17	Byes, etc.	22
Butler, b Mynn	5		
Hawkins, c Baker, b Hillier	15	Total	266

SECOND INNINGS.—Barker, not out, 29; Fenner, not out, 19; Butler, b Hillier, 0; byes, etc., 10. Total, 58.

Time was when I could have passed a good examination in the history of the scores made by old Etonians, who had learnt 'to handle the willow' within sight of Willowbrook, at Eton. But memory is apt to be treacherous, and my friend, the Rev. Sir Emilius Laurie (*the* Bayley of my time) has given me some very interesting particulars with reference to his career as a cricketer, as well as his observations on Mr. Frederick Gale's 'Notes on the First Half Century of the Canterbury Cricket Week.' A paragraph in that work is headed 'The Conceit of an Old Boy'; here it is:

'May I mention, rather conceitedly perhaps—but it is the conceit of an old boy—two incidents? On the morning of the Winchester and Eton match, the day before Emilius Bayley made his great score against Harrow, I saw him at "Lord's" defending his wicket against five Marylebone bowlers with the greatest ease.

In his second innings against Winchester he had scored 14 runs in grand style, when a very quick ball ran up his bat and "rocketed" between the wickets. Bowler, wicket-keeper, or point might have gone for it, and probably would have collided. I was standing "short mid-off," my regular position, and shouted in agony: "Let me come—let me come! I've got him!" And they made way for me, and to my eternal joy I just got my hands to the ball and fixed it there. This occurred fifty years ago, and my shoulders, I think, are still sore; for a thin white jersey was a poor protection against ten pairs of hands of my comrades, who danced round me like so many Red Indians, and slapped me on the back.'

On this, Sir Emilius remarks in a letter to me: 'In that Winchester match to which Mr. Gale refers, it was not exactly as he describes it. The ball was a long hop to the off, and I should have let it alone, but I didn't, and paid the penalty. We were in for the runs, and, with fairly good luck, could have got them, as we did next day against Harrow. I remember it all as if it were yesterday.'

The match between Kent and England in

1844 was a memorable one, and Sir Emilius remarks: 'After our big Kent innings, the first England wickets went down for nothing, and the match was considered lost by England. Someone said in my hearing, "It's 100 to 1 on Kent." Richard Cavendish said, "No match is lost till it's won. I'll take 100 to 5;" and it was bet and lost, England winning by nine wickets. I went in first for our second innings, and saw all our side out for 44. The Kent people thought we had sold the match, which, of course, was nonsense, but Alfred Mynn was hissed in Maidstone market.

'I met Randolph in the train last week, and we talked much cricket. He and George Yonge bowled for us in 1841, and they bowled Harrow out in the second innings for 35.

Harrow: First innings	-	-	98
,, Second innings	-	-	35
Total	-	-	133
Eton: First innings	-	-	308

I kept wicket, and well remember how the balls came spinning down and taking the top of the bails. We were not a good eleven, but there were one or two who could get runs occasionally. I have looked through the Upper Club Book, and see that I began with 93 on May 1, and wound up at the end of July with 41 and 34, bowled Redgate, to whom you refer. I believe that I was the first to engage an outside professional; he came for a fortnight at two guineas a week, and bowled a fastish, well-pitched, and straight ball, when sober.

'One curious incident I remember. The late Lord Q—— (then Lord D——) played in our game after twelve, in June, 1840. After four we saw him gallop up the Slough road, and the cause of the flight was eagerly discussed by Eton and Windsor gossips. His absence from the Playing-fields involved a fine of 2s. 6d., and the Sunday after he came back to his regiment at Windsor, I went up to get the 2s. 6d. He was under arrest for going away without leave, and his room was full of officers, cross-questioning him about his flight to Gretna Green on the Saturday previous.

'In Harrow v. Eton the same year, Harrow was in for the runs, and the match was running close. Poor Lord D—— was too excited to stay on the ground to *see* the finish, and he hired a cabman to drive him two miles away, and then to bring him back; on his return, he found that we had won. He rode down Portland Place and Regent Street cheering at the top of his voice. I rode with him, and well remember the strange exhibition.

'On another occasion, Robert Grimston said that Harrow was losing because he had not on his "lucky breeches," and he actually went to Grosvenor Square and changed his trousers to a pair of old brown ones; but no good came of it. Poor Bob! he was the incarnation of pluck, but very superstitious, and had never walked under a ladder in his life, and was very angry one day with me for doing so. But I must not weary you with old-world shop.

'One story more. In a masters' match with some club, three boys were taken in to play. I was getting runs (50 I think I got). My dear father was looking on, surrounded by a bevy of masters, and he made them a short address: "You masters ought to do my son's verses for the rest of the half for winning your match for you." "You needn't trouble yourself about that," said Cookesley; "they are always done for him as it is." And so they were—by little George Sumner, now a Bishop.'

This famous cricketer is a real authority for the often-quoted story of Hawtrey and Finmore. The originators of a practical joke, resuscitated in my own time, were Edward Thring, about as good a schoolmaster and strict a disciplinarian as ever lived, and Henry Coleridge, who made Obedience the ruling principle of a long and honoured life.

These grave and reverend seniors enjoyed in their day a practical joke played upon the headmaster as keenly as we, their successors, did in later times. When a majority was bent upon mischief, the refusal to aid and abet the ringleaders was voted disloyal. Over-propriety and caution were generally snubbed. Thus, when Beamont, a contemporary of mine (honoured as boy and man by everyone who knew him), refused to smoke, when all his comrades, at the risk of their skins, were compelling clouds in Botham's garden 'after 4,' the guilty ones avenged themselves by gibbeting him with an epigram and a bad joke :

> 'Beamont is a Pharisee,
>   And that is very sad, you see.'

Thring's and Coleridge's revolt against law

and order was thought a very spirited affair. The Protagonists were flattered by a close copy of the original thought, which inspired a sixth-form boy, some years afterwards, to repeat the old joke on the same victim, and without variation. The eye-witness of the farce, when first represented, shall speak for himself:

'Do you know the story of Thring (captain of the school) tying a string round the handle of the bell, just behind Hawtrey, and passing the string under Hawtrey's chair to little Henry Coleridge on the other side? First pull, up came Finmore. "Did you ring, sir?" "No." Second pull. Ditto. Much pressure and pinching to make Coleridge pull it a third time, but he did so. Again Finmore, asserting that it had been rung three times. Hawtrey looked about him, and caught sight of the peccant string. "Thring, did you *ring* the bell?" "No, sir, I didn't *ring* it." "Thring, I'm ashamed of you — contemptible subterfuge!" I was in Hawtrey's division at the time, and saw it all.'

A friend and contemporary has supplied me with his recollections of 'Fireplace'; they are clearer and fuller than my own. Old collegers, the survivors of the mysteries in Long Chamber, will recognize the pre-Raphaelite accuracy of his description.

FIREPLACE.

'We fifth-form collegers looked forward to our supper as the jolliest part of the day: not that regulation supper in Hall at eight o'clock, consisting of cold breast of mutton or cheese, but the supper in Fireplace at 10 p.m., which was a regular institution from October 11 to Easter. Five bedsteads were arranged as a "triclinium" around the Upper Fireplace in Long Chamber, on which we sat and ate our own provisions, in "messes" or parties of our own choosing, if we had any; or if not, we cadged as "hungry wolves" on those who had been more provident than ourselves.

'The construction of the fire was a fearful and wonderful mystery, supposed to be handed down from very ancient times; but this must have been a myth, as no fireplace existed in Chamber earlier than 1784. We made the fire in turn—that is to say, every Jew had to make three fires first, and then the colleger of older standing. The ceremony began with "putting on the top crust" at 7.45 p.m., and raking out the dust; the time between Hall supper and prayers was occupied by further feeding and humouring the fire, and carefully measuring with rug-strings three, or, if possible, two big coals which would go right across above the top bar. These coals were supplied extra, and had to be paid for by the victim of the evening. After prayers, this magical headpiece was put on, and at 9.15 the "captain in" was requested to poke the fire from below.

'The same ceremony was repeated at 9.30, after which the "Captain of the Fireplace" was appealed to, to judge the fire. Woe to the unlucky wight whose "top row" gave way during the poking! his fire was certain to be condemned, unless a good-natured sixth-form kindly smashed it in for him, in which case the fire must be judged good. If it was not "let off" or declared up to the mark, the same boy had to do the same thing all over again the next night, and so on till he had learned how to make a proper one.

'Supper began at 10, and lasted half an hour; at 10.30 the three lags put the bedsteads back in their places. Sometimes we sent a message to the sixth form, who were supping

HARRY ATKINS, COLLEGE SERVANT.

in Lower Chamber, to ask if we might sing, and the answer usually came back, "Yes—half-holiday," meaning that we need not be in bed till 11 instead of 10.45. We then sang, or rather roared in chorus, several traditional songs, with plenty of time in them, chiefly about drinking, poaching, and sea life, the sixth-form and Liberty helping us, till time was up.

'On occasions we had a "governor," that is, a four-and-a-half cask of beer, or sometimes even two, provided by subscription (the sixpences given by the bursar on Threepenny-day were always immediately taken for this purpose), or given by the sixth-form, or some old colleger who was sleeping in. Then it was always a whole holiday, and we never went, or were helped, to bed till all was finished.

'On very special occasions, such as a victory over the oppidans at football, or a "resignation" coming for a popular captain, there would be a "lush," when every mess brewed its punch, or egg-flip, in washhand-basins, and drank it out of tooth-mugs—it was equally divine nectar to us.

'Harry Atkins, the college servant, made everything tidy the next morning, and claimed a shilling from everyone who had caused him extra trouble.

'The materials for these orgies were mostly provided on tick by a system of "Christopher bills," countersigned by a sixth-form, who seldom omitted to take toll of the goods thus purchased on his own responsibility. Mine host of the Christopher had pledged himself to the headmaster not to supply spirits to Eton boys; but this little difficulty was easily got over by the bill presented bearing the signature of a tradesman, whose initials happened to be identical with those of one of the sixth-form, who borrowed the rest of the name for the occasion. The money for the bills was collected by the sixth-form on the first day of the next half, and, of course, any defaulter would get no more bills backed, besides a licking into the bargain.

'One can readily understand the sadness that possessed our souls on first moving into the "new buildings" in September, 1845, when all these pleasures became mere memories of the past.'

An article on 'Eton Masters Forty Years Ago' appeared in the *Churchman*, December,

1886, and though a decade has elapsed since its publication, the author's views have for me the same value now that they had when they first came under my notice. His series of short monographs comprises, with one exception, the whole body of the assistant masters who were in office when I first went to Eton. On the whole, I agree with his criticisms and distribution of praise and blame; anyhow, my friend, from his antecedents and his distinguished career at school and College, is far more qualified to speak on educational topics than I am. I offer him my cordial thanks for allowing me to reprint his article.

ETON MASTERS FIFTY YEARS AGO.

'Shall I always be a hearer only? shall I never retaliate?' says Juvenal. Something of this sort have I felt when reading of schools and schoolmasters. Much has been written of late years about schools. Stories of school-life by former boys, a week or a day at school by present boys, criticisms of schools in magazines and newspapers, advice tendered by parents, by masters, by some who have some knowledge of the subject, by many who have none—all this we have had in plenty. Writers have given their opinions freely about the schoolmasters of their own school and time.

But their tone appears to me to have been too fault-finding. Out of the whole, truth might be gathered; but many may fail to gather it. For, though a sensible reader will discount the opinions of the schoolboy author who, proud to find himself in print, will rush in where older persons would hesitate, will decide questions trenchantly and pass judgment on his masters confidently, the general public is apt to forget that these boy-writers are commonly not among the best of the school; nay, sometimes not even average boys, but, by their own confession, indolent and careless. So that a great and important part of the boys have never been heard—the wiser part, who have been, probably, too modest to write and criticize their elders. And of the older chroniclers and critics too many write chiefly to grumble and to air their own pet theories; their remarks about their schoolmasters are often needlessly severe and unfair; they make no allowance for time, and often blame their masters where they should blame themselves.

Especially in my own Public School—Eton—has this been the case. Its masters of some forty years since have hardly received fair measure. From some accounts readers might be left under the impression that they were mostly harsh, unenlightened, narrow, indolent, and self-indulgent, the reverse of which I hold to be the truth.

There are, we know, historians who draw a line and say, 'English history begins here; there was none before.' In like manner as to Public Schools, their system and teaching: some seem to believe that before Arnold Public Schools were not, or were not worth anything. No one wishes to deny the great good that Arnold did; but why need we think that there were no sensible and conscientious schoolmasters before him, or where his influence had not penetrated? *Vixere fortes ante Agamemnona multi.*

Arnold's influence cannot have been great (if it was felt at all) in modifying our system in my school-days, which began before his death. No doubt many of our masters knew of the work he was doing, and honoured him; but there were reasons which would make them, as a body, rather anti-Arnoldian in theology and politics; and little that we had could have radiated from that Warwickshire centre.

Yet, in spite of this, our Eton masters were conscientious men, deservedly liked by their pupils, for whose good they worked to the best of their powers—nor were these powers contemptible. Such was my opinion of them as a boy (though, of course, I did not formulate it thus); such has been my maturer opinion in looking back upon my school-life; and such is my opinion still, after thirty years' experience of teaching and of other public schools and masters.

In this opinion I do not suppose I stand alone; but more are found to blame than to defend those times and teachers: the middle-aged writer about a school nowadays is often the reverse of Horace's old man, being *Culpator temporis acti se puero, censor castigatorque seniorum.* So, out of gratitude to dear old Eton and the preceptors of my youth, I am moved to be not only a reader, but a writer, on these matters, and to jot down a few memories of those to whom I owe much. Though I name no names, those of my own time, or nearly so, will know of whom I speak; but I feel sure my remarks will neither outrage the memory of any dead nor offend any living.

King Henry's School was my only one. Preparatory schools were then rare: boys went to Public Schools younger, and so were in them longer. I myself entered Eton well prepared by my father, and had good home advice and encouragement all the time I was there. No doubt this saved me from some difficulties and temptations, and might have led me as a boy or as a young man to underestimate evils from which I myself was exceptionally guarded. But it does not follow that one possessing these advantages, who afterwards has much experience of schools and teaching, is in advanced middle age an incompetent judge of the general merits of his school and schoolmasters.

The industrious old boys have at least as good a claim to be heard as the average or idle. And as we then spent a longer time at our Public School, and passed under many masters—perhaps through nearly all the classical staff—we became more imbued with the traditions of the school, and got a better knowledge of its masters than is given by the three years and a half which is now the average duration of a boy's Public-School life.

I was eight years at Eton, passed under eleven form-masters, and can quite well recall my time with each. Some, of course, impressed me more than others; doubtless some were better teachers than others. But what I feel bound to say is that at no time did I think I was learning nothing from them; there was not one whom I did not respect, not one of whom I do not recollect traits of kindness, carefulness, helpfulness to those under him. And this is just what I miss in many books about school-days—a due recognition of such a general debt to schoolmasters.

Particular masters are praised—are even over-praised; but the generality are slightingly spoken of, if not severely censured; whence the reader is left to infer that they did their duties in a very perfunctory manner.

I shall try to sketch some of the pastors and masters of myself and contemporaries as they appeared to me then, and still do appear, not giving any minute account of my own school-life or of our school-system generally; for the former was not eventful or out of the way, and of the latter enough has been written. Eleven in number were my form-masters. Of the eleven four are still living. With many I had later acquaintance; but my school impressions about them are clear, nor have they been much changed by my subsequent knowledge.

Well do I remember my first lesson up to my first master. He taught his form in a ground-floor room under the Upper School, towards the north-west corner of the schoolyard. He must have been quite a young man then, and was small of stature; but to a boy of eleven no master appears young or small. To me he seemed formidable at that first morning lesson —Greek grammar, I think it was. However, he did nothing to me that justified dread either then or afterwards during our mutual experience: we remained good friends. It was, of course, humble work that he did with us; but he did it well. And if easy in quality, in quantity (as I now know) the work of any of our then masters must have been great. A lively manner had this, my first pedagogue; we have often met since, and I am glad to say he still lives. His scholarship he has well proved by some classical editions of considerable merit.

From him I passed upwards to one with whom I remained a longer time than the usual half-year, the regular term of a boy's sojourn in one of the forms of the lower part of the school. For when I with his division moved up, he moved up also.

We liked him very much, and I remember how pleased we were when we heard that he was to be promoted with us; and this was not because he was over-indulgent: he was an excellent disciplinarian, but just. Alert and vigilant he was: I remember but one occasion of his being absent in mind. He was hearing us say by heart our Ovid—twenty lines. The custom was for each boy to say but a few lines, beginning where the last left off, and then to be dismissed. I began to say; my hearer had, I think, some note or paper to look at which put him in a train of thought; I went on through the whole score of lines without any hesitation, and then, like Cock Robin, when I came to the end I began again.

The same words recurring in the same voice roused him from his reverie, and he pronounced the usual 'Go!' Afterwards he made some kind remark to my father on my good memory.

A very good scholar this master was, as I came to know afterwards; at the time I probably did not appreciate this. Very handsome I thought him, and dignified. He had the character of being rather too lenient with his pupils, not forcing much work from the unwilling; but he had several distinguished pupils during my time. Afterwards he was appointed to the headmastership, accepting it rather under pressure at a difficult and critical time, when there was a general clamour for changes. If he did not satisfy all opinions, refusing to advance as fast and as far as some wished, he, at all events, gained credit for straightforward honesty in doing what he thought best for the school, and ruled firmly with justice and courtesy.

With my third master I reached the Remove, a part of the school in which geography lessons were a prominent feature; and a sore trial to many were 'Description' and 'Mapmorning.' Our worthy and kind form-master was especially noticeable and imitable in the lessons, his voice and manner being somewhat peculiar. We used to laugh at him and at certain often-recurring phrases. But at whom and at what will not boys laugh?

According to my remembrance I did well under his teaching; and, though I did not much like the maps and their accompaniments, I yet had dinned into me somehow a fairly lasting knowledge of the 'contagious countries.' It is by his geography lessons that we who were under this master shall always remember him: we shall not easily forget his feeling appeals to us as 'miserable boys'; his wonder whence we had crept into his division. Doubtless, poor man, he was sorely tried at times by our dulness, bad memory, or thoughtlessness. I remember, when revisiting Eton from Cambridge, how I and a fellow-undergraduate stole up to the open window of his class-room to listen for the well-known tones and demand for the modern name of Troy or an Asiatic mountain-chain.

Number four was 'my tutor.' What this means a Public-School boy, especially an Etonian, knows. Perhaps the outside world now know, or think they know, for in magazine articles, newspaper letters, etc., the tutorial system has been discussed, criticized, and (as I think) undeservedly abused. But into the question of its merits we will not enter.

Of my tutor I necessarily saw and knew more than of any other master. I liked him, so did his pupils generally. From the beginning to the end of my eight years at school, I was continually learning much from him. If he made us work hard, he also worked hard for us. But as a form-master he was terribly strict, and not liked, perhaps with some reason. He was so exacting that I believe there must have been cases where dulness, not idleness, got too severely punished; for it sorely taxed me (who was neither dull nor idle) to come up to his requirements, especially on the geography mornings, and I had one or two narrow escapes of severe punishment when it would have been really undeserved.

But probably in those times form-masters were over-weighted with too many boys; they had therefore no time to find out the exact powers of each; and my tutor thought it juster and better on the whole to err on the side of strictness. At any rate, with his pupils he was reasonable; he would not tolerate idleness, but he could find out what they were really able to do, and worked them accordingly. And for his promising pupils, when preparing for particular examination or scholarship, he grudged no extra time and trouble. Nor did he confine his sympathy and presence with us to pupil-room. He was often on the river, and at the bathing-places when we 'passed' for swimming. And I remember some pleasant excursions with him up the river to Cliefden or Marlow in the summer term.

And while speaking of my tutor's work with us, I would say a word or two on the religious teaching and influence at a public school. Some have blamed public schools severely on this head: have asserted that before Arnold there was of Christian teaching nothing, or next to nothing. I cannot subscribe to this judgment. Doubtless there was room for improvement: *e.g.*, in the matter of sermons, we might with advantage have been more frequently addressed by our headmaster, by other masters, by younger preachers. Yet I can still recall some good and impressive sermons. To one preacher (still living) many of us listened with interest, and (which is more) did things that he told us to do. But religious influence would come chiefly through the tutor; and I certainly do not admit that it was as nothing.

Of my own tutor I feel bound to record one fact: how carefully and conscientiously he prepared us for Confirmation, taking each boy separately. I remember how serious and impressive were his words at the beginning, how thorough the instruction that followed. Nor can I look upon as valueless, in a religious or spiritual point of view, the Greek Testament or other Divinity lessons with tutor or in form. How these things impressed other boys, or bore fruit in them, I cannot pronounce judgment. All I contend is that serious advice and religious teaching were given to those who would hear and learn; our masters did their duty; for what our tutor did for his pupils, others no doubt did for theirs.

My next step up the ladder brought me to a master for whom, both as a master and on other accounts, I have always had a great respect. On entering his form one found a change in the work; and there was, I think, a difference in his teaching; he went more outside the actual school lesson in the way of illustration from history and literature. I am far from saying that our other masters did not suit their teaching to their class, making it higher and more advanced for the higher forms; they did so, no doubt; but I seem to have noticed it especially in this case of my fourth step upwards.

A year or so after I was in this division I came under this same master in another relation; he was our superintending master in College, and there he was much liked by us as a kind adviser and friend. He used to come round the corridors in the evening—I think I see him now, a remarkably upright figure, bearing a little lamp in hand—and would chat pleasantly with us in our rooms. He resigned his mastership to keep a promise of joining a friend in missionary labour at the other side of the world, in New Zealand.

Perhaps my time under my next three masters was my least progressive time at Eton, yet not through their fault, but my own, for I was less industrious; and besides this, being high in the school for my age, I was rather victimized by bigger and older dunces in my boarding-house, helping them in their work to the detriment of my own. This is a thing hardly to be prevented in a Public School; but, if it go not too far, it is not an unmixed evil that forward boys should have, as it were, the drag put on to some extent, while they also learn by teaching others and seeing and helping them over their difficulties.

But to return to these three masters. The first was certainly a good and careful scholar; he had some distinguished pupils, and was reckoned a very good tutor; but in his form-teaching he was rather dull, and unawakening in manner. Afterwards he became Headmaster, then Provost, and filled both positions with credit and honour. Above him came a master who was generally liked, a courteous and gentlemanly man. He used especially to enforce neatness and finish, and to check rambling, diffuse and slovenly work.

Next to him was one whom I recollect as particularly kind to my brother and myself, to whom he gave some specimens from his collection of stuffed birds, as we were keen young naturalists. He had been a fine cricketer in his youth, and was often to be seen looking on in Upper Club; once or twice I remember to have seen him batting well in practice or in a match. I believe he had weak health; he died at Eton as a master before I left the school.

And now I rose to the division of one whom I liked much, and from whom I learnt much—more, I think, than from any one form-master before. It is true that I was under him longer than I had been under any other; for, as one rose towards the top of the school, promotion became slower. A very clever man he was, but eccentric—indeed, so much so, that we boys applied to him the monosyllable 'mad.'

He was a decidedly good and stimulating teacher, gave one new ideas, especially about the connection of words and philology, little attended to at that time. Energetic he was, and almost violent in manner at times; enthusiastic, and devoting great pains where he thought them well bestowed. To myself he was very kind on more than one occasion. I have a book given me by him as a prize for a special verse copy. Such prizes, it was said, he often promised, but generally forgot to give; however, I am an instance to the contrary.

That he failed to make his mastership and his house a success financially, and left the school in consequence, does not, of course, lessen my debt of gratitude to him as a teacher.

Tenth in order and penultimate was my next master. Of him, too, I had a long experience —as had all boys who rose quickly and reached his division while young, having to wait for admission to the headmaster's division. Of this master's teaching I have not such a favourable remembrance as of some others—in fact, I do not agree with the estimate of it given in several notices since his death by grateful pupils ; for he is exalted above his colleagues— spoken of as decidedly in advance of them. As form-master he was not so to my apprehension or that of many others ; and I was beginning to be able to judge.

Being now old enough to understand reasons for work, I worked, and got on well with him ; but I did not think then, nor do I think now, that as a teacher he was above my other masters, or even equal to some. His teaching did not seem an advance on the form below ; he was particular, not to say crotchety, about some little things, and seemed to me to aim too much at enforcing his own views. But he had many pupils who won distinction both at Eton and afterwards; and I do not wish to disparage his general merits. For he was a man widely known, had many interests besides those of the school, initiated and generously helped many good works. It is only as a master that I think his zealous friends have unduly extolled him at the expense of others—rather as if he was the only enlightened, liberal-minded, and conscientious tutor among far inferior colleagues.

And now I come to our Head — 'The Doctor,' a well-known name, which I will not scruple to give, Dr. Hawtrey. Long did he reign over our school, resigning the ferule to take the Provostship about a year after I went to College. That he was a polished scholar and gentleman is beyond all question; nor were these unimportant points in a school like ours. Less minute and precise in scholarship he was than some of our day; but many of these appear to me, in analyzing the parts, to have lost enjoyment of the whole. Indeed, the generation to which our then chief and my own father belonged, as well as some of my own generation, did, I feel sure, enjoy their classics more than our juniors do.

Of this Headmaster's teaching and influence over his division I have always thought highly. The willing and intelligent boys gained much, learnt to take wider views of things, heard illustrations from many a language and literature. It is true there was not much driving of the laggards in that form; the aim was rather to lead the van than to bring up the rear. 'Somebody must be last' was the consolatory remark with which our Head used to meet a somewhat derisive titter of ours at the last name read out in the examination list. I have no doubt he wittingly gave up the forcing principle, thinking it did not become the Headmaster of a great school to be like one of Pharaoh's taskmasters. Thus it happened that triflers could and did trifle. Indeed, not only in the Doctor's division, but throughout much of the school, there was more freedom and more chance of shirking work than is now the case either there or elsewhere. A minimum was required, but a minimum easy to get through somehow; and boys were left more to themselves.

Perhaps less work, on the whole, was got out of them (though of this I am not sure as regards Eton of late years and Eton then); and for some boys the system had disadvantages. But there are counterbalancing disadvantages in the high-pressure system, where every corner of a boy's time is filled up, and he is never, even out of school hours, otherwise than superintended, lectured, and directed. Such was not our Eton system; such, indeed, is still not the Public-School system as compared with private schools; but it may tend more and more to become so, as new studies rise up and popular clamour demands that each and all shall have a place in the Public-School curriculum But whither am I diverging? Our 'Magister Informator,' at all events, went on the old plan, and worked it, on the whole, well. And I, with doubtless many others, feel grateful to him for his teaching and influence during the latter part of my school-life.

I have thus given my impressions about eleven form-masters. Some two or three of the classical staff there were who taught forms below the fourth form, in which I entered. Also there were non-classical, or extra, masters;

but attendance on these—even on the mathematical—was at that time optional, and they were not in the same position as the classical masters, an injustice which has since been rectified.

Of two extra masters I retain an affectionate remembrance. One was our French master, a courtly-looking old gentleman, in dress and manner quite of the old régime. I used to go to him for lessons when quite young, some time before I entered the school—indeed, on entering the school, or soon after, I discontinued my French with him, it being thought that I should be overpressed by adding this to the regular lessons. But when I afterwards took up the language again, the early foundation thus laid stood me in good stead. The old gentleman was sorry to lose me for a pupil, having predicted for me the Prince Consort's prize, then lately established. He was a pleasant teacher and a friend of my father's. Long years afterwards I came upon a blotting-paper interleaved book of exercises done in those early days.

My other extra master came at the end of

my Eton course. He was the German master; but I learnt from him not German, but Hebrew. Most liberal he was of his time and trouble, was an enthusiastic Hebraist, and always glad to see me at any odd moments I could spare. I learnt from him for more than two years, till I left for College, being for the greater part of the time his only Hebrew pupil. He knew other Oriental languages besides Hebrew, Syriac and Arabic certainly, and perhaps more. Also he and his family were very musical.

Such are my reminiscences of my school and schoolmasters. Too favourable a picture some will deem it; yet, looking back as I do with the light of many years' subsequent experience in the same line, I am confident that it gives quite as truthful an impression of Eton then as do some descriptions that are more carping and critical.

A working boy well cared for sees the best side. Granted; but some of the indolent who have written saw only the worst. Some boys (it may be said) will learn from anyone. True; but also some from no one. And then, repentant as they grow wiser, those of this kind (or something like it) put upon their masters and their school faults mainly their own. Nor would anyone be right in supposing me to have been an all-work-and-no-play model boy; I took my fair share of everything that was going. I have confined myself in this paper to the masters and their work with us; but I have memories of and could be garrulous about Eton cricket, football, fives, the river, the surrounding country.

And again, let none suppose I have penned these reminiscences to prove that our system was faultless, our masters superhumanly perfect, or to complain of all change. 'The old order changeth, yielding place to new;' no sensible person would deny that changes were needed at Eton as elsewhere, or that good has been done by some reforms. But it is a pity when we cannot mend and reform without disparaging the generation on whose foundation we build, on whose work we improve, without supposing that with us were born both wisdom and conscience. And about the masters of our time, I repeat my conviction that, whereas outsiders might from some accounts infer that they were unenlightened, indolent, and self-seeking, they were as intelligent, hard-working and conscientious as any body of masters in the present day.

With masters thus respected and liked, it may well be that boys were less ignorant and idle than a younger age is prone to believe. More leisure they had to be idle; but under good influence leisure uncontrolled is not always abused to idleness—nay, it may be and is turned to good account in various ways. While, on the other hand, the boy with his time over-filled is apt by a kind of reaction to give all his leisure (almost as a matter of conscience) to the very opposite of work. Having thrust upon him, as he thinks, too much wisdom, he runs into the more foolishness. The bow bent over-much, when loosed, recoils the more. But the learners of my own time I neither blame, praise, nor estimate in any way—'that which we were we were.' With our teachers I think we had no reason to be dissatisfied, and so I pay them this debt of gratitude, for I honour the maxim of the old school in Aristophanes,* whose words I freely paraphrase:

> 'Remember not each petty fault, forgetting all the good,
> Of older men who fed thy youth with wisdom's sacred food.'

FLOREAT ETONA.

On a recent retrospect of Eton College.

Here is the old familiar place,
There are the Castle's strength and grace;
Here are the Playing-fields, there is the wall;
Here is the Chapel, and there is the Hall;
Turrets and pinnacles orderly ranged;
The stones remain, but the living are changed.

Fifty years have passed and gone.
Where are my schoolfellows? Hardly one
Remains of the race that rowed with me,
Or wielded the willow skilfully,
Or fought with the gloves or single-sticks
In eighteen hundred and forty-six.

Twenty arms, supple and strong,
Lifting the *Royal Ten-oar* along;
Close behind her, blue as the sky,
Dashes the valiant *Victory*;
Then the *Prince* and *Britannia* and all
Follow the *Monarch* to Surley Hall,

---

* Ar. *Nub.*, 999:
μηδ' ἀντειπεῖν τῷ πατρὶ μηδέν, μηδ' Ἰαπετόν καλέσαντα
μνησικακῆσαι τὴν ἡλικίαν ἐξ ἧς ἐννεοττοτροφήθης.

Hark! the multitudinous noise,
The thronging feet of a thousand boys
Hurrying on to the beautiful ground,
Where the poet's elm-trees stand around,
Where the world is playing a match with Eton,
And the world, as usual, is soundly beaten.

'*Mater Etona vale!*' says the boy
As he leaves her bosom in hope and joy.
'Farewell, Eton!' again we say,
In the last dim glow of a fading day.
'Live with thy children brave as of yore—
Live and flourish for evermore.'

A. H. A. HAMILTON.

THE END.

BILLING AND SONS, PRINTERS, GUILDFORD.
G., C. & Co.

www.ingramcontent.com/pod-product-compliance
Lightning Source LLC
Chambersburg PA
CBHW021424300426
44114CB00010B/637